Pleasures and Pastimes in Medieval England

Pleasures and Pastimes in Medieval England

COMPTON REEVES

New York   Oxford
Oxford University Press
1998

Oxford University Press

Oxford New York
Athens Auckland Bangkok Bogotá Bombay
Buenos Aires Calcutta Cape Town Dar es Salaam
Delhi Florence Hong Kong Istanbul Karachi
Kuala Lumpur Madras Madrid Melbourne
Mexico City Nairobi Paris Singapore
Taipei Tokyo Toronto

and associated companies in
Berlin Ibadan

First published in the United Kingdom by Alan Sutton Publishing Limited,
an imprint of Sutton Publishing Limited.

First issued as an Oxford University Press paperback, 1998

Oxford is a registered trademark of Oxford University Press
198 Madison Avenue, New York, New York 10016

Library of Congress Cataloging-in-Publication Data available.

ISBN 0-19-521423-4 (paperback)

1 3 5 7 9 8 6 4 2

Printed in Great Britain

Contents

Colour Plates

Preface

This book began with an invitation to present the Keynote Address before the Annual General Meeting of the Richard III Society, American Branch, in 1989. That luncheon talk was published by the society as *Delights of Life in Fifteenth-Century England*; the printed lecture was seen by Alan Sutton Publishing Ltd and the result was an invitation to do this book. The publishers bore with exceeding kindness delays in producing the manuscript caused by my academic responsibilities and the unwelcome distress and distraction of parental death, parental illness and surgery, domestic move, and a further litany of disturbances I have no wish burdensomely to elucidate. It has been a gift to me as the author that the book is not devoted to a depressing topic.

Traditional training as a documentary historian does not truly prepare a person to seek after the pleasures and pastimes of the past. We, it seems, are expected to do more 'serious' things with our energies. Happily, 'serious' scientists are discovering how therapeutic laughter and recreation can be. As the following pages will reveal, I have pursued the guidon of many a scholar into one field of research after another only slightly known to me as a traditionally trained historian. I hope that my followership has been worthy of their leadership. To aspiring researchers I can say that no subject discussed in this book has been explored and explained to its uttermost, and that there is much yet to be learned about the pleasures and pastimes of our medieval ancestors, even those of the fourteenth and fifteenth centuries upon whom these pages concentrate most heavily.

Several present and former students, people of perception and good humour, have talked with me about this project and even read drafts of some chapters, and it is a pleasure to acknowledge the assistance of Gil Bogner, Paul Gorley, Bill Kimok, Laura Kinner, Susie Rohrbough and Mike Zempter. Friendly colleagues who gather at the International Congress on Medieval Studies at Kalamazoo, and my long-time mentor Brynmor Pugh have been most encouraging.

For my sons
David and Adam

ONE

Literature

Following the authority of the Roman poet Horace, whose *Ars poetica* stated that literature could be informative and a guide to wisdom, or a pure pleasure, medievals were prepared to accept that literature was potentially both. They might have been most comfortable on moral grounds with literature which was intended for edification, but literature simply for pleasure was acknowledged. Pleasure might come from a pleasing style, involving such things as the metre and rhyme of poetry or the use of rhetoric; pleasure might come from the story itself, the presentation, a humorous tone or any number of other devices.

It would be impossible in attempting to discover what sorts of literary pleasures were available to readers and hearers in late medieval England to provide anything like a comprehensive description of all the literature produced by contemporary or earlier writers in England or elsewhere that was within reach. What suits our present purposes better is a survey of the major types of literature available, together with some examples, and giving greater attention to the contents than to the style. The spread of literacy in the later Middle Ages generated a demand for reading matter. Devotional works, romances, ballads, chronicles, and histories circulated in copies more workaday than de luxe in their quality of workmanship.

Romance

English success in the French wars of the fourteenth century carried implications for the literary form of the chivalric romance. War and romance enjoyed comradeship. Edward I and his grandson, Edward III, both warrior kings, made the most of the prestige of King Arthur. Edward I, for example, was present at Glastonbury Abbey in 1278 for the reinterment in front of the high altar of what were believed to be the remains of King Arthur and Queen Guinevere. Some seven decades later, Edward III founded the Order of the Garter. The literary side of these events was the category of romance literature known as the 'Matter of Britain', which is to say, the whole cycle of tales which developed around King Arthur. The stories were of Welsh origin, and were spread and romanticized in the French-speaking world in the course of the twelfth century. Great encouragement and further fame was given to the King Arthur legend by Geoffrey of Monmouth in the 1130s when he wrote the substantially unhistorical *History of the Kings of Britain*. The reading and hearing of chivalric romances was a common pastime of the English nobility in the later Middle Ages, and Arthurian stories were central to this entertainment.

Medieval English romances were stories with happy endings, written mostly in verse, of the adventures of noble men and women. The earliest examples of this enduringly popular form of literature appeared in the thirteenth century. A manuscript of about 1250 preserves the romance *King Horn* as well as *Floris and Blauncheflour*. The former tells a primary story of the losing and regaining of a kingdom and a lesser story of Horn's love for Princess Rymenhild. The latter are royal lovers who are separated and who experience assorted exotic adventures before being reunited. A romance of princely love and adventure along the same lines as *King Horn* but somewhat later in composition is *The Lay of Havelok the Dane*. Romances dealing with King Arthur were especially suited to the English milieu. 'Sir Gawain and the Green Knight' and Malory's *Le Morte Darthur* are mentioned in context elsewhere, but they are classics. One of the earliest English Arthurian romances is *Arthour and Merlin*, which tells of Merlin's role in the gaining of the crown by Uther, the birth and coming to rule of Arthur, and stories of some of his battles.

Most of the medieval English Arthurian romances focus on individual knights, with Gawain predominating. *Syre Gawene and the Carle of Carlyle* of around 1400 would be one example which includes the themes of a beheading and an imperious host. In some of the Gawain poems, the action builds around the performance of a vow, or vows, as in the case of *The Avowing of King Arthur, Sir Gawain, Sir Kay*, and *Baldwin of Britain*, which dates from about 1425. Around the middle of the fifteenth century the theme of the loathsome lady is exemplified in *The Wedding of Sir Gawain and Dame Ragnell*. Stories of other knights are often adapted from French models, such as *Lancelot of the Laik*.

Dozens of popular English verse romances were composed from the thirteenth century onwards, and a great many medievals over

A scene from English romance: Sir Gawain kneeling before Arthur and Guinevere (from the only surviving manuscript of 'Sir Gawain and the Green Knight') (British Library Cotton Ms. Nero A X, f. 130)

the generations would have been entertained by the stories, instructed by the ideals imbedded in the tales, and familiar with the strengths and weaknesses of the assorted characters.

PROSE ROMANCE

Very few English romances were written in prose until long after the romance genre was well developed. A few were produced before 1450, but most appeared over the following six or seven decades. The prose romance with the most enduring fame is *Le Morte*

The Swan Knight: a misericord from Exeter Cathedral of a knight seeking adventures in a boat guided by his brother who takes the form of a swan (Conway Library, Courtauld Institute of Art)

Darthur, which Sir Thomas Malory completed in 1469–70, and which William Caxton printed in 1485. Caxton divided Malory's text into twenty-one books, broken down into 506 chapters. Malory, however, organized his work around eight tales, and he called the entire thing *The Whole Book of King Arthur and of His Noble Knights of the Round Table*. The first tale is about how Arthur became the undisputed King of Britain, the second is about foreign conquest, and the third is made up of several episodes, with special emphasis upon the chivalry of Sir Lancelot. The hero of the fourth tale is Gareth, brother of Gawain, while the fifth tale, the longest, is filled with tournaments, quests and adventures. The world of romance is in full flower in the fifth tale, which is concluded with the Grail theme. This is continued in the sixth tale, wherein various knights go in pursuit of the Grail. In the sixth tale the Arthurian world is beginning to decline, and in the seventh tale the decline continues, with the adulterous affair of Sir Lancelot and Queen Guinevere narrowly escaping discovery. In the last tale, the affair is discovered, and Guinevere and Lancelot ultimately die good deaths as penitents in the religous life and, following his own adventures, the wounded Arthur is taken away to the Vale of Avalon.

Other prose romances do not measure up to the standard of *Le Morte Darthur*, but some appropriate examples should be mentioned. The prose *Alexander*, which was written sometime in the first half of the fifteenth century, takes fortune as its main theme, while penance was the theme of *Robert the Deuyll*, written early in the next century. Prose romances like *The Sege of Thebes* and *The Sege of Troy*, written in the fifteenth century, were based upon standard romance subjects drawn from episodes of antiquity. The prose *Merlin*, to mention just one more example, was translated in about 1450 from the thirteenth-century French *Estoire de Merlin*, and relates the history of Merlin from his conception, through various adult political and counselling roles, to his ultimate imprisonment.

Chaucer

Geoffrey Chaucer (died 1400) employed Arthurian material in two of the stories included in *The Canterbury Tales*: *The Squire's Tale* and *The Wife of Bath's Tale*. Thought of primarily as a poet, he also wrote such prose pieces as the *Treatise on the Astrolabe*, *The Parson's Tale*, *Boece* (a translation of Boethius' 'Consolation of Philosophy'), and *Melibee*. Chaucer put the *Treatise on the Astrolabe* together for his young son, and the work became the standard handbook in English on the use of that scientific instrument. He also translated from French the popular poem of courtly love, the *Roman de la Rose*.

There have doubtless been many more words written about

Geoffrey Chaucer (British Library Harley Ms. 4866, f. 88)

Chaucer than he himself penned, but a cursory orientation is necessary here to illuminate his life and literature. Chaucer was a Londoner. His father, John, was an important vintner, and Chaucer spent his life in business and in royal and aristocratic service (including fighting in France in the army of Edward III and being captured in the failed siege of Reims). He was a Justice of the Peace and sat in the Commons. His writing was an avocation. An indication of the circles in which Chaucer was moving by the late 1360s is to be found in his poem *Book of the Duchess*, which is an elegy of over 1,300 lines for Blanche of Lancaster, wife of John of Gaunt, Duke of Lancaster. Chaucer was already associated with John of Gaunt when Blanche died in 1369, and it should be remembered that extending patronage to a writer was beneficial to a lord's prestige. A significant poem from the 1370s was his *Hous of Fame*, a dream-vision left unfinished even after more than 2,000 lines, whose underlying theme is the familiar idea that all earthly things, including fame, are transitory. An important work from the 1380s is the *Parlement of Foules*, another dream-vision of 699 lines written for St Valentine's Day. The gist of the poem takes the myth that birds gather before the goddess Nature on St Valentine's Day to choose their mates, and in this playful context Chaucer discusses different kinds of love. The *Legend of Good Women* was also a dream-vision written in the 1380s, which is a series of stories about good women, many of whom were betrayed by unworthy or wicked men.

The influence of the 'De Consolatio Philosophiae' by the Roman philosopher and senator Boethius is evident in Chaucer's *Troilus and Criseyde*, although there is also influence from the *Filostrato*, written by Chaucer's Italian contemporary Giovanni Boccaccio (died 1375). Troilus was the son of the Trojan King Priam and Criseyde was the daughter of Calkas, a deserter priest, and a widow. The poem is a love story, a philosophical discussion on sexual love, free will, and much more, set against the background of the Trojan War. *Troilus and Criseyde* was completed in 1386, and by then Chaucer was thinking about *The Canterbury Tales*. The framing device was to be a pilgrimage from Southwark, across the Thames from London, to the shrine of St Thomas Becket in Canterbury Cathedral with the pilgrims participating in a storytelling contest to ease the tedium of the journey. *The Canterbury Tales* engaged Chaucer through the 1390s, but it was not brought to completion: a return journey from Canterbury was not written, and not all of the pilgrims tell stories. The twenty-four tales offered Chaucer an opportunity to present different literary genres, such as the beast epic (*The Nun's Priest's Tale*), the legend (*The Pardoner's Tale*), the racy fabliaux (*The Miller's Tale* and *The Reeve's Tale*), or the courtly romance (*The Knight's Tale*).

Mandeville

Mandeville's Travels purports to be the account of Sir John Mandeville, a knight from St Albans, who set off from England in 1322 upon a journey which took him to the Holy Land and on into Asia. The author of this work was, in fact, probably French and he

Illustrations from Anton Sorg's second Augsburg edition of *The Travels of Sir John Mandeville*, 1481

put together the wide range of travel information, both fictional and factual, without leaving France. Such ugly historical facts were unknown to medieval English readers. The book was a popular source of information about the marvels of the Far East until well into the eighteenth century, and it was especially the more fabulous material that was attractive. Other examples of travel books are John Capgrave's travelogue for Rome, written about 1450, and William Wey's itineraries for travellers to Jerusalem and to the shrine of Saint James of Compostella, written in the 1450s.

Trevisa

John Trevisa was probably born at Trevessa in Cornwall in the early 1340s. He studied at Oxford, became a priest, made his literary mark as a translator, and was dead by 1402. The translations from Latin into English for which Trevisa is best known are the 'Polychronicon' by Ranulph Higden, the 'De Regimine Principum' by Giles of Rome (Aegidius Romanus), and the 'De Proprietatibus Rerum' of Bartholomaeus Anglicus.

Lydgate and Gower

Two poets whose reputations have been eclipsed by that of Chaucer are John Lydgate (died about 1450) and John Gower (died 1408). Lydgate was a monk at the Benedictine abbey of Bury St Edmunds who wrote more poetry than William Shakespeare, although his 145,000 surviving lines are today mostly of interest to literary specialists. In his own day Lydgate was lavishly patronized and greatly admired for such works as 'The Troy Book' and the 'Life of Our Lady', both of which he dedicated to Henry V, and 'The Fall of Princes', which he dedicated to Henry's younger brother, Humphrey, Duke of Gloucester. John Gower is a reminder that the literary world of late medieval England was trilingual. His three major works are each in a different language. The 'Speculum Meditantis' (or 'Mirour de l'omme') was written in French, and is a searing denunciation of the iniquities of Gower's day, from the rapacity of lawyers to the profligacy of the clergy. The 'Vox Clamantis', in Latin, was written for a learned audience and was dedicated to Archbishop Thomas Arundel of Canterbury. It drew heavily from Ovid, and is in part a criticism of the clergy, the laity, and the nobility, the three estates of society, and in part a book of advice for a prince. The English 'Confessio Amantis', which runs to some 33,000 lines in octosyllabic couplets, is a collection of exemplary tales of love. The framework of the poem is the action of the poet, Amans, making his confession to a priest of Venus.

Latin Historical Prose

There was an ongoing late medieval interest in preserving a record of historical events in the principal language of scholarship. Probably the finest English historian of the thirteenth century was Matthew Paris, the monk of St Albans whose writings ceased in 1259. His best-known book was the 'Chronica Majora', but he was also capable of turning out saints' lives in French verse and illustrating his writings. Other Latin chroniclers of the century included Bartholomew Cotton, a monk of Norwich, and the Dominican friar, Nicholas Trivet, whose 'Annals' provide a vivid description of the coronation of Edward I in Westminster Abbey in 1274. The principal account of the greater part of the reign of Edward I's markedly less dynamic son, Edward II, was the 'Vita Edwardi II' ('The Life of Edward II'), written by a canon of Hereford, John Walwayn. A London view of the early fourteenth century is provided by the 'Annales Londonienses' and the 'Annales Paulini' ('The Annals of Saint Paul's'). The long reign of Edward III (1327–77) was noted by such chroniclers as Geoffrey le Baker, Thomas Gray, Ranulf Higden, Henry Knighton, and Adam Murimuth. The 'Historia Anglicana' by Thomas Walsingham is an important account running from the end of the reign of Edward III to the year 1422. Chronicles for the reign of Edward III's grandson and successor, Richard II, include the 'Historia Vitae et Regni Richardi' ('The History of the Life and Reign of Richard') and the 'Chronicon' of Adam of Usk, who had a part in the deposition of King Richard in 1399. The recording of history in the English language was displacing Latin as we move into the fifteenth century, and we may conclude this abridged survey of Latin historical writing with Thomas Otterbourne's 'Chronicon Regum Angliae' ('Chronicle of the Kings of England'), which is of value for the first twenty years of the century, and the anonymous 'Chronicon Angliae Temporibus Ricardi II, Henrici IV, Henrici V, et Henrici VI'.

English Historical Prose

The various continuations of the Anglo-Saxon Chronicle ceased to be kept in the mid-twelfth century, and the writing in English of historical prose only resumed in the late fourteenth century with

Matthew Paris's marginal depiction of the abbey church of St Albans and Fawkes de Breauté, from the 'Chronica Majora' (The Master and Fellows of Corpus Christi College, Cambridge, Ms. 16, f. 54r; photograph: Conway Library, Courtauld Institute of Art)

such works as the English translation of Higden's 'Polychronicon' made by John Trevisa and the anonymous translation of the 'Brut', based upon an Anglo-Norman version, which in turn was based upon Geoffrey of Monmouth's 'Historia Regum Britanniae'. The 'Brut' and its continuations proved to be the most popular piece of secular writing in England in the Middle Ages, and it had a great impact on the conception of the English past. Keen interest was taken in the events of the time, and civic chronicles, for the most part anonymous, were written about happenings in London. In particular for fifteenth-century London could be mentioned the 'Great Chronicle'; 'Gregory's Chronicle', an anonymous chronicle called nonetheless after a City mayor of the 1450s named William Gregory, and 'The Main City Chronicle'. The years of Edward IV's reign from 1461 to 1474 were narrated in John Warkworth's 'Chronicle', and a political biography was produced by John Rous in 'The Pageant of the Birth, Life, and Death of Richard Beauchamp, Earl of Warwick'. These are but some of the major English prose writings of a historical sort available in the later Middle Ages.

Informative English Literature

With the expansion of opportunities for education and literacy in the late medieval period, especially marked in the fifteenth century, there was an increased desire for information of many kinds to be made available in English. 'The Pricke of Conscience' was a popular didactic guide for morality, and pious tales were brought together in such fifteenth-century works as the 'Gesta Romanorum' and the 'Alphabet of Tales'. An example of an astronomical treatise is the anonymous English translation of the 'Exafrenon', attributed to Richard Wallingford, Abbot of St Albans, who was famed for the astronomical clock he constructed. The 'Secretum Secretorum' enjoyed great popularity in England and Europe, and was cast in the form of a book of advice written by the quintessential philosopher, Aristotle, for the quintessential emperor, Alexander the Great. It existed in many versions and adaptations, which included political and moral advice for rulers, astrology, and physiognomy, and more than a dozen English translations were in circulation. 'The Libel of English Policy', an anonymous work, argued for an orderly commercial policy and the importance of a navy to control the surrounding seas. Lapidaries, or treatises about stones, continued as they had for centuries to attract readers who were especially interested in any magical, medicinal, or protective properties belonging to different stones.

Several textbooks were written in English to assist students in learning Latin grammar, and textbooks were also written for arithmetic, such as the 'Crafte of Nombrynge' from the early fifteenth century. Glossaries which were designed to explain in English the meaning of French or Latin terms circulated for the use of lawyers, those who used plants for medicinal purposes, and others with special interests, and English–Latin and Latin–English dictionaries were also produced in the fifteenth century. Books on courtesy were useful to those with social aspirations, and some of those that appeared are discussed in this book in association with etiquette at meals (pp. 155–61). Books on cookery, gardening, and hunting are also discussed elsewhere.

Several manuals on chivalry were available in English before the justly famous 'Book of the Ordre of Chyvalry' was printed by William Caxton in 1484. William Worcester, secretary to the experienced English commander Sir John Fastolf between 1438 and 1459, wrote the 'Boke of Noblesse' in the 1450s. It advocates ongoing war with France in a sort of militaristic nationalism, but tells of episodes of ancient warfare, stories from the Anglo-French war, and the attributes to be found in successful knights and commanders. Caxton's 'Ordre of Chyvalry' had its most remote ancestry in the thirteenth-century 'Libre del ordre de cavaleria' by the Catalan Ramon Lull. Christine de Pisan's 'Livre des fais d'armes et de chevalerie' was translated into English with only slight alterations in the text by William Caxton in 1489 as 'Book of Fayttes of Armes and of Chyvalrye'. Christine was interested in defensive militarism for the protection and peace of Christendom. The first of the four books into which her work is subdivided owes a great debt to Vegetius. The whole genre of military manuals is conveniently represented by the continuing popularity of the high ranking Roman Flavius Vegetius Renatus' fourth-century 'De Re Militari', which was the ultimate primary source for medieval military manuals. The earliest translation into English was in 1408 for Thomas, Lord Berkeley, who was fighting at the time with Prince Henry against the Welsh followers of Owain Glyndŵr. A verse paraphrase of Vegetius was written in English between 1457 and 1460 in the midst of the strife we know as the Wars of the Roses. The author of this 'Knyghthode and Bataile' is unknown, but he was an ecclesiastic and a supporter of Henry VI.

Some curious instructional literature from the later Middle Ages includes a treatise on sailing, a treatise on lacemaking, several works on chiromancy (palmestry), and a great many works of the almanac type, particularly those of the astronomical sort that could be consulted to determine the best times for planting crops or garden plants, or for carrying out medical procedures such as surgery or phlebotomy. Recipes were to be found for such things as making ink, making dyes of assorted colours, making soap, glue, parchment, and other items. A few readers were also able to consult works on alchemy, such as the 'Speculum Lucis' ('Mirror of Light') by Albertus Magnus (died 1280) or the 'Liber de Consideratione Quintae Essentiae' (known also as the 'Liber Lucis'), written around 1350 by Jean de Roquetaillade, which circulated in both Latin and English.

Several writers engaged in the activity of tendering advice to princes. In a fairly loose sense, this type of literature is categorized as 'mirrors for princes', and most were more inclined to offer moral advice than specific suggestions about the art of government. One of the most popular works on the subject of how a prince was to behave was 'The Regement of Princes' by Thomas Hoccleve. Hoccleve was born in about 1368 and lived until 1426. Throughout his working life he was a clerk in the Privy Seal office, one of the major administrative departments of the English government. His avocation was the writing of poetry, and the 'Regement' of some 5,460 lines was his most ambitious effort. It was composed in 1411–12 for the benefit of the Prince of Wales who was later to become Henry V. The title, 'The Regement (that is, Rule) of Princes', or its Latin equivalent, 'De Regimine Principum', was not an uncommon one, having been used earlier by the famous Thomas Aquinas. The 'Regement' is largely derivative in its ideas, and Hoccleve did not attempt to present his thoughts as original. The main source was 'Chess Moralised' ('Liber de Ludo Scacchorum') by Jacob de Cessolis, and his other major sources were the ever popular 'Secretum Secretorum' and the 'De Regimine Principum' of Egidio Colonna, known also as Giles of Rome. Hoccleve was interested in the duties of a king rather than the way a king might accomplish his ends. There is more on what an ideal king should be than on what he should do. The 'Regement' is in effect a general plea for virtue in government that employs many popular sermon themes in its moralistic and religiously dogmatic counselling of Prince Henry.

Hoccleve's 'Regement' fits into an established tradition of concern for the behaviour of princes. It followed such works as Geoffrey Chaucer's *Tale of Melibee*, the seventh book of John Gower's 'Confession Amantis', the Wycliffite 'Tractatus de Regibus', the 'De Quadripartita Regis Specie', and Richard Ullerston's 'De Officio Militari'. It anticipated John Lydgate's

Thomas Hoccleve presenting 'The
Regement of Princes' to Henry,
Prince of Wales (later Henry V),
c. 1412–13 (British Library
Arundel Ms. 38, f. 37)

fragmentary translation of the 'Secretum Secretorum', two anonymous works known as the 'Tractatus de Regimine Principum ad Regem Henricum Sextum' and 'The III Consideracions Right Necesserye to the Good Governaunce of a Prince' (a mid-fifteenth-century English translation of a fourteenth-century French work), George Ashby's 'Active Policy of a Prince', and many other literary works.

Legal Literature

English common law, one of the great creations of English civilization, has produced a vast bank of literature. An honoured name in that genre is the judge Henry de Bracton (died 1268), author of 'De Legibus et Consuetudinibus Regni Angliae' ('Concerning the Laws and Customs of England'). Bracton's treatise was well organized and demonstrated thorough familiarity with the principles and practices of English and Roman law, and it gained quick acceptance. No books of such estimable quality as that of Bracton appeared soon after. Lawyers seemed to expend their energy in the practice of the law rather than in thoughtful written analysis of it. Then in the later Middle Ages there appeared Thomas Littleton and Sir John Fortescue. Littleton rose in the legal profession to become a judge of the central common law court of Common Pleas in 1466, a position he held until his death in 1481. Littleton's 'Tenures' was not written in Latin but in French, and dealt with the area of common law concerned with real property, an exceedingly important and complicated branch of law. Though a specialized work on land law, it has been recognized as one of the classic books of English legal literature.

The fame of Sir John Fortescue (died about 1479), who rose to be Chief Justice of the central common law court of King's Bench, was confirmed primarily by three treatises. He wrote the 'De Natura Legis Naturae' ('On the Nature of the Natural Law') between 1461 and 1463 to argue the claim of the House of Lancaster to the English throne through an appeal to natural law. It is both political theory and political partisan argument. Fortescue's 'De Laudibus Legum Angliae' ('In Praise of English Law') was written while in exile in France as a book of instruction for the also exiled son of Henry VI and Margaret of Anjou, Prince Edward of Lancaster, who was to die in the Battle of Tewkesbury in 1471. Fortescue discusses fundamental principles of English law in the book, distinguishes between English and civil (that is, Roman) law and asserts that English law is superior to all others. It is rich in legal detail, a lucid book of instruction for a layman, and it came to be widely used by lawyers. It was probably in 1470 that Fortescue composed the 'Monarchia' or 'The Governance of England'. A main theme in this work was the contrast between limited English government and absolutist French government, and he eloquently defended the rule of English law and the institution of Parliament.

A third fifteenth-century legal writer of distinction to be noted was a Doctor of Canon and Civil Law, William Lyndwood, who died in 1446 as Bishop of St David's. Lyndwood was active in royal service as a diplomat and Keeper of the Privy Seal in addition to being involved in the administration of the English Church. As a legal writer he made his mark in canon law. In Lyndwood's day the body of canon law of the western Church consisted of the 'Decretals of Gregory IX', promulgated in five books as an official collection of binding canon law in 1234; the 'Liber Sextus' of 1298 and the 'Clementinae', which was officially added in 1317. In addition to this universally binding body of canon law there existed rules and customs of regions and localities which were considered to be valid so long as they did not contradict the laws of the universal Church. Archbishops and bishops as legislators could, as it were, add appendices to the universal law of the Church, but the Pope was the sovereign legislator for the Church as a whole. It was to the legislation of the archbishops of Canterbury, effected in provincial councils, that Lyndwood directed his attention. Beginning with the legislation of Archbishop Stephen Langton in the Council of Oxford of 1222 and continuing to the legislation of Archbishop Henry Chichele in his own day, Lyndwood gathered, organized, and digested what he believed to be the most important and useful of the provincial statutes of fourteen archbishops. This work was brought to completion before a journey on diplomatic business to Portugal in 1422. Upon his return to England, he began writing a glossary on the statutes he had collected, relating them carefully to the common law of the Church. The glossary was no brief commentary; it exceeded many times over in length the collection of provincial canons. This work of scholarship, informed by long experience as a practitioner of canon law in the archdiocese of Canterbury and dedicated to Archbishop Chichele, is known as the 'Provinciale, seu constitutiones Angliae'. It was a practical and useful book, and Lyndwood provided it with an index to make it still more serviceable.

Were we to wonder if Lyndwood was pleased with the 'Provinciale', it should be noted that he directed in his will that a copy be safely chained for ready consultation in the Chapel of St

Stephen at Westminster where he wished to be buried. Interestingly, in the nineteenth century the body of an ecclesiastic with a crosier across his chest was accidentally revealed by workmen in St Stephen's Chapel, and almost certainly it was that of Lyndwood. The crosier is to be seen in the British Museum, and we have drawings made by a nineteenth-century antiquarian before the body was interred at Westminster Abbey to suggest the appearance of England's most distinguished medieval canonist.

Alliterative Poetry

After a period of dearth, unrhymed alliterative poetry reappeared in the middle of the fourteenth century with such examples as 'William of Palerne' and 'Winner and Waster'. The movement continued with the production of such works as the 'Destruction of Troy', the 'Siege of Jerusalem', and an epic portrayal of the deeds of King Arthur, the 'Morte Arthure', which was later used as a source by Sir Thomas Malory. This alliterative movement is memorable in particular for four glorious anonymous works. One of these is the chivalric romance 'Sir Gawain and the Green Knight', two are homiletic poems, namely 'Purity' and 'Patience', and the dream-vision 'Pearl'. These four works have come down to the present because of a single manuscript written in about 1400. The long alliterative poem 'Piers Plowman' attributed to William Langland, by contrast, exists in three versions, known today as 'A' (1360s), 'B' (1370s), and 'C' (1380s). 'Piers Plowman' achieved considerable circulation, and was in part an attack upon the political and ecclesiastical establishments.

Spectacles

A handy technological innovation that was available in the later Middle Ages to those able to afford them was spectacles, and for people needing them they would have been a boon in the pursuit of the pleasures of reading.

A pair of spectacle frames that have been dated to about 1440 were found in the mid-1970s during excavations in the City of London at Trig Lane, and they are now in the collection of the Museum of London. This example was made in two pieces, each cut (it would appear) from the flat posterior surface of the metacarpal bone of a bull's front leg. Each piece of bone frame is a circle with a handle-like extension. The frames are not complete, and the circular lenses, which would have been about 30 mm in diameter are missing, but the two pieces are fastened together with an iron rivet through the ends of the two handle extensions. The two pieces, then, would pivot on the rivet, and could be clamped on the nose of the wearer to hold the lenses before the wearer's eyes. A similar pair of riveted spectacles were carved on a gargoyle in St Martin's Church, Salisbury, and another example in art would be the fresco portrait of Cardinal Ugone, dated 1352, in the Chapter House of the church of St Nicholas at Treviso in Italy. Three sculptured figures, dating from the first decade of the sixteenth century, wearing spectacles of a bow type in which the frames are a single piece with an arch over the nose of the wearer are to be seen in Henry VII's Chapel in Westminster Abbey.

The Trig Lane spectacles have generated some plausible but unproven speculation. It is supposed that the lenses were plano-convex, and that they were used for magnifying. It is also supposed that by bringing the two parts of the frame together so that they overlapped, it would not only be convenient for storage but the two lenses could also be used in combination. Furthermore, it is speculated that the three holes near the lense in each side of the spectacles were not mere decoration, but could function like 'pinholes' to further assist the vision of the user.

The invention of spectacles is credited to Italy in the later decades of the thirteenth century. This useful invention soon appeared in England, and spectacles, probably of the riveted type, appear in the inventory made of the possessions of Bishop Walter

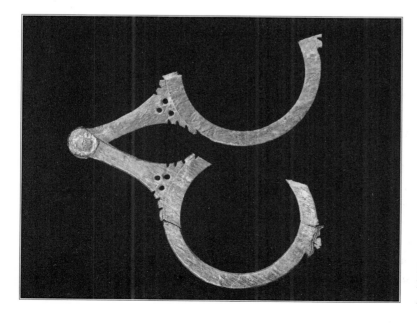

Bone spectacle frames from Trig Lane, London (Museum of London Archaeology Service)

Stapeldon of Exeter after he had been killed by a London mob in 1326. How quickly spectacles became common is not yet known, but if the frames were not made of precious metal they seem not to have been too costly a luxury. It is likely that most spectacles were imported from the Low Countries, and the earliest record found thus far of a spectacle maker in England places him in Southwark in the late 1450s. The Worshipful Company of Spectacle Makers of London did not appear on the scene until the seventeenth century.

TWO

Art, Architecture, Music and Dancing

The products of artists and craftsmen created tension in the medieval social fabric. There were those who pointed to the danger of idolatry, noting that simple folk might not understand that a painting or sculptured image of a saint was just a symbolic representation and was designed to stimulate devotion to the saint in heaven, and not to be itself an object of veneration and prayer. Others would point to the resources expended in the creation of mere material things when there were hungry, needy, and homeless people all around. Charity, some argued, should be directed to helping the unfortunate, not to creating artefacts for aesthetic delight. To counter such opinions, the idea of visual representations to teach the unlettered was repeatedly put forward. No justification was offered for the creative urges, both lofty and mundane, of artist and patron. The creations of artists and craftsmen were appealing and gave pleasure to many, even if they did not have absolute theological respectability.

Artists themselves got little credit for their genius. The creative gift was assumed to have come from God, and God was thanked. The collaborative nature of much medieval creative art also meant that the contribution of the individual artist was easily obscured in the group effort. The artist was a craftsman, and the craftsman was an artist and the skill resided in his mastery of the production techniques of whatever he might be making. Originality did not especially appeal to the medieval aesthetic, but fine craftsmanship, quality materials, and colour did. Medieval art did, of course, display originality, and even humour. Consider the mazer, or drinking bowl, in the shape of a swan owned by Corpus Christi College, Cambridge, which was made probably in the second half of the fourteenth century, and is a trick device that can spill its contents into the lap of the unwary drinker who tilts it to his lips. Medieval art was Christian art, and was intended for the glorification of God, not the artist. Moreover, the fame or credit for the creation of a work of art was inclined to be visited upon the patron with a deep purse, not the artisans who carried out the plan.

The greatest patron of artists and craftsmen in the later Middle Ages in England was the Crown. Masons, carvers, carpenters and painters would be obvious craftsmen for employment by the Crown, but goldsmiths engraved seal matrices and the dies for striking coins, while embroiderers provided fine cloth, limners illustrated books and stationers sold them. The arts were interdependent, and complemented one another. Artists who were skilled in a particular craft would be accustomed to consult and collaborate with craftsmen in other media, as the building of a church, for example, would require masons, woodcarvers, painters, glaziers, carpenters, and perhaps others as well, such as tilers. The place where most people would have been exposed to the greatest amount of art would have been the parish church, which would have been decorated through the efforts of every sort of artist and craftsman.

Architecture

People living through the eras of creativity we are examining did not know such terms as Romanesque and Gothic for architectural styles. The term Romanesque (Roman-like) is used to indicate the artistic and architectural style from the disintegration of the Roman Empire until the development of the Gothic style in the mid-twelfth century, and varied greatly over time and place. The old style did not suddenly disappear with the development of the new, but the slow shift from Romanesque to Gothic is one of the great stylistic changes of the medieval period. Romanesque architecture displayed massiveness and volume and, while flavoured by the Roman past, was not simply a continuation or imitation of Roman building forms. A substantial building to which the term Romanesque would be applied has thick walls containing few windows to carry the weight of the building, together with heavy columns and rounded arches. The columns and arches along the sides of the nave of Durham Cathedral, built around 1200, display these features, although the stone vaulting of

The columns and arches along the sides of the nave of Durham Cathedral exemplify features of the Romanesque style, while the stone vaulting suggests the Gothic style (Conway Library, Courtauld Institute of Art; © Canon M.H. Ridgway)

the nave is better described as Gothic. The shallow, rounded arches characteristic of the Romanesque style transfer weight and stress outward and require thick walls for support. The higher, pointed arches characteristic of the Gothic style transfer weight and stress downward and allow for lighter walls that can be opened up with more windows. The walls of a Gothic building are characteristically given additional support from the outside by the technical innovation of the flying buttress, which further eases the weight on the walls. Ribbed vaulting is another typical engineering feature of the Gothic style and delicacy, detail, and light are qualities associated with it.

In the later Middle Ages, it is clear that architects pursued the twin goals of creating uniform interior spaces in the buildings they designed, and using decorative schemes to give unity and to be part

The evocative ruins of Rievaulx Abbey clearly suggest the horizontal lines characteristic of Early English Gothic (© RCHME Crown Copyright)

of the function of the architecture. A fully complete and decorated Gothic building would truly be a mirror of the world, a *speculum naturale*. A building which reflected the creative powers of God for all to see was a piece of public art, a mechanism for the instruction of the viewer, and an expression of the Christian assumptions that shaped the way people saw and understood the world they lived in.

EARLY ENGLISH

No style of art remains permanently satisfying. It is to be expected, then, that even within the style we know as Gothic there were changes and developments, and it assists us in our understanding of the pleasure medievals derived from the art around them if we follow the guidance of art historians who have reflected upon Gothic art and categorized its phases in England. The first phase of Gothic in England, unfolding for about a century after 1200, is called Early English. The earliest cathedrals built in this style, and both in fact were begun somewhat before 1200, were Wells and Lincoln. A characteristic to be seen in Early English is an emphasis

Opposite: The Lady Chapel at the east end of Lincoln Cathedral contains the ruin of the shrine of St Hugh (© RCHME Crown Copyright)

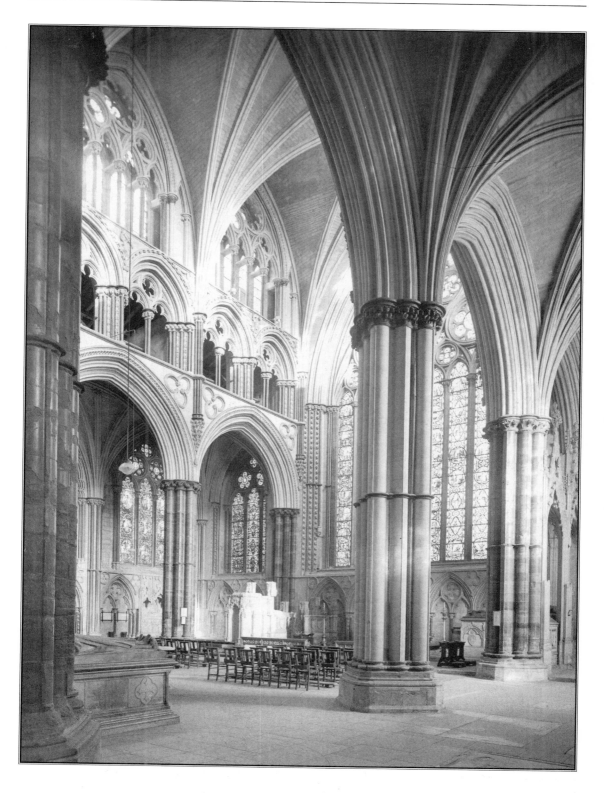

upon the horizontal line. For example, at Lincoln Cathedral within the nave the viewer's eye is drawn by the horizontal line emphasized along the walls at the base of the arches of the triforium and clerestory. The strong horizontal lines of the triple-tiered choir and the steady march of simple pointed arches to be seen in the ruins of the Cistercian abbey of Rievaulx in Yorkshire offer another example. The star vaulting (with short ribs added between the main ribs to produce star shapes) in the nave of Lincoln Cathedral is another characteristic of the Early English phase of Gothic, although not so defining as the horizontal lines. Star vaulting would continue to develop until it reached its apogee in the middle of the fourteenth century at Exeter Cathedral, which boasts the longest uninterrupted Gothic vault in the world.

Wells Cathedral, like Lincoln, marks the beginning of building in the Early English style of Gothic (Conway Library, Courtauld Institute of Art)

The vaulting is but one of the compelling features of the Ely Cathedral Lady Chapel, built in the Decorated phase of Gothic (© RCHME Crown Copyright)

DECORATED

The Early English gave way to what is known as the Decorated phase of Gothic and, as the name given to it implies, decoration is the primary feature. This style ran to about 1350, and its characteristics are such things as traceried windows, curves and angles as opposed to straight lines, and decoration on all surfaces. The choir of the church at Tewkesbury Abbey is a fine example of windows of the Decorated style and the geometrical tracery of the windows of the Lady Chapel at Wells Cathedral, built around 1320, offer another good example. At Ely Cathedral the Octagon, a timber vault and lantern spanning the crossing of nave and transepts built by the royal carpenter William Hurley, and the Lady Chapel are other examples of Decorated. The Lady Chapel at Ely is a flurry of decoration: sculptures once painted in bright colours, pinnacles, gables, tracery, and ogee arches. The polygonal ground-plan of the Chapter House at Southwell Minster in Nottinghamshire affords a good example of the use of angles, with one result being the oblique play of light through the windows.

PERPENDICULAR

The Decorated style of Gothic was followed in the middle of the fourteenth century by what is called Perpendicular, the final flowering of the Gothic age. The style derives its name from the characteristic slender, straight, vertically subdivided piers. Arches are more cusped than pointed, and windows are virtually high rectangles subdivided by vertical tracery with geometric designs at the top. There is an element of stark simplicity and restrained dignity about the Perpendicular. The wide arches and large windows give to a building in the Perpendicular style a sense of space and light. The nave of Canterbury Cathedral would be a familiar example of late fourteenth-century Perpendicular, and an excellent example from the following century would be the chapel of King's College, Cambridge, founded by Henry VI (reigned 1422–61). At Oxford the Divinity School (now part of the Bodleian Library) or the quadrangle of Magdalen College would be other familiar examples. In the north of England, York Minster offers imposing examples of fifteenth-century architecture and craftsmanship, although the choir of the minster begun in the 1360s was the first Perpendicular building in the north. Both west towers of the minster, together with the central tower and the central lantern from which it rises, were constructed in the course

The Divinity School at Oxford is an example of the Perpendicular phase of Gothic (Conway Library, Courtauld Institute of Art)

of the fifteenth century. Within the minster, the stone screen with its statues of fifteen English kings from William the Conqueror to Henry VI is a regal example of free-standing sculpture. The Great East Window, dating from the first years of the century and glazed by John Thornton of Coventry, is a treasure because of its colourful beauty as well as its sheer size, for it is the largest single medieval stained glass window to survive in England. It would have been a callous worshipper indeed in York Minster about the middle of the fifteenth century who failed to be both delighted and struck with reverential awe when gazing at that window in the bright light of a clear summer morning. Enough additional stained glass from the fifteenth century survives in such places as the parish churches of York and Norwich and Oxford colleges to impress us with the importance of that art in adding a dimension of pleasure and beauty to worship.

As well as collegiate buildings and cathedral churches like Canterbury and York, many parish churches were also built in the Perpendicular style as expressions of faith and displays of wealth and current architectural fashion. A few of the very many examples still to be seen would be Long Melford, Lavenham, and Southwold, all in Suffolk; or Salle in Norfolk; St Mary Redcliffe, Bristol; or, in Gloucestershire, St John the Baptist, Cirencester, Northleach church, and St James, Chipping Camden. A late and magnificent expression of Perpendicular is Henry VII's chapel in Westminster Abbey, built early in the sixteenth century. The chapel also exemplifies the English invention of pendant vaulting, which seems to hang in the air. English architects had long been drawn aesthetically to the development of patterns in vault ribbing. Similar to the star vault was the net vault, in which the vault ribs were built so as to form triangle and lozenge shapes rather than stars. As construction techniques matured with the increase in the number of ribs, the ribs and webbing between the ribs were combined into a single structure of stone, and vaults could be given various shapes. This resulted in fan vaulting sometime after the middle of the fourteenth century, a style of vaulting ultimately constructed so that it seemed to squeeze out cones of decorated stone towards the floor, such as are seen in Henry VII's chapel. The vault of the Henry VII Chapel is extremely ornate, with deeply cut tracery and long pendants drooping from the centre of each cone. The decorative fan vaulting is in fact held in place structurally by transverse arches, invisible above the tracery.

Sculpture in the Perpendicular era could be idealistic or realistic. The tomb effigy of Edward III is an idealized representation of a wise old king, while that of his queen, Philippa of Hainault, who died in 1369, is an effigy taken from life. In fact, Philippa commissioned the white marble effigy for her tomb two years before her death, and it is the earliest realistic effigy portrayal of a person in England. Effigies tended, like that of Edward III, to be stereotyped representations of the qualities of the person being memorialized.

Edward and Philippa's grandson, Richard II, who succeeded Edward III, was an enthusiastic patron of the arts. He supplied the money for the completion of the nave of Westminster Abbey, which had been long in the building and then, having a lofty notion of his regality, turned to work on a secular hall that would complement Westminster Abbey. The Great Hall in the Palace of Westminster stood close by the abbey, and had been built by William II at the end of the eleventh century. Westminster Hall was reworked under the patronage of Richard II to be a glorious symbol of kingship. Windows in the Perpendicular style were added, and other changes were made under the leadership of two outstanding figures in the history of English building arts: the king's master mason, Henry Yevele, and the king's carpenter, Hugh Herland. Herland's oak hammer-beam roof is a masterpiece of the highest order, and the earliest example surviving in England. It is constructed with support braces fixed into the existing walls, upon which stand the hammer-beams projecting horizontally into the open space of the hall, and the main arch braces rest upon the hammer-beams.

A favoured motif of fifteenth-century art was the fate of the soul after death which explains the fashion for founding chantries, where chaplains would say Masses and other offices for the contented repose of the souls of those individuals designated by the founders. The notion was often reflected in art that even persons enjoying the utmost eminence in this life would, just like the most lowly of mortals, be reduced by death to food for worms. The Dance of Death (*danse macabre*) whereby all are equally brought down was a theme of art and literature. Paintings of the Last Judgement, and funerary effigies of skeletons and decaying corpses, all suggest perhaps a preoccupation with, or at least the devotion of considerable mental energy to thoughts of death. One of the two effigies of Alice, Duchess of Suffolk, made in the 1470s for Ewelme church, is a representation of a distinguished elderly lady, and the other is of the same woman as a decaying corpse. The tomb of Sir John Golafre in Fyfield, Berkshire, displays a shrouded skeleton, as do the paired memorial brasses of Richard and Cecilie Howard in

The Dance of Death: a vivid representation of the three living and the three dead kings, early fourteenth century (British Library Arundel Ms. 83, f. 127)

Aylsham, Norfolk, and Ralph Hamsterley is represented in his brass at Oddington, Oxfordshire, as a shrouded skeleton infested with worms.

When facing death or other crises, the Virgin Mary was thought of as the best of intercessors. The Virgin as Annunciate evoked an attitude of humility in a powerful way. The chantries of Henry V at Westminster Abbey and Richard Beauchamp, Earl of Warwick at St Mary's, Warwick, are dedicated to the Annunciation. It is an iconographic curiosity concerning the Virgin that the artistic scene of St Anne teaching her daughter, the young Virgin Mary, to read was invented in England in the fourteenth century, and never became common in other parts of Christendom. With the increasing popularity of chantries, the interior of parish churches where chantries were established underwent changes. For example, the area set aside for the chantry might be isolated by a screen, and an altar would be put in place for the chantry priest to perform his duties. Carpenters were employed in many churches in the course of the fifteenth century to carve rood screens, that is, screens decorated with a crucifix to separate the nave and choir. Rood screens were not only carved of wood or stone, but were also commonly painted and gilded. Wooden ceilings were much more usual than stone vaults in parish churches, and after about the middle of the fifteenth century the style of angel roofs developed, which were hammer-beam roofs with a carved angel mounted at the end of each hammer. Wooden ceilings might themselves be painted.

Artful Craftsmanship

Goldsmithing ranked higher in prestige than painting in England during the later Middle Ages. St Dunstan, the tenth-century archbishop of Canterbury, had a reputation as a worker in precious metal, and when the Goldsmiths' Company of London was founded in 1327, St Dunstan became the patron saint. The seals which were used to give authenticity to documents survive in considerable numbers, and are a testimony to the engraving skills of goldsmiths, but very few of the objects created by late medieval goldsmiths have escaped being melted down.

Another medium for engraving was memorial brasses. The leading English workshop for memorial brasses in the late fourteenth century was in the churchyard of St Paul's, London. The marbler, literally one who works in marble, would have a variety of designs for his customers to select from, or customers could have a distinctive design produced. The memorial brass of Abbot Thomas de la Mare, engraved in about 1360 for St Alban's Abbey, exemplifies the finest craftsmanship in this medium. Memorial brasses increased in popularity in the fifteenth century, at least in part because they were less expensive than three-dimensional tomb effigies.

The first luxury art exported from England to gain fame was *opus anglicanum*, the production of which was centred mainly on London. Music and alabaster carving would in the fifteenth century join in repute with this fine, silk embroidery. *Opus anglicanum* was a desirable luxury because of its beauty, the preciousness of the materials, and the fine workmanship. Ecclesiastical garments, either as vestments for the clergy or altarpieces, provided most of the demand for the work, but there are records of secular commissions. Examples which have survived, such as those in the British Museum or the famous 'Leopards of England' in the Musée de Cluny in Paris, are mostly ecclesiastical. Styles in colour and design changed over time, but the method of stitching did not. Silk threads of many colours and threads of precious metal wound around a silk thread core were attached to the embroidered surface by the method called 'underside couching'. In this method a piece of gold thread, for instance, would be placed against the backing cloth, often velvet or heavy silk, according to the design being created, and then attached by means of a linen thread coming from the underside of the backing cloth, looping over the gold thread, and then running back through the background cloth to anchor it. The tiny loops of linen couching thread are invisible from the surface of the embroidery. When coloured silk threads were used in the embroidery design, a split stitch was used.

A virtual industry in alabaster sculpture grew up around a few quarries, especially near Nottingham, in the later Middle Ages, and alabaster figures were sold around England and even abroad. Alabaster is gypsum, a softer material than marble, and this moderately translucent stone lent itself nicely to stone effigies, images of saints, and altarpieces. The effigies of Henry IV and Queen Joan in Canterbury Cathedral are among the best-known examples, and a vast collection of alabaster carvings is to be seen in the Victoria and Albert Museum. Smaller alabaster carvings were frequently mounted in wood frames and were used in private dwellings as well as in chapels and churches. It was the practice to paint and gild alabaster figures, so their appearance was vivid and colourful rather than cool and pale.

People would have seen more of the work of woodcarvers than of carvers in alabaster. Choir stalls, roof bosses and beams, screens, pews, pulpits, misericords, and many ordinary implements of life were enhanced by the woodcarver's skill. Some fine examples of roofs still exist: there is the elaborately decorated roof over Weare Giffard Hall, Devonshire, the Law Library at Exeter, and the great hall at Eltham Palace in Kent. Eltham Palace was the major domestic building project of Edward IV, and the design of the great hall is credited to the king's chief carpenter Edmund Graveley.

The collective nature of some artistry can be nicely illustrated in the process of producing an illuminated manuscript. It is often thought that this category of craftsmanship was the work of monks, although monks were not especially active as craftsmen because their time was considered better employed in the work of God. The exception to this general rule would be in the production of books, and even here monks were less and less involved after the late twelfth century. The preparation of the animal skin was a technical process that required knowledge and skill, and the ink had to be made, pigments acquired and, if the skin was to become a page in a book, all the materials, tools, and skills of the binder would be brought into play. A collective decision would be reached initially about the layout of the page. The scribe would then write in the text, and hand it on to the painters for illustration. Any gold would be put on first, followed by colours and highlighting. Several painters, under the direction of a master, might work on a single picture, decorated letter, or marginal illustration. The page might then be passed on to the binder. The involvement of so many hands in the bringing of a piece of leather from animal skin to finished work of art would be multiplied dramatically in the labours required for the creation of something huge like a parish church.

In the era of Decorated architecture, manuscripts were also being produced with an abundance of painted marginalia, such as those produced by the painters known as the East Anglian school, of which the early pages of the St Omer Psalter would be an example. The Luttrell Psalter, which affords wonderful insights into everyday life through the work of its decorative artists, was done around 1340. The wall-paintings on dry plaster from about 1330 in the Great Chamber (or Painted Chamber) of Longthorpe Tower near Peterborough in Northamptonshire are another expression of a lively attitude towards decorative pictures.

A detail from a wall-painting at Longthorpe Tower, depicting King Reason and the Wheel of the Five Senses. These are represented by the animals around the wheel (Conway Library, Courtauld Institute of Art)

Whether the Longthorpe paintings are characteristic of early fourteenth-century house decoration for those in comfortable economic circumstances or not is impossible to know, for they are unique survivors, and they are also the most complete set of medieval mural paintings in England. The surviving fragments of the wall-paintings done in an oil medium from the royal chapel of St Stephen in the Palace of Westminster, dating from the 1350s, show wall-paintings in a different context. These paintings are two-dimensional decorations, undisturbed by the bother of perspective. The wall-paintings in the cottages in Silver Street, Ely, or the religious wall-paintings in 68 Piccott's End, Hemel Hempstead, suggest that people of more modest means were able to realize their desires to surround themselves with decoration and colour. More than half the medieval wall-paintings known to survive in England have been found in the second half of the twentieth century.

Toward the end of the fourteenth century there was a revival of the thirteenth-century fashion of having lavishly decorated service books for use in churches. One example is the missal that Abbot Nicholas Litlyngton of Westminster had made for his abbey church. The 'Litlyngton Missal', still in the possession of Westminster Abbey, was completed in the mid-1380s, and was the work of a professional scribe, Thomas Preston, and a group of anonymous illuminators. Another splendid example is the Sherborne Missal (or Mass-book), made for the Benedictine abbey at Sherborne in Dorset in around 1400. The scribe was a Benedictine, John Whas, and the illuminator was a Dominican friar, John Siferwas. Siferwas is known to have been the master of a workshop of manuscript painters, as was his contemporary Herman Scheere, who may have been a Carmelite friar. Scheere's work included the psalter and book of hours created under the patronage of John, Duke of Bedford (died 1435) (see p. 58).

Artful craftsmen did not normally write about their work. A German monk named Theophilus wrote 'De Diversis Artibus' (Of Diverse Arts) in the early twelfth century, and from the perspective of posterity it is fortunate that it has survived. It might be called a craftsman's manual, and such a work was a rarity because craftsmen learned their skills through apprenticeship rather than by studying books, and so were under no particular compulsion to write about their methods. Theophilus' book, which was written for the uninformed, offers rare and useful insights into the methods of medieval craftsmen. There is no evidence that this work had wide circulation in England, but the things he described, such as metalworking techniques, were broadly similar all over Europe. The theoretical treatise on architecture by the Roman writer Vitruvius, 'De Architectura', was known in England, and some medieval copies still survive. Another book, 'Pictor in Carmine', was a practical book of iconographical designs which would have been useful to painters of walls or manuscripts, designers of stained glass windows, or those wishing to commission such works.

Music

The music of medieval England must not be approached as if it were isolated from music in the rest of Christendom. The Church, especially, encouraged the development of music unhindered by political boundaries. Aristocratic courtly and chivalric culture, of which music was a part, also ignored political boundaries, and some skill in music was expected of an aristocrat.

Music was integral to the fabric of life, and because the Church was so central to life, we should expect much of medieval music to be of a sacred character. There was, however, what we must call secular music as well as sacred music, but very little notated secular music survives from medieval England. Aristocratic patronage was directed to religious music in England, whereas in France and Italy, for example, patronage was being given to secular lyric poetry and to secular music reflecting courtly culture. In England, secular music was rarely notated before the thirteenth century. It was fairly simple music, and was part of a lively oral song tradition in which improvisation was a matter of routine. Work-songs to ease the performance of tasks were a part of life. The Privy Seal clerk and poet, Thomas Hoccleve, complained in the early fifteenth century of the difficulty of being a scribe, saying that artificers could sing and talk while they worked, but not so clerks like himself:

> We stowpe and stare up-on the shepes skyn,
> And keepe must our song and wordes in.

As secular music became more complex and as people wanted to conserve repertories, it began to be written down. Pricksongs were songs written with notation as well as words, and books of pricksongs were becoming increasingly common in the age of Thomas Hoccleve.

Most secular lyrics sung in medieval England were never written down. 'Sumer is icumen in' is one of the rare survivals, and it

'Sumer is icumen in': one of the most famous of English medieval musical compositions (British Library Harley Ms. 978, f. 11v)

surely must be the most famous of English medieval musical compositions. The date of this composition, preserved in the British Library (Harley Ms. 978), is a matter of controversy. A modern English version of the text would be: 'Summer has come, loudly sing cuckoo. Now is the seed growing and the meadow flowering and the forest springing to life. Sing cuckoo. The ewe bleats after the lamb, the cow lows after the calf, the bullock leaps, the buck breaks wind. Merrily sing cuckoo. Cuckoo, cuckoo, well dost thou sing cuckoo, never cease now.' The 6/8 rhythm is characteristic of the church music being written in the last quarter of the thirteenth century. Unfortunately, not enough evidence survives about English musical culture around the end of the thirteenth century to be able to say how typical or unique 'Sumer is icumen in' happens to be.

Church music tended to be more complex than secular music, and that together with the desire to perform it as flawlessly as possible in a sacred setting, encouraged notation, as would the amount of music in circulation. Little importance was placed on authorship, and most music before about 1400 is anonymous; thereafter the habit of attaching a name to a composition grew slowly. Much music seems not to have been produced as a creative art, but to fill the needs of a choir-master or singer or instrumentalist in need of a repertory.

Music as a distraction from the activities of life was not a part of the medieval legacy. Rather than using aesthetics to evaluate music, the medieval mind would have given perhaps greater weight to function, that is, how a piece of music was used in the liturgy of the Church or how effectively it announced the arrival of some noble personage. Music was viewed more as a potentially powerful method of communication than as an autonomous art-form.

The Minstrels' Gallery at Exeter Cathedral, constructed in around 1350. It depicts twelve angels, playing contemporary instruments: a citole, bagpipes, recorder, fiddle, harp, trumpet, primitive organ, gittern, tambourine and shawm (The Dean and Chapter of Exeter Cathedral)

To take some instances, it was accepted by medical practitioners and medical theorists that medicine and music intersected. Music could alter moods, could aid the healing of wounds by stimulating the tranquility of the patient's mind, and might even be an antidote to poison. If joy was the cure for melancholy, then music therapy was a source of joy. To listen to loud or discordant music during a meal was simply to invite indigestion. Music that aroused ire was prescribed for patients with paralysis. If body and soul were united by a musical harmony, as Boethius suggested, the proper sort of music could be selected to benefit every human activity. The authoritative treatise 'De Musica' by the late Roman scholar and political leader Boethius, figured not only in the curriculum of faculties of arts in medieval universities, but also in the curriculum of faculties of medicine. Music was one of the seven liberal arts, and thus central to the intellectual world. The association of the beat of the pulse with music is readily appreciated. (Medieval physicians took the pulse either at the wrist or at the brachial artery in the upper arm.) Proper bodily harmony was vital to such a procedure as a phlebotomy, and here music and medicine and astrology would all intersect. In hunting, the music of the horns informed the hunting party of the stage of the hunt. It was also suggested by the fourteenth-century 'Sir Gawain and the Green Knight' that the more rhythmic the progress of the hunt and kill, the more healthful to eat would be the prey. The *shivaree* was the stimulating, erotic music played for a newly married couple as they went off to bed, and it was believed that the music would aid and promote the consummation of the marriage. Medieval music was not intended for abstract aesthetics.

PLAINCHANT

Melody and rhythm were of paramount importance in medieval music. Most medieval music was structured around a single melodic line, that is, it was monophonic. Beginning in the thirteenth century some composers branched off into polyphony, in which two or more lines of melody would be heard at the same time and so combined that they would be pleasing to the ear when heard simultaneously. Throughout the Middle Ages, monophonic music would have been that most commonly heard. The emphasis in medieval music upon rhythm is an aspect that differs from later music, which tends to substitute tone for rhythm, as it tends to substitute harmony for the melody of medieval music.

The development of medieval music was profoundly influenced

by the Church, and plainchant or plain-song, the monophonic music sung in churches, was the principal form of church music. In the public worship of the Church, most texts were sung rather than spoken, because the practice made the words more audible and because it added dignity. The plainchant repertory of some churches gained influential eminence, such as the Salisbury Use and the Use of York.

Plainchant notation appeared around AD 800, and probably contributed to the constant growth of plainchant repertory. The expansion of existing pieces of plainchant was known as troping. The term troping was borrowed from rhetoric, and in essence it was the adding of words and music to the existing plainchant. An example of a new form of plainchant was the invention of the 'sequence' in the mid-ninth century. Sequences were poems set to melodies, and this musical form encouraged collaboration between poet and composer. Another way of enhancing church services was to introduce new, non-liturgical pieces of music into the service, and in late-medieval England these pieces were called *conductus*.

POLYPHONY

As an art form, polyphony probably began in Carolingian lands in the ninth century as a means of adorning the plainchant used in worship services. Monastic communities were especially important in contributing to the development and spread of polyphony. The earliest form of polyphony for singing in church services, now known as organum, added a voice a fifth or a fourth below the plainchant melody which was sung simultaneously. The principal plainchant melody was known as the *cantus firmus*, or fixed melody, and the voice that sang it came to be called the tenor, or holding voice. The term 'tenor' therefore described function and did not come to designate a voice pitch until the sixteenth century. As polyphony developed, other melodies were added around the *cantus firmus*, which we might think of by such terms as soprano, alto, or bass. By the late twelfth century polyphonic music was spreading out of the Church into the secular world, and the earliest form of secular polyphony was the motet. The motet was created in France, and it had greater prominence there than it did in England. In essence, the motet is a song made up of several interwoven voices with the tenor as the foundation voice. Each voice had either its own text or its own syllable division, but all voices would sound together in consonance. The motet grew to be both musically and textually complex, for the different voices sometimes sang different words. The motet, while it became a secular form of polyphony, was almost always in Latin and for liturgical use, and was a prominent musical form in England by around 1300. Polyphony also made its way into secular music by way of improvisation during performances. An Oxford student from Holland in the middle of the fourteenth century, Johannes Boen, commented on the English fondness for impromptu polyphony in folk music.

There is no certain indication that any distinctly English style of polyphonic music developed before the middle of the thirteenth century, and a fair amount of polyphony, in fragmentary form, has survived from the late thirteenth and early fourteenth centuries. English music emerged slowly from the broad European musical context known as the *ars antiqua*. An earlier form of polyphony, known as the *organum purum* declined in the thirteenth century, and thereafter the word *discantus* (discant or descant) comes to be used for any kind of polyphony. The term 'English discant' is used for the three-part polyphony of the fourteenth and fifteenth centuries.

For late medieval English music the Old Hall Manuscript is an important document. It was produced in the early fifteenth century, and takes its name from the library of St Edmund's College, Old Hall, near Ware, where it was once kept; it is now in the British Library (Additional Ms. 57950). The manuscript contains the works of at least twenty-five composers, and is the largest surviving source in England for early fifteenth-century church music. The three basic polyphonic forms found in the music of the Old Hall Manuscript are chanson, English discant, and motet. These forms dominated English, and European, music generally during the first half of the fifteenth century.

English music went through such a creative period in the early fifteenth century that it gained an audience abroad. Among the most important figures in this time of intense musical activity were Lionel Power (died 1445) and John Dunstable (died 1453). Power first comes into the historical record as the instructor of the choristers in the chapel of the household of Thomas, Duke of Clarence (died 1421), the brother of Henry V. Power's compositions are included in the Old Hall Manuscript, and one theory is that the manuscript was compiled for Clarence's chapel. The course of Power's career after the duke was killed in the French war is not well documented, but he did have an association with the music of Canterbury Cathedral. Dunstable also had association with the Royal House of Lancaster, being in the service of Joan of Navarre, wife of Henry IV, and later of Humphrey, Duke of Gloucester, brother of Henry V. The compositions which can be

A Gloria, to be sung during Mass (British Library Additional Ms. 57950, f. 22)

ascribed to these two composers are almost all for sacred Latin texts.

John Dunstable was a noteworthy composer of votive antiphons, the first example of which is found in the Old Hall Manuscript. It is a liturgical form consisting of the antiphon, a versicle and response, and a prayer. The votive antiphon flourished until the Reformation, and was a Latin poem (or sometimes a prose text) sung or recited to honour an object of devotion or a saint, as Dunstable's 'O Crux Gloriosa' honours the Holy Cross or his 'Beata Mater' honours the Virgin Mary. The votive antiphon grew out of the custom of turning a devotional Latin poem into a polyphonic conductus. Polyphony was used for services other than the Mass. In fact, the one Magnificat by Dunstable to survive is the earliest English musical setting by an identifiable composer.

The Old Hall Manuscript is, for the most part, a collection of polyphonic music to be sung during Mass. Nearly all Masses had texts in common for those items in the Mass known as the Ordinary: Kyrie, Gloria, Credo, Sanctus, and Agnus Dei. Power and other composers developed the idea of relating all five elements of the Ordinary to one another musically, and in doing so created what is known as the cyclic Mass. The method employed was to use one cantus firmus as the base setting for all five elements, rather as in the manner of the motet. A single plainchant cantus firmus provided a basic unity for the music of the cyclic Mass, but did not hinder the free development of the music from that aesthetically satisfying base setting. The idea of the cyclic Mass was picked up as a composition technique in England and on the Continent. The cyclic Mass continued to be used by such English composers as Walter Frye (died about 1475), John Plummer (died 1484), and Robert Fayrfax (died 1521), until the Latin rite disappeared in the Reformation era in 1559. A more general aspect of late medieval English music that broadly influenced European music were the qualities of euphony and a fullness of sound.

The isorhythmic (that is, same rhythm) motet had a brief popularity beginning in the later fourteenth century, which largely culminated with the talent of John Dunstable. This was similar to any other medieval motet in that it was held together by the cantus firmus, and above the tenor a duplum and a triplum declaimed complimentary but different texts on the general theme of the motet. There might even have been a contra-tenor singing in a fourth voice and sharing the tenor's range. The eleven isorhythmic motets we have from Dunstable were seemingly all written for specific feast days. Another English composer of this intellectually demanding musical form was John Benet (died about 1450), from whom three isorhythmic motets survive.

INSTRUMENTS

A great variety of musical instruments was available in medieval England. The harp was a common stringed instrument, plucked with the nails. As many as twenty-five strings, usually made of sheep-gut, were usual, and the instrument made a brighter sound than the rich-sounding modern harp. The psaltery was also an open-stringed instrument. The metal strings were plucked with a quill plectrum held in each hand, and there was a string for each note. It is thought that the harpsichord, which appeared late in the Middle Ages, was developed as a mechanized psaltery. The psaltery itself certainly developed into the dulcimer at a later stage. The lute, like the psaltery, was plucked with a quill plectrum, and the gittern was basically a small lute. The gittern might be considered the northern equivalent of the southern European guitar. The citole, which was made in several forms, usually with four strings like the gittern, was a complementary stringed instrument, as was the fiddle, a fourteenth-century English example of which is in the collection of the British Museum. The fiddle was a stringed instrument of various shapes, played with a bow. Essentially a tenor instrument, it was therefore very important for the music of the late medieval period. The rebec was a stringed instrument suited for pitches higher than the fiddle. The rotta was a late medieval revival of the ancient lyre, while the symphony, later known as the hurdy-gurdy, was a stringed instrument with one or two strings tuned to produce a drone. It was sounded by turning a rosined wheel across the strings (as if continuously bowing) with one hand while playing keys which 'stopped' the strings with the other hand.

Wind instruments included the straight trumpet and, by the late fourteenth century, such reed instruments as the shawm and its larger version, the bombard. The bagpipe, which is still with us, was not always made with a drone bass pipe to emit one continuous tone. The organ was a wind instrument provided with bellows. The positive organ was portable, but needed to be placed in position to be played, and the musician required an assistant on the bellows. The portative organ was smaller, with tiny pipes, and was usually supported by a strap over the standing player's

Opposite: Marginal figures in this decorated page from the Luttrell Psalter are shown playing a pair of hand bells, a portative organ with drone pipes at treble end and reversed keyboard, a bagpipe with conical chanter and trumpet drone, a symphony, and nakers (The Luttrell Psalter (f. 176), British Library, Additional Ms. 42130), East Anglian, *c.* 1340

Musicians play (left to right): bagpipe, symphony (hurdy-gurdy), cornet or recorder, portative organ, kettledrums, gittern, harp, fiddle and psaltery (Bodleian Library, Oxford, Ms. Douce. 18, f. 113v)

ciones eorum.

Exaltate dominum deum nostrū:
et adorate in monte sancto eius: quo
niam sanctus dominus deus noster.
Ubilate deo omnis terra: seruite do
mino in leticia

Introite in conspectu eius: in exulta
cione

Scitote quoniam dominus ipse
est deus: ipse fecit nos ɿ non ipsi nos.
Populus eius ɿ oues pascue eius
introite portas eius in confessione
atria eius in ympnis confitemini illi.
Laudate nomen eius quoniam

shoulder, or upon the knee of the sitting player, and the player could work the built-in bellows with the left hand while applying the right hand to the keyboard. By the fifteenth century organs had been developed that covered three octaves, rather than one, and were fully chromatic, as suited an age of polyphonic music.

Percussion instruments included pairs of small kettledrums suspended from the player's waist, called nakers, and the tabor, a small cylindrical drum with a snare, or strand of gut, running across the drumhead. The timbre, ancestor of today's tambourine, cymbals, chime bells, pellet bells, clappers, rattles, and the triangle, were some of the other percussion instruments.

MUSICIANS

Professional musicians were thought of rather like craftsmen. The musical theorist and philosopher, the *musicus*, was on a higher level than the instrumentalist. Minstrels added a colourful and zestful element to an immense variety of occasions. Some were simple musicians who entertained when and where they could, while others were established professionals who moved on circuits among aristocratic households. The minstrels Henry V took with him to war in France were paid 12*d* a day, twice what an archer was paid and the same as the master surgeons. The tradition of the harp-playing minstrel who told stories while playing was ageless, and Henry V and his queen, Catherine of Valois, were both patrons of harpers and practitioners of the art.

When Edward I arranged to celebrate the knighting of his son, the future Edward II, in 1306, no fewer than 175 minstrels gathered at Westminster for the occasion. Many of these were itinerant minstrels, others were in the service of wealthy households, and twenty-seven were members of the Royal Household. The minstrels in the Royal Household were of equal rank to the royal huntsmen and falconers, who were anything but menial servants. The only woman paid as a minstrel in 1306 was not a member of the Royal Household, but she was a professional acrobatic dancer, who was called by what must have been the stage name of Matilda Makejoy.

Minstrelsy as a rule included a degree of jesting. Tricks could be crude or flashy or athletic. Acrobatic dancing, balancing, tumbling (which could range from high athleticism to buffoonery), juggling, contortionism, dancing on stilts, or performing with animals were all part of the circus-like routine. It was not unusual for a noble household to employ a jester, which strictly meant a story-telling

Opposite: A bagpipe player accompanies a female acrobat. In the initial (above), a harp is being plucked

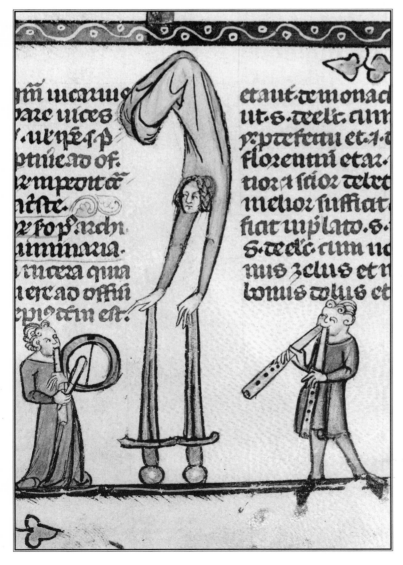

Above: An acrobat doing a handstand while a boy musician plays, from the Alexander Romance (Bodleian Library, Oxford, Ms. Bodl. 264, f. 90r)

Left: Fourteenth-century acrobats. From a manuscript illuminated by a monk of St Bartholomew's Priory, London (British Library Royal Ms. 10 E IV, f. 58)

minstrel, as a comic entertainer. Narrative songs about the lives and deeds of saints and princes formed the repertory of minstrels. There was a hierarchy among minstrels, from those at the bottom who barely survived as jugglers, puppeteers, and humble musicians to the well-to-do professionals at the upper end of the scale, who performed as drummers, trumpeters, harpists, fiddlers, narrators, or whatever in the service of the secular and ecclesiastical nobility. Romances were one kind of narrative song heard in medieval England, and ballads were another. A thirteenth-century example of a ballad is 'The Bargain of Judas', which tells a story of how Judas was given thirty pieces of silver by Christ to buy food for the disciples, was robbed of the money, and then betrayed Jesus to Pilate to recoup the missing silver.

Minstrel bands employed by civic corporations were known as waits. They would dress in the livery of the town, and originally their main task was as watchmen on the city gates. With trumpets or shawms, which were loud and had carrying power, the waits could blow the hours or sound warnings. In prosperous towns such as London and York, waits in the late Middle Ages had become more than watchmen, they were professional and entertaining minstrels, and were symbols of civic pride and prestige.

Dancing

Dancing at the amateur level was ordinarily round-dancing or processional, and was of ancient lineage. Carols (*coreae* in Latin) were the principal form of secular music in medieval England, and they are the musical core of the entertaining chain- or carol-dance. The carol-dance was usually performed by a circle of dancers, with hands clasped or arms linked, who would take a few steps to the left as their leader, normally standing in the middle of the circle, sang a stanza of a song. The dancers then marked time with treading steps as all sang the chorus (or burden). This basic dance could be varied in many ways, from dancing in line to miming the story of the carol, and the carols might be stories about heroism, romance, or religion. For the most part, carols seem to have been joyful. Carolling could be done outdoors, and the churchyard was a favourite venue, or indoors in a lordly hall. Churchmen repeatedly repudiated carols and the lascivious songs that were being enjoyed in churchyards when minds and hearts ought to have been inclined to more spiritual matters. Carols prompted confessors to impose penances for sins of voice, sins of movement, and sins of touching.

As music and text, the carol had a long monophonic ancestry,

Dancing and making music distract peasants from the cares of life (Bodleian Library, Ms. Douce. 93, f. 28)

mostly unrecorded. The polyphonic carol comes to light in the fifteenth century, and was a musical form almost unique to England. The text of a carol might be English, Latin, or both, or even a mixture of English, Latin, and French. Beyond question the most famous among surviving polyphonic carols is 'Deo gracias, Anglia', written in thanksgiving for the stunning English victory under the leadership of Henry V over the French at Agincourt in 1415.

The carol-dance was not the limit of dancing activity. The basse dance was performed on the ground without springing into the air, and was a late medieval refinement of the processional dance or open carol-dance. The pavane was a fast-moving variation on the basse dance, and called for displays of many manners of steps and elaborate costumes. Additionally, display dancing became fashionable in late medieval courtly circles after its importation from Italy and Burgundy.

THREE

Fashion, Ornament and Craftsmanship

O ne source of sensual delight, which involved colour and display, was clothing. For those who could afford them, the latest styles in fashionable dress were an expression of position, pleasure, and wealth. The enjoyment of nice clothing became so pronounced, in fact, that the social establishment attempted to restrict certain types of clothing to designated strata of society. Several ordinances were attempted, with no success whatsoever, before the first effort at a comprehensive sumptuary statute was passed in 1363. It, too, was a model of failure in the realm of enforcement (it was repealed the year after its enactment), just as it was the model for subsequent efforts to regulate the dress of the various classes of the king's subjects.

In the decades before the statute of 1363, the clothing styles which were in vogue had been evolving. In the first quarter of the fourteenth century, utility seems to have been the major determining factor in clothing, with distinctions being primarily in the quality of fabric. A noble gentleman wore velvet and fur, and his gowns tended to be voluminous. In the fourteenth century robes of voluminous character were gradually abandoned by most men, but were preserved in the distinguished dress of lawyers, academics, or the formal attire of the king. Men often wore a coif, a close-fitting bonnet tied under the chin, which covered the hair (which often reached the shoulders) and ears, and over this a hat was worn. Women wore as an outer garment a surcoat, and beneath it an outer gown over a tight-fitting kirtle. The sleeveless outer gown was split at the sides, and thus showed the sleeves and sides of the kirtle. At the waist or slightly lower a girdle or belt would be worn with a pouch attached for carrying items. A common hairstyle for women was to part it in the centre, and weave it into plaits doubled over the ears or enclosed in a net, which might be decorated.

The hood worn by men underwent many changes in style in the later Middle Ages. It began as a simple cowl with a point at the back, pulled on over the head with sufficient cloth to form a gorget to protect the neck and shoulders. Then the point of the hood was elongated with a pipe of material called a liripipe, that sometimes was an appendage of considerable length. In some styles, the liripipe was wound round the head and the gorget perched atop the head like a cockscomb. All sorts of creative draping evolved from the simple cowl in the course of the fourteenth and fifteenth centuries.

In the second quarter of the fourteenth century the clothing of stylish men and women assumed a more figure-fitting cut and shape than had been the rule earlier. The clinging lines were often managed by lacing the garments down the back from neck to waist. Belts and buttons were becoming more decorative. The tight-fitting tunic, or cote-hardie, was worn by both sexes of the upper classes. The cote-hardie was buttoned down the front and might reach mid-way down the thigh, perhaps further, and under it men would wear a gipon or doublet, which also fitted closely, and beneath that an undergarment. The hose were tied with strings to the gipon and were sometimes particoloured and styled as tights, called chausses. A man's shoes had pointed toes of ever

Musicians in tight-fitting tunics and pointed shoes perform for the dancers in the Garden of Mirth (Bodleian Library, Ms. E Mus. 65, f. 3v)

increasing length, and the shoes were either buttoned up the front or buckled over the insteps.

The cote-hardie usually had sleeves that fitted tightly from elbow to wrist and were often decorated with buttons. It was often worn with a decorated belt, perhaps even jewelled, which rested at hip level. The earlier fashion for long pendant sleeves gave way to the attaching of tippets just above the elbows of the cote-hardie; the tippet was a detachable piece of silk that hung like a long streamer. The cote-hardie could be made of gorgeous material and decorated with jewels, and some chose to have ornamental edging, which was said to be 'dagged' (that is, scalloped or pointed). Over the cote-hardies cloaks or mantles were worn when appropriate, and they might also be dagged. Particoloured clothing became more fashionable around the middle of the century.

The dress of women tended not to be so extravagant as that of men, except in the variety of head-gear. A wimple of some sort, which covered the chin, throat, and breast, was worn by many women throughout the fourteenth century. Despite the declining fashion of the wimple, some form of head covering, even if just a veil or hood, was worn. The nebule head-dress appeared around 1350, and consisted of a cylindrical case of woven wire which framed the face across the forehead and down the cheeks. The nebule head-dress allowed women to show their hair, which could be decoratively styled. Soon women were also exposing their necks with low-necked dresses. Sleeve tippets that sometimes reached the ground were being attached to dresses, but this style disappeared after about 1380, as did the nebule head-dress.

Folk without the means to be extravagant in dress could at least use more colour in their clothing. Working men wore tunics, usually reaching to the knees, with a cord around the hips from which hung a square bag, the gypciere, which was used to carry tools or other items. Men wore the coif still or the hood. Peasant women are usually portrayed wearing loose-fitting gowns with tight sleeves, aprons, and hoods.

The last quarter of the fourteenth century was an exciting time for aristocratic clothing in England. King Richard II, who loved luxury and extravagance, set the example. The houppelande, a gown that was shaped rather like a bell with a hole in the centre through which the head protruded, was worn in varying lengths by men and women. Both men and women continued to wear the tight-fitting tunic beneath the houppelande. For women, the houppelande was given a wide opening and was often worn with a wide belt, often embroidered, reaching from the waist up to just

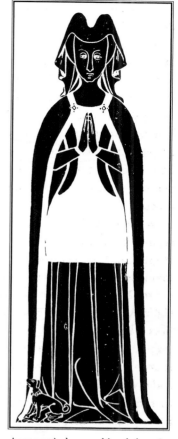

A woman's dress and head-dress in the mid-fifteenth century, a memorial brass from the tomb of the wife of T. Sherneborne, at Shernbourne, Norfolk, 1458

beneath the breasts, giving a new high-waist appearance. This was also the beginning of the use of gigantic and ornate head-dresses for women, which increased in size and embellishment, and which continued to be stylish throughout the fifteenth century. Women also wore purses suspended from their belts, with small daggers attached to the outside. The houppelande in the form worn by men sometimes had a neck so high the ears were covered, and it varied in length from thigh to ankle. (In the early fifteenth century, the collars on some houppelands reached the top of the head.) The toes of shoes became longer than ever, and in extravagant cases even needed to be anchored to the knees with gold or silver chains to prevent the wearer from taking an undignified nosedive. Men of style began wearing a head-covering called the chaperon, which took on many forms, with lengths of cloth being wound about the head like turbans, and ornamental dagging draping down.

A fashion innovation of about 1400, which remained popular with some men for about twenty years, was the bag-sleeve, buttoned at the wrist and tight at the armhole, and as voluminous as possible in between. Sleeve styles, however, had great variety in this era: tight with a gathered puff at the shoulder, bell-shaped, extended to such length that they had to be knotted to avoid dragging on the ground, or full and turned back to the elbow to display a fur lining. Women engaged in sartorial exaggeration with their head-dresses and the width of their skirts. The steeple head-dresses of gigantic height and adorned with an elongated veil, and so often thought of as typical of the clothing of aristocratic medieval women, were stylish in the 1420s and 1430s. The taste for extravagant fashion gradually eased, as fashions are inclined to change, but the centenary of the sumptuary act of 1363 was marked by another of 1463, and there is no indication that the statute of Edward IV's reign had any more impact on how people chose to dress than had the statute of Edward III's reign. It should be noted that there were further efforts at sumptuary legislation in 1477 and 1483: if not successful in regulating his subjects' apparel, Edward IV was at least persistent.

FURS

Furs had a special place in the fashions of the later Middle Ages. In the thirteenth and fourteenth centuries, folk with elegant pretensions wore the fine northern squirrel skins called *miniver* and *gris.* A robe lined with these skins was indeed a step above the more accessible lambskins used by a great many people to keep warm. Towards the end of the fourteenth century tastes in furs were changing, and the highest rank fell to the northern variety of marten called sable, the pine marten, and the black lambskins known as budge (from south-west Europe). Squirrel, rabbit, and lesser furs came to be seen as appropriate for more humble folk. Passing into the sixteenth century, such furs as lynx, mink, and fox became the height of fashion. By the mid-sixteenth century, furs were losing out to rich fabrics as status symbols. One result of this was that the vocabulary for the various grades and types of furs became unfamiliar, and when a French version of the Cinderella story was written in the seventeenth century, her slipper lined with *vair* became a slipper of *verre.* Thus a slipper lined with squirrel fur became a slipper of most improbable glass.

MILITARY COSTUME

To outline the development of military costume is a more straightforward enterprise than to outline what happened to its civilian counterpart. Unlike civilian costume, there is less Englishness about military costume because it had similar currency throughout Europe. The development of armour is a highly detailed and technical subject. Broadly, it might be said that the eleventh through to the thirteenth century was the era of mail, a type of armour made either from rings punched out of a sheet of metal or from wire links formed by riveting individual loops of wire. A shirt of mail might be made of thousands of these rings or links. It would be heavy to wear but flexible enough not to be frightfully uncomfortable. It was made up of hood, shirt, leg pieces, mittens, or whatever it was possible to acquire for protection in combat.

The fourteenth century might be considered an era of transition from mail to plate armour. As the name suggests, plate armour was made from plates of iron that would vary in shape and thickness according to the part of the body they were designed to protect. The armourers' craft gradually developed greater skill in the production of plates until by the fifteenth century one might speak of the age of plate armour when the entire body was finally encased in plate. A dramatic way to illustrate the changes would be to progress from the chain mail portrayed on the warriors in the Bayeux Tapestry, to the memorial brasses of English knights: Sir John D'Abernon (Stoke

An English manuscript, *c.* 1450, showing a knight being armed for combat (The Pierpoint Morgan Library, M. 775, f. 122v)

D'Abernon, Surrey, *c.* 1277), Sir Roger de Trumpington (Trumpington, Cambridgeshire, 1289), Sir Robert de Bures (Acton, Suffolk, 1302), Sir Robert de Septvans (Chartham, Kent, 1306), Sir John de Argentine (Horsheath, Cambridgeshire, 1360), Sir Robert de Swynbourne (Little Horkesley, Essex, 1391), Thomas de St Quintin (Harpham, Yorkshire, 1445), Sir Robert Staunton (Castle Donnington, Leicestershire, 1458), Sir Thomas Grene (Grene's Norton, Northamptonshire, 1462), and Sir Humphrey Stanley (Westminster Abbey, London, 1505). The magnificent tomb effigy of Richard Beauchamp, Earl of Warwick (died 1439), in St Mary's Church, Warwick, displays in detail the plates of armour, front and back, and how they were fastened in place.

ECCLESIASTICAL COSTUME

Ecclesiastical vestments changed little during the Middle Ages, and resembled the Roman models from which they were developed. The cope was the semi-circular vestment worn by high ecclesiastics reaching from the neck to the floor and closed in the front with a broad tab of cloth. We may think of the cope as analogous to the cloak worn by the laity. There is a lovely fifteenth-century cope of *opus anglicanum* in the Durham Cathedral Treasury. The cope was used in the later Middle Ages as a processional vestment, and was not worn by the priest as he celebrated Mass. The chasuble, on the other hand, was a Mass vestment. Its Latin name, *casula*, little house, suggests a full, circular garment that covered the entire body, with a hole for the head. Chasubles were often made of fine materials enhanced with decorative embroidery. Beneath the chasuble was worn an undertunic, the alb of white linen. All officers of the Church wore the alb, not just priests. The albs of priests and higher dignitaries of the Church were decorated with panels of ornament, known as the apparel. Apparel would be attached to the alb on the breast, the back, each cuff, and front and back at the foot of the garment; six in all.

Over the alb a deacon assisting at the Mass would wear a silk dalmatic, or upper tunic. A sub-deacon would wear a linen tunicle over his alb. The dalmatic and tunicle are shorter than the alb. Dalmatics and tunicles worn by bishops and abbots were edged with a fringe. Another ecclesiastical vestment was the amice, originally a hood worn on the head, but which by the later Middle Ages had evolved into a collar. A celebrating priest would carry in his left hand an embroidered maniple, which had evolved from a practical towel used to wipe the face during Mass. Senior ecclesiastics also wore a stole, a long embroidered band that passed around the neck and was crossed over the chest and held in place by a girdle at the waist, the ends of which hung to near the bottom of the alb. A high ecclesiastic, like an archbishop, would wear a mitre on his head which was often decorated with precious jewels. An archbishop would also wear around his shoulders a pallium, a narrow white band which came from the Pope and was a symbol of his office. Gloves and beautiful slippers would also be a part of the garb of an archbishop. In contemplating the visual splendours of the age, one must not neglect the high ecclesiastic in full vestments, encased from foot to mitre in sumptuous and richly decorated attire.

A Franciscan friar, from Matthew Paris's 'Chronica Majora' (The Master and Fellows of Corpus Christi College, Cambridge, Ms. 16, f. 71r; photograph: Conway Library, Courtauld Institute of Art)

PROFESSIONAL COSTUME

Some professions had distinctive attire. Academic dress was in many ways similar to ecclesiastical costume, such as the cape and hood. The three rankings of scholar, bachelor, and master or doctor could be distinguished by slight differences in attire. Judicial garb was another category of distinctive costume. Judges appointed by the king wore grand robes (usually scarlet in colour), and all judicial costume included a closed gown with narrow sleeves, a cape over the shoulders, a distinctive mantle, a coif, and a skull cap.

Display and its Pleasures

Philippa was the daughter of Henry of Bolingbroke and Mary de Bohun, and was their sixth child. She was born at Leicester on 4 July 1394, and her mother died in childbirth. In 1406, at the age of twelve, Philippa went off to join her husband, King Eric of Denmark, Norway, and Sweden. The display associated with Philippa's move to Scandinavia holds interest for our present concerns. She was sent off with a wedding dress, a tunic and mantle, to be worn with a long train of white satin adorned with velvet, miniver, and ermine. There were five other gowns, including one of gold cloth and another of red velvet, embroidered with pearls. Four of these gowns warmed the princess with miniver and ermine. There were numerous other garments as well, as such as a cap of beaver furred with ermine, three pairs of boots, numerous pairs of shoes, a sumptuously decorated and appointed bridal bed, two additional beds, a carriage, silver items for Philippa's chapel, and even a folding iron chair. There were many other items issued from the royal wardrobe for the young woman and her extensive retinue, but no personal jewellery was included in the surviving inventory.

Philippa's brother, John, Duke of Bedford (1389–1435), died in France, at Rouen. Before his final return to France in July 1434 he stored many items in England. Sir Robert Whittingham (died 1452), Bedford's receiver-general, had charge of five chests containing 338 pieces of gold and silver plate from Bedford's household and chamber, stored in Bedford's house in Walbrook in London. This was just a fraction of the material wealth Bedford had accumulated. His rich dresser for state occasions, for example, was a separate item altogether from the plate in his chamber, and separate from the ordinary household plate. For a formal occasion, the wealth of a man like Bedford would be put on display on what was called a dresser or buffet. It might be a free-standing piece of furniture or, as with Bedford's, a temporary structure built of stepped boards, covered with luxury textiles, and perhaps augmented with a canopy. The number of shelves and the amount of plate on the dresser, together with what was used on the banquet table, proclaimed the wealth and honour of the householder.

Detail from The Bedford Hours showing the Duke of Bedford (British Library Additional Ms. 18850, f. 256v)

Bedford's dresser displayed 128 pieces of plate (5 gold, 69 silver-gilt, 54 silver cups, ewers, bowls, pots, spice-plates, and goblets), and it was the normal usage to put the largest pieces on the bottom shelf and range them upwards until the most precious and valuable would be shown on the top shelf. The plate from the dresser was valued after his death at over £848. The rich cupboard was in London when he died, but he was not without table plate for his use in France.

Among his possessions was an 'ars-girdel', one of those belts worn about the hips which had become fashionable in the second half of the fourteenth century and was still being worn in Bedford's day, which was decorated with twenty sapphires and the same number of large balas rubies as well as 120 pearls. There were also such things as the four small silver saucers for blood-letting. The only item of goldsmiths' work in Bedford's collection at the time of his death which is known to survive today is the Royal Gold Cup, now in the British Museum.

In a household such as that maintained by the Duke of Bedford, an important way to display magnificence was with expensive textiles — silks, satins, velvets, tapestries and furs — and embroideries, including *opus anglicanum*, to be used for secular and liturgical purposes. A man like John of Bedford also had the status symbol of a private chapel for which he had splendid vestments for the serving ecclesiastics and rich textile hangings to complement the chalices, cruets, crosses, pyxes, holy-water buckets and sprinklers, patens and candlesticks. A 'chapel' in a textile sense meant matching sets of vestments for several priests, lectern hangings, an altar cloth, altar hangings, and copes in the range of colours for the liturgical year. John of Bedford was also a book collector and a patron of manuscript illumination; the Bedford Psalter and the Bedford Book of Hours are now in the British Library collection.

John of Bedford's nephew was King Henry VI. A financial account for the fiscal year 1452/3 survives for Henry's wife, Margaret of Anjou. Margaret's treasurer of the chamber and master of jewels, Edward Ellesmere, submitted an account that, among other things, indicates the New Year's gifts made by Margaret. Many were jewels, sending her deep into debt in January 1453. Gift-giving was important to social prestige, and jewels were a form of investment and a source of collatoral as well as items of beauty; in 1453 Margaret was focused upon developing friendships.

GOLDSMITHERY

Despite the name, goldsmiths worked not only in gold, but in silver and even in copper alloy which was decorated by such techniques as enamelling and gilding. There is no evidence of gold being mined anywhere in Britain from the end of Roman occupation until the sixteenth century. The jewels used by goldsmiths were prepared by jewellers, and precious stones mainly came from the East in the medieval period. The London Company of Goldsmiths acquired a royal charter in 1327, and by 1368 its membership numbered 135. Most English goldsmiths in the later Middle Ages were laymen such as those in the Company of Goldsmiths, and the monastic goldsmiths characteristic of an earlier age were very few in number. The London Goldsmiths were a livery company, which is to say that on special occasions the members wore distinctive clothing, or livery.

Goldsmiths used various methods in the decoration of the surface of precious metal objects, such as embossing (where the goldsmith used a hammer and punch to work from the back side of the metal), chasing (working from the front), engraving (gouging slivers of metal from the front), stamping patterns with a steel punch, applying patterns by soldering wire filigree on the metal surface, enamelling (which was rather like pouring hot glass of assorted colours into a prepared metal surface, allowing it to solidify by cooling, baking it in a kiln, and polishing it), or gem-setting. Silver and copper alloys were gilded in two ways, both methods using mercury to dissolve gold into an amalgam which would be applied to the object. This was then heated, evaporating the mercury and leaving the gold adhered to the object.

Gold and silver leaf were used to decorate wood, stone, or parchment surfaces. The leaf was made very laboriously by placing pieces of metal foil (which often started out as coins that were hammered thin) between pieces of parchment (goldbeaters' skin). Then, with assorted hammers, the goldbeater slowly worked the sandwich of alternating layers of malleable metal and parchment until gold or silver leaf of even thickness was produced. Painters used powdered gold and silver in their work.

Precious stones were valued for beauty and rarity, and were used as amulets. The gems most frequently prized were sapphires, rubies, pearls, turquoises, emeralds, and diamonds. The beauty of diamonds depends so much upon the difficult skill of cutting that diamonds did not achieve the degree of preciousness associated with them today until the nineteenth century. Diamonds were often left in their natural crystal shape, or split in half to make a pair of pointed diamonds. More elaborate cutting of diamonds was being done by the end of the medieval period, but there is no evidence yet of English craftsmen doing such work. Other non-metallic materials used for medieval jewellery included jet, coral, amber, garnet, beryl, and rare shells. Most precious stones were imported into England, although jet, reputed to have power over evil, could be found at Whitby in Yorkshire. It is mentioned elsewhere that precious stones were often credited with medicinal or magical powers.

Surviving medieval gems seem irregular in shape because they were polished to bring out their brilliance. Jewellers polished stones with abrasives like sandstone or saliva and tile dust or oil and emery sand. The operation was done by hand or using a lathe operated with a fiddle-bow. If a gem was pierced, it was done with a steel bit, again powered with a fiddle-bow. When gems were cut it was normally to produce cameos and intaglios.

Gems were normally mounted by goldsmiths either with collar settings, four-pronged claw settings, or petal-shaped settings. Pearls were frequently pierced with a drill so that they could be sewn on clothing or strung together, and on jewellery they were mounted on a metal tang through the hole in the pearl.

A fine example of the goldsmiths' art is the wedding coronet of Margaret of York, sister of Edward IV who, in 1468, became the bride of Charles, Duke of Burgundy. The coronet is today in the treasury of Aachen Cathedral. It is small (12 cm in diameter) and high, and was probably worn high on Margaret's head to enhance her flowing blond hair. The coronet is gold and decorated with enamelled white roses, pearls and precious stones. The enamelled letters in red, green, and white would spell out 'Margaret of York' if all were still present. The centre and front of the bridal crown is distinguished by a diamond cross, above which an impressive pearl is set in a white rose. The lower edge of the coronet is decorated with gold 'C' and 'M' motifs joined by lovers' knots.

Goldsmiths were directly involved in the engraving of the dies used in the production of the coin of the realm. English coinage in the later Middle Ages was made primarily of silver, but a gold penny was minted under Henry III in 1257, and intermittently thereafter gold coins were minted in England. The gold coinage of Henry III was an unsuccessful experiment. Goldsmiths were generally also the craftsmen who from the twelfth century onwards engraved the seals with which impressions were made in soft wax to authenticate documents.

The seal of Thomas Brundish, goldsmith, *c.* 1350 (PRO, E329/434)

The votive coronet of Margaret of York (Cathedral Treasury, Aachen)

The shrine of St Thomas at Canterbury, plated with gold and decorated with precious stones, was among the most impressive products of English medieval goldsmiths. Unfortunately it was totally obliterated by that premier destroyer of traditional religious practices and furnishings, Henry VIII.

PRECIOUS JEWELLERY

Jewellery ranked among the precious treasures gathered by people to enhance their pleasure. It would be of great benefit to our perception of English medieval jewellery if more examples had survived to the present. For example, no royal jewellery from the thirteenth century exists today. One popular item of jewellery in the thirteenth century was the ring brooch, frequently used to fasten a garment at the neck. The ring brooch came into fashion in the twelfth century, and remained popular throughout the remainder of the medieval period. Such a piece could be made of gold or silver and be decorated with stones and inscriptions. Various examples of these brooches have survived. A gold one set with four garnets alternating with four sapphires is in the

A gold thirteenth-century ring brooch, either French or English, set alternately with red rubies and blue sapphires *en cabochon* and punched decoration between them. On the back is an inscription of love (British Museum, MLA AF 2683)

Gold brooch set alternately with three chalcedony cameos and three cabochon rubies. The cameos probably date from the mid-thirteenth century but the brooch was more likely to have been made *c.* 1320–40. Found at Oxwich Castle, Wales (National Museum of Wales, Cardiff)

collection of the Manchester City Art Galleries, but probably the most remarkable example is the Oxwich brooch (found at Oxwich Castle in 1968) in the National Museum of Wales at Cardiff, which is a ring of twelve pieces of gold soldered together, and set with three cameos and two rubies (a sixth stone is missing).

Rings were another popular item of jewellery, and some of the best surviving examples that can be presumed to be English work have been found in the tombs of English bishops. The rings of Archbishops Sewal de Bovill (died 1258) and William Greenfield of York (died 1315) are both set with rubies, while the gold ring found in the grave of Bishop Henry Woodlock of Winchester (died 1316) is set with a sapphire, as is the very impressive gold ring of Archbishop William Whittlesey of Canterbury (died 1374), which has enamelled shoulders of flowers and foliage.

The wearing of jewellery like brooches, decorated belts, gold and silver chains, and rings became so popular that sumptuary legislation of 1363 attempted, with utter lack of success, to regulate what strata of social and economic society might employ different sorts of decoration about their persons. Later in the fourteenth century gold jewellery decorated with white opaque enamel came to be highly stylish among the wealthy, and the spectacular Dunstable swan jewel of about 1400 in the British Museum is a surviving representative of the fashion. The gold base is shaped into a swan of white enamel, and there are traces of black enamel on the legs and feet. The swan was found in 1965 at the Dominican friary at Dunstable, and the pin and catch to fasten the jewel to a garment are still in place as is the gold coronet around the swan's neck, to which a gold chain ending in a ring is attached. The swan was a badge associated with the Tony and Bohun families; the first wife of Henry Bolingbroke, who became the first Lancastrian king, Henry IV (reigned 1399–1413), was the wealthy heiress Mary de Bohun. The Dunstable swan jewel is likely to have been a livery badge. The swan was also used as a livery badge by their son before he became King Henry V (reigned 1413–22). The method of enamelling employed on the Dunstable swan jewel is known as *email en ronde bosse* (encrusted enamel), which was developed in the fourteenth century.

One inventory that shows what precious jewels a nobleman might possess is the document associated with the Frenchman

The Dunstable swan jewel, an example of opaque white enamel over gold, probably made by a London goldsmith, *c.* 1400 (British Museum, MLA 1872, 12–16, 1.6)

Guichard d'Angle (died 1380). He served the English in Edward III's war with France, and King Edward made him a Knight of the Garter and Earl of Huntingdon. While at Ospringe, Kent, in 1377, on a journey from Dover to London, d'Angle was robbed of goods which were inventoried. The list included a girdle and pendant of gold, a gold eagle, another eagle made of large pearls with a wreath of pearls around it, yet another eagle of smaller pearls, a gold clasp in the image of St George with a large sapphire and an emerald and large pearls, another clasp with sapphires and rubies and pearls, rings, brooches, his seal and signet seals, and many other jewels and items of gold and silver. A jewel from about this time which does survive is the Founder's jewel belonging to New College, Oxford. The Founder's jewel is a silver-gilt brooch in the shape of the letter 'M'. The double arch of the 'M' is decorated with gems, and in one of the arches stands the Archangel Gabriel while in the other stands the Virgin Mary.

Wealthy customers were hardly restricted to buying what the goldsmiths were inspired to create. For instance William Curtys, Abbot of Bury St Edmunds, placed an order in 1430, with the London goldsmith, John Horwelle, for an enormous new crozier that was to weigh 12 lb 9¼ oz. On one side of the crozier head was to be depicted the Assumption of the Blessed Virgin, and on the other the Salvation of the Virgin. Around the head were to be placed in twelve niches (called tabernacles) the twelve apostles, and in the crook of the staff a tabernacle boasting an image of St Edmund. The goldsmith was to get £40 for his work.

Badge-brooches like the Dunstable swan jewel and the white hart that was used by King Richard II had political significance in addition to being items of adornment. Collars of livery served also in both political and decorative ways. John, Duke of Bedford established a short-lived order of chivalry about which very little information survives. There are no extant statutes, and it may have been no more formal than an association of those who had accepted Bedford's livery collar and bound themselves in allegiance to the duke. An interest in jewellery calls attention to the duke's portrait in the Bedford Book of Hours. He is wearing a collar of alternating S-shaped links and Bedford's root badge. The pendant is an eagle, another of his badges, perched upon a root.

One of the most famous collar devices was the 'SS' developed by John of Gaunt, Duke of Lancaster. It is theorized that the 'S' stood for *souvenez* (remember), but when Gaunt's son became Henry IV the 'S' easily came to mean *souverain*, and the three Lancastrian kings dispensed collars of varying value bearing the 'SS' device to

Silver collar of SS consisting of a chain of forty-one letters of S meeting in an ornamental arrangement of buckles and links ending in a fluted ring, *c.* 1440 (Museum of London)

A secular silver cup, *c.* 1400–50, long preserved as a chalice at Lacock Church, Wiltshire (British Museum)

retainers and persons they wished to honour. In 1983 a nearly complete silver collar of this design was discovered under several feet of Thames mud at London near the location of the medieval Winewharf. This collar is a chain of forty-one cast S-shaped links, and is thought to date from about 1440, the middle of the reign of Henry VI. Each letter has two pairs of loops so that it can be joined by rings to adjacent links, and the central letter (the twenty-first) has a hook on the back so that it can be secured to the clothing of the wearer behind the neck. The chain of letters joins in the front with ornamental buckles hooked to a trefoil-shaped tiret, from which hangs a fluted ring. The collar, about 2 ft in length, is in the collection of the Museum of London and, although impressive, it is not among the most sumptuous recorded: even a knight would probably have been given a richer one.

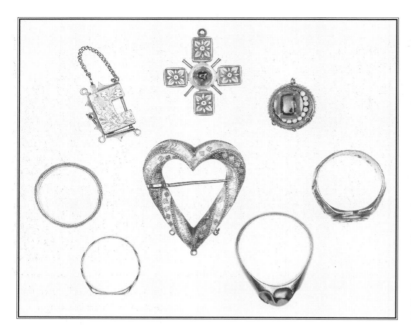

Part of the hoard of gold jewellery buried at Fishpool, Nottinghamshire in early 1464. The jewellery is elaborately decorated with black-letter inscriptions, engraved flowers and foliage and enamelling (British Museum, MLA 1967.12)

Most of the work produced by goldsmiths, such as rings, fittings for belts and knives, brooches, cups, and bowls, was for secular use. Surviving examples today tend to be examples of ecclesiastical goldsmithery because in many cases these things had a more protected existence. One sample of secular gold jewellery is known as the Fishpool hoard. This can be dated from coins as having been buried at Fishpool, Nottinghamshire, early in 1464 and includes four rings, a roundel with a sapphire in the centre, a brooch, a locket, and a cross. A silver cup made for secular use in the first half of the fifteenth century, which was long used as a chalice in Lacock Church, Wiltshire, can be seen in the British Museum. A most unusual piece of surviving goldsmiths' work, apparently for the use of an ecclesiastic, is known as the Middleham Jewel because it was found at Middleham, Yorkshire. It is a gold devotional jewel, a portable reliquary, made to be hung around the neck. It is dated about 1450, and contains a large polished sapphire above which is engraved ANANYZAPTA, a protective against falling sickness or epilepsy. On the same side is an engraved representation of the Trinity, and the inscription ECCE AGNUS DEI QUI TOLLIS PECCATA MUNDI TETRAGRAMMATON (Behold the Lamb of God that takes away the sins of the world). The reverse side of the jewel has an engraving of the Nativity scene, and a surrounding border of saints.

The Middleham Jewel (now in the Yorkshire Museum, York) is a rare gold and sapphire reliquary pendant, late fifteenth century (British Museum)

A misericord, originally from the church of St Nicholas, King's Lynn, depicting a woodcarver at work in the company of his apprentices and dog (The Board of the Trustees of the Victoria & Albert Museum)

Craftsmanship

In the days before the industrial manufacture of exact multiple copies of goods, when every pot or spoon or spade was at least slightly different from every other pot or spoon or spade, people of necessity developed an eye and an appreciation for craftsmanship and the materials from which items were made. It is probable that the medieval eye took pleasure in even simple and inexpensive items that were skilfully crafted from everyday materials, and held such things precious.

Most wood, of course, was consumed as fuel. Yet commonplace and valued objects made of wood were to be seen everywhere. Houses and bridges and wharfs, ships and walls were everywhere made of wood. The tools, vehicles, and mills of agrarian workers; the shields, bows, arrows, engines of war, and saddle frames of the warriors; the utensils, furniture, gadgets, spinning wheels, toys, looms, chests, and armoires of householders; the font covers, pulpits, screens, and misericord seats were all over England made for the most part of wood. It must have been rare for anyone to have had no cherished wooden possession.

METAL GOODS

Tools and other items made of iron were necessary commonplace products for society. The iron ore, which was the source of the material worked by the indispensable smith, was found in most counties of England, but the most important medieval sources were the Forest of Dean, the Midlands, and regions in the northern counties. Further supplies of iron were imported from the Continent. Iron ore was first processed by smelting at a bloomery to get a more pure form of iron oxide. The iron that came out of the process was called a bloom, and the size of the bloom depended upon the size of the furnace and the bellows (whether hand pumped or water-powered) that forced the draught of air in to raise the temperature of the charcoal smelting fire. The smith took the bloom of iron and worked it into objects of wrought iron, cast iron, or steel of one form or another. To produce a piece of steel of even quality and hardness that would take and hold an edge as a weapon or tool required great skill. The skill and cost involved in producing a large piece of high-carbon steel explains why agricultural tools like spades and scythes were made almost entirely of wood with a cutting edge of steely iron attached. The products of smiths were to be found at every turn, from simple objects like nails and horseshoes to the delicate wrought-iron works of the clock in Salisbury Cathedral, which dates from 1386 and is the oldest surviving clock in England.

Smiths achieved a high level of technical skill in the thirteenth century. The development of strong dies and curved punches as tools to make stamped and cut-out designs made possible the precise repetition of decorative motifs. Examples of the decorative iron work that would have been seen in late medieval England survive today primarily in churches, on such items as doors and chests. The grille over the tomb of Queen Eleanor at Westminster Abbey was made in 1293–4 by Thomas of Leghtone. The doors to the chapter house vestibule at York Minster and the west door of Lichfield Cathedral are attractive examples of late thirteenth-century wrought-iron work, as is the chest from the Church of All Saints, Icklingham, Suffolk. Around 1300 tastes changed in favour of geometric tracery designs carved out of wood, and iron decoration became less fashionable. Smiths began to work with chisels and files on cold iron, and produced such work as the grille for the tomb of Bishop Roger Mortival of Salisbury, made in 1330. New decorative ironwork in the later Middle Ages consisted of such things as tomb railings and door rings, as carpenters took over the making of decorations for doors and chests that had earlier been the speciality of smiths.

The tinning of copper alloy and iron for culinary and other decorative wares provided attractive items for many households. Tin was commercially mined in medieval Britain, and was both used domestically and exported. When tin was alloyed with copper, the result was bronze, which was itself a useful metal for making valued articles. Lead ore of two kinds was mined in medieval England, and black ore (lead sulphide) yielded considerably more lead as well as more silver as a by-product than did the white ore (lead carbonate). Both types of ore were processed by smelting. Lead was produced in the mining of silver, yet it had its own practical use in such areas as constructing roofs and guttering. Lead was also used decoratively for things like souvenir badges and holy water flasks collected by pilgrims to various religious shrines. When tin was alloyed with lead or copper (or both), the result was pewter, an important material in late medieval England for making such things as pitchers, plates, and salt cellars. English pewterware was made in sufficient quantity and of appropriate quality to be exported even before the London pewterers were granted their ordinances in 1348. Pewterware

English pewter cruet, fifteenth century (Board of Trustees of the Victoria & Albert Museum)

Holy water flask, thirteenth century, found on the Thames foreshore; a souvenir of a pilgrimage to the shrine of St Thomas at Canterbury (Museum of London)

would have been among the precious consumer goods of many English households.

NON-METAL GOODS

More humble people, who would have been unable to acquire gold and silver plate and jewellery, may have had ceramic objects among their precious possessions. Pottery was such an ordinary thing that potters were classified as peasantry rather than being grouped with craftsmen of various sorts, and the making of pottery was, for some, only a part-time occupation. In the later Middle Ages pottery that was decorated with incised lines or with applied ornament (modelling) or by some other means, such as being shaped to resemble a person or animal, was increasingly appreciated. Pottery and tiles were produced all over medieval England because suitable clay was generally available. In the late medieval period, wheel-made pottery was very common and handmade pottery was still being produced. Some pottery was glazed and some was not. Jugs, for instance, were normally glazed, while more functional cooking vessels and bowls were not. A finely glazed jug would have been the centre-piece on the table, and a person might have pointed with pride to a floor or roof made of glazed tiles.

Medieval pottery 'face jug' for the table (Museum of London)

Pavement tiles were made by using a stamp to create a depressed pattern in the moist clay which would then be filled with a clay of contrasting colour before firing. It was not a decorative art which most households would have found affordable. The designs created were of animals, plants, heraldry, or other decorations on individual tiles. A series of tiles with different designs could also be laid in a floor in such a way as to create a composite picture or design. The late thirteenth-century tiles discovered at the site of Chertsey Abbey in Surrey are an impressive example, and various examples can be seen in the Medieval Tile and Pottery Gallery in the British Museum.

Another product of extractive industry was brick. Some householders would have been able to boast brick chimneys and brick-lined hearths, as these became increasingly common in the fifteenth and sixteenth centuries. Perceptive observers would have noticed that a higher standard of brick building was introduced into England in the early fifteenth century. We may suppose that Henry V regarded it as highly desirable when he rebuilt Sheen Palace with brick and stone.

Leather goods would also have held pride of place in some

The tanner (Bodleian Library, Oxford, Ms. Douce. 5, f. 7r)

English households. Tanning and tawing were elaborate, messy, and smelly processes which produced a rough dried leather. The tanner or tawyer then sold this product to the currier, who smoothed the rough leather, shaved it to an even thickness, and oiled it so that it was ready to be crafted. Using such techniques as stitching, gluing, cutting to shape or moulding, leather could be formed into shoes, purses, gloves, leather-covered boxes, bottles, buckets, harnessing for animals, armour, sheaths, saddles or any number of other things. Cordwainers and corvesers made new shoes, and cobblers repaired or remade old shoes, though towards the end of the Middle Ages, these terms were replaced by the general 'shoemaker'. So many things could be made of leather that it is not difficult to imagine people taking pleasure in it. The antlers and bones of certain of the animals whose hides were turned into leather goods yielded decorative items: buttons, combs, beads, handles for knives and swords, playing pieces for games, and tuning-pegs for musical instruments.

Glass windows or a glass vessel or two might have ranked among the precious objects in some late medieval English households. Medieval glass of English manufacture nearly always had a distinctive green colour resulting from the slight percentage of iron oxide present in the sand from which the glass was made in Surrey and Sussex, the most important English centres of the medieval craft. Most coloured glass used in England was imported. Good supplies of wood and fire-clay for crucibles were also fundamental ingredients, along with the sand, for the making of glass. Window-glass and vessel-glass were both made by glass-blowers working with molten glass. Glass objects frequently used included goblets, linen-smoothers, hanging lamps in which oil was burned, and the urinals so central to medical diagnosis. The modern patient going to consult a physician equipped with a list of symptoms and questions is the descendant of the medieval patient setting off for consulation carrying a glass urinal in a cylindrical wickerwork case with cover and loop-handle.

The household wealthy enough to acquire a lantern would appreciate the horners' craft. One type of lantern was made with an iron frame to hold translucent leaves of horn through which the light of a candle could shine. Horners soaked animal horns to separate the sheath of horn from the inner material, then boiled the sheath to soften it, slitting it along the inner curve. Then they pressed the sheet of horn flat before polishing, trimming, or even splitting it into several thinner sheets. Such leaves of horn were used as window-panes, and horn was also used to make items like tumblers, spoons, springs for composite crossbows, or the inkhorns treasured by scribes as tools of their trade.

FOUR

Games, Drama and Heraldry

Numerous games were available to both adults and children in medieval England. Many of these are recognizable today as the predecessors of games such as noughts and crosses, backgammon and blind man's buff. Sadly the rules and strategies of others have been altered to such an extent that the original game is unknown.

Children's Games

Some children's games were in essence easier and softer versions of adult games, as with marbles, a version of bowls played by adults. Playing shuttlecock was a more gentle game than tennis, and was played with a cork stuck with feathers rather than the hard ball used in medieval tennis. William fitz Stephen spoke of London schoolboys late in the twelfth century playing at disputation or formal debate, which was a very serious matter for advanced students and masters. Children also imitated adult ceremonies and rituals, like playing at celebrating Mass or imitating a noble procession. Other games played by medieval children are still being played today: hide-and-seek, follow-the-leader, whipping tops, skipping, swinging on swings, catching butterflies, upping and downing on a see-saw, blowing cherry stones out of the mouth, running, acrobatics and balancing, wrestling, tag, walking on stilts, and blind man's buff, which medieval children knew as hoodman blind. In this version the eyes of the child who was 'it' were covered simply by turning a hood around backwards so that the opening for the face was at the back of the head. Hot cockles was also a blindfold game in

Medieval boys play blind man's buff (Bodleian Library, Oxford, Ms. Douce. 276, f. 49v)

Girls catching butterflies in their hoods (Bodleian Library, Oxford, Ms. Bodl. 264, f. 135r)

which the player whose eyes were covered, and who knelt or stood with his or her hands held behind their back, had to guess correctly who had struck the outstretched hands in order to pass the blindfold on to another player.

Dicing

Dicing was an ancient game, and one of pure chance, so long as it was played honestly. In its earliest form dicing was done by rolling bones, and this continued through the Middle Ages, but play with cubic dice began long before the medieval era and was widespread in late medieval England. Dice games were numerous, and tend to be difficult to explain because the rules changed and were in any case seldom recorded. Hasard was a commonly played game with two dice and varying rules in which participants and onlookers bet on the outcome of the throws. Some dice games, like raffle, used three dice. The way to win at raffle was to throw all three dice alike or, failing that, to throw a pair with higher value than one's opponent. Crooked dice were far from unknown, quarrels over dice games were often violent, and even as a relatively crude form of gambling, dice play was popular, even addictive.

Akin to dicing was cross and pile, which took its name from the farthing coin of Edward I, which had a cross on one side while the other was called the pile. Games in which two players toss coins to the ground in front of them, calling out 'heads' or 'tails' ('cross' or 'pile'), with the winner calling correctly how the coin will land, and thus winning the coin of the other player, are still

Misericord from Gloucester Cathedral: Two youths are playing a game of chance with three dice; the one on the left has two discs and the one on the right three (Jack Farley)

played. Also related to dicing was queek, which was played by rolling or throwing pebbles onto a chequered board with bets being placed anticipating the pebble landing on a light or a dark square.

Board Games

A very popular game known to medievals as tables was the ancestor of today's backgammon. It existed in some two dozen forms, but basically the players used dice to determine the movement of the counters over the board. The game involved both luck and skill, in which each of the two players tried to clear his counters from the board while blocking his opponent's efforts to do the same. Archaeological refuse pit excavation on the site of the early Norman castle in Commercial Road, Gloucester, revealed a nearly complete board and a full set of thirty playing pieces for a game of tables. This game set, lacking dice, is thought to date from the eleventh century, and is made with bone plates for the board and bone playing pieces. The thirty tablemen are decorated with such motifs as Samson and the lion, a centaur with a bow, a

Gloucester tablemen. They appear to be, from left to right: Sagittarius, the Virgin, a figure with a fish and fowl (City Museum & Art Gallery)

hooded archer, and a seated harpist, but there is no certainty about the relationship of the decoration, if there was any, to the playing of the game.

Another very popular board game was merrills. In its most simple form the board had nine holes, and the play was like the pencil and paper game of tic-tac-toe or noughts and crosses: each player had three pieces, and they took turns putting them in holes in the board, trying to get three in a row while blocking their opponent. Playing surfaces with nine small cup-like indentations have been noticed in such places as the benches in the cloisters of Westminster Abbey, and at the cathedrals of Canterbury, Norwich, and Chichester. This game, also called three men's morris or smaller merrills, had many possibilities for variation and expansion. One evolution was into a more complex game with an expanded board, each player having nine pieces, and involving the capture of one's opponent's pieces: the winner being the first player to capture seven of his opponent's pieces. This is nine men's morris or larger merrills and is laid out with three squares of eight holes each, one inside the other, and simple but precise rules governing the vertical and horizontal movement of the pieces. Merrills became even more complicated with the addition of yet more

Two women play what appears to be draughts (Bodleian Library, Oxford, Ms. Bodl. 264, f. 60)

Chess being played in a walled garden (Bodleian Library, Oxford, Ms. Bodl. 264, f. 258v)

pieces and diagonal movement on still larger boards and one form of it, fox-and-geese, was played by Edward IV. The board for fox-and-geese looked like five smaller merrills boards put together in the form of a cross, and there was one playing piece, the fox, directed by one player, which was pitted against thirteen to seventeen other pieces, the geese, which were guided by the other player. The fox needed to capture geese by jumping over them before the geese could pin the fox up and prevent him from further movement. A fox-and-geese board has been found cut on the cloister benches of the Benedictine abbey at Gloucester (now the cathedral).

The board game that outclassed all others was chess. A game of strategy and war that reflected the world of real politics, it was, by the late Middle Ages, being played by all ranks of society in spite of, or perhaps because of, its aristocratic aura. Chess came to Christendom from the Muslim world, and it reached England in the aftermath of the Norman Conquest. In a courtly European context the chess pieces, which because of Islamic prohibition against artistic representations of the human form had few distinguishing characteristics, became a political microcosm of pieces with clearly defined features: king, queen (a counsellor or

assis nous a ia ses engiens fait drechier
cour en pocs lost gtre val cel uergier
a vos ij neueus mandau auancier
Quains iiij iors venroit entor ces murs lanch
v alles dist cassamus naies soing desinaier
Quen uostre secors uient alixand dalier
sont en sa cpaigne x mille chenalier

Two medieval board games: chess (above) and merrills (below) (Bodleian Library, Oxford, Ms. Bodl. 264, ff. 112r, 60)

vizier in the Muslim game), bishops (formerly elephants), knights (formerly horses), castles (formerly chariots), and a retinue of retainers (the infantry of the Muslim army). In Europe the movement of some of the pieces changed, with the bishop and queen gaining more freedom of movement, for instance, and the queen finally emerging as the dominating piece on the board. The game evolved in different ways over time, but it became and remained popular. To play chess well required intellectual strengths and practice, and the game became a fixture in the education of noble boys and girls. England's first printer, William Caxton (died 1491), printed as his second book 'The Game and

Playe of the Chesse', his own translation into English of the 'Liber de Ludo Scacchorum' by Jacob de Cessoles, a Dominican friar of Rheims, who wrote his treatise in the late thirteenth or early fourteenth century. The game of draughts, which in part was derived from chess and was played on a chess board, was given some attention in medieval England, but it gained no particular popularity until the seventeenth century. Draughts was developed in the twelfth century in southern France.

Cards

The game of cards took hold quickly when introduced into England in the fifteenth century. The game came from Muslim India by stages to Italy, Spain, and France, where King Charles VI had a painter decorating cards for his use in 1393. The first clear reference in England to the game of cards is a letter written by Margery Paston on Christmas Eve 1461, wherein the game is mentioned as if it were commonplace. Two years later, in a protectionist statute, Edward IV prohibited the importation of

A late medieval game of cards (British Library, Additional Ms. 12228, f. 313v)

playing cards as an encouragement to home manufacture. The London Company of Makers of Playing Cards was not incorporated until 1628, and no medieval English playing cards are known to survive. Whatever the particular game, cards required strategy and skill, and afforded an opportunity for the exquisite anguish of gambling. The cards themselves were made of ivory, parchment, or wood, with the designs and images put on and coloured by hand. The finest of early packs of cards must have been beautiful and costly productions. A legacy of the medieval design of cards is that the queen of all standard English suits today is a stylized representation of a contemporary portrait of Elizabeth of York, daughter of Edward IV and wife of Henry VII, who holds in her hand the white rose of York.

Drama

Dramatic performances in medieval England were in character almost exclusively religious, and are normally categorized as miracle, mystery, or morality plays. Stories from the scriptures and teachings of the Church presented as plays were greatly enjoyed. When these plays were performed by members of 'misteries', that is, trade or craft guilds, they were called mystery plays, and when they were performed by professional or amateur actors who were not representing any trade or craft guild, the plays were termed miracle plays. In morality plays, which never gained the popular following of the mystery or miracle plays, the characters were allegorical representations of the virtues and vices, and the action was the struggle between the representatives of good and evil. The idea behind the morality plays went back at least to Prudentius (died about AD 405), the finest Christian Latin poet of the late Roman Empire whose enduringly popular 'Psychomachia' was an allegorical depiction of the spiritual contest for the soul of humanity between the virtues and the vices. The plays 'Mankind' and 'The Somonynge of Everyman' are powerful and entertaining examples of morality plays surviving from late medieval England.

Miracle plays were first presented individually as early as the twelfth century, and were normally in Latin and performed by clerics. Plays in English performed by the laity came later. In time, sponsorship by guilds and series of plays performed sequentially resulted in the cycles of mystery plays associated with towns such as Chester, where they first appeared in the third quarter of the thirteenth century, Wakefield in Yorkshire (the Towneley plays), Coventry, Leeds, Lancaster, Newcastle-on-Tyne, Beverley, Preston,

Kendal, London, and York. A popular time for the performance of cycles of plays, following the example of Chester, was the feast of Corpus Christi, a moveable event which fell in May or June, founded by Pope Urban IV in 1264 to honour the sacrament of the eucharist. Extensive parts of only four of the play cycles survive: those connected with Chester, Coventry, Wakefield, and York. Various numbers of plays were used in each cycle to tell biblical stories from the Creation to the Last Judgement. The Chester cycle was made up of twenty-five plays, the N-Town cycle of forty-one, that of Wakefield thirty-two, while the largest cycle of mystery plays to survive to the present time comes from York, with forty-eight plays and a fragment (a list from 1415 notes fifty-seven plays). The feast of Corpus Christi fell on a day with the many hours of daylight needed to get the full cycle in. At York the plays were performed on flat-topped pageant-wagons with four wheels which were rolled through the streets of the town, the wagons stopping in turn at each designated station for the performance of a particular play. The spectators simply remained in one spot and watched each play as it came to them. As enterprising bourgeois capitalists, the property holders at the stations charged the spectators fees. The number of stations rose from twelve when the cycle was early in its development to sixteen in the middle of the sixteenth century when the plays were nearing their end, which came in 1580. The Coventry performance (the 'Ludus Coventriae'), on the other hand, was presented in one place, which must have been an undertaking requiring masterful planning. Only part of the Coventry cycle survives, and it is therefore difficult to analyse it effectively in terms of performance.

Single plays, such as a Christmas interlude (a general medieval term for diverse sorts of dramatic entertainments), were being performed at York by the 1370s, and the Corpus Christi cycle was developed fully in the first half of the fifteenth century. Richard II visited York when the plays were being presented in 1397, and was the only recorded royal viewer of the York cycle, but the Coventry plays were seen by Margaret of Anjou, wife of Henry VI, in 1457, by King Richard III in 1484, and by his supplanter, Henry VII, in 1486 and 1492. Plays were clearly an important cultural pastime for the people of York and Coventry and the other towns where they were performed in the later Middle Ages. They were a means of religious instruction as well as entertainment. They were also a source of honour for those who put them on, both the rulers of the town and the participants, and for the town in which they were performed.

The symbolism which links the notion of the body of Christ of which all believers partook and became a part, and the body of citizens who collectively were encompassed by the presentation of the plays, would have been apparent. The public events of Corpus Christi Day in most towns which staged plays began with the celebration of Mass, followed by the consecrated host, the Corpus Christi, being carried through the town accompanied by those of importance, dressed in symbols of office or guild livery, and processing in hierarchical order to the church where the body of Christ was placed. Only at this point would the secular aspects of the day's activities begin, highlighted by the presentation of the plays. The play cycle at York was so time consuming that the Mass and procession were held on the day following Corpus Christi.

The cost of putting on the plays was borne largely by the members of the guilds which sponsored them and by persons not in guilds who were doing business in the city, who were charged fees. Members of the guilds sponsoring the different plays were often the actors, and the activity had the potential for building camaraderie through co-operative effort. The lavishness of the pageant-wagons, the scenery and other stage properties, and the costumes, redounded to the honour of the sponsoring guilds. Such manifestations of honour on occasion led to clashes among guilds over precedence and prestige, a ludicrous way to mark a religious festival geared towards unity and concord.

LITURGICAL DRAMA

Liturgical drama was an occasional part of church life. These Latin plays presented during worship services were not supplanted by the better-known mystery plays, but existed simultaneously until the time of the Reformation. They were used to give emphasis to aspects of worship, and were especially common at Easter and Christmas. With the similar intent of religious instruction for the faithful, were saints' plays in English, based upon the lives of saints, of which examples survive dealing with St Paul and Mary Magdalene.

Mumming

Mumming was a form of popular dramatic entertainment in which a champion was killed while fighting and was then brought back to life. Mumming plays may have grown out of ancient ceremonies associated with the agricultural year, because all of the examples

ont lost mdoise crie / z se gaumentent tuit Que li slex phelppon / vanatabee
Eignozs dust castam? as ceualiers greiois az e uoie en son dangier / ne alui accozde
Demain nous asseurra / clarus le mdois C ar il a tout le mont sougit z enchante

Mumming in long-tailed hoods
(Bodleian, Ms. Bodl. 264, f. 129)

that have been collected from Scotland and Ireland as well as from England are seasonal, and also contain the elements of death and resurrection. The actors were male, and wore disguises of various sorts. The many examples of mumming ceremonies are conveniently grouped into three types. In the 'Hero-Combat' type protagonist and antagonist engage in combat, one is killed, and then is revived by a third character. The 'Sword Dance' type has at least five participants with one dancer being ritually subdued by the rest, all armed with mock swords. The antiquity of mumming plays is a matter of scholarly dispute, but mummers in costumes of festive disguise were certainly on the scene. Morris dancing was akin to sword dancing, the enemy being the Muslim Moor. This entertainment became popular in England in the fifteenth century, but there is no positive association with the Muslim Moors, the Spanish Arabs. The 'Wooing Ceremony', the third type of mumming, is indigenous to the East Midlands and includes a death and resurrection element, but more central to the action is the wooing of an actor disguised as a woman, who is successfully courted by a clown. By the fifteenth century, mummings were being called disguisings.

Pageants

Pageantry was a source of delight for many observers, and incorporated a powerful element of drama. City guilds and corporations enhanced their prestige, honoured dignitaries, and entertained citizens with pageants. The great and the wealthy of the kingdom moved about at all times surrounded by followers and presented a display of magnificence which exemplified their power.

Even the grief of the great was an occasion for display. Blanche of Lancaster, an eminent heiress whose marriage in 1359 to John of Gaunt made her husband the supreme private landowner of his day in England and opened the way for him to become Duke of Lancaster, died of plague on 12 September 1369. Thereafter, until his own death in 1399, John of Gaunt commemorated the anniversary of her death in eloquent fashion. There would be two more duchesses later in his life, but he determined that his remains would be laid to rest beside those of Blanche in the tomb designed by Henry Yevele, one of the finest of medieval England's mason-architects, in St Paul's Cathedral, London. It so happens that a detailed financial account survives for the anniversary services celebrated in 1374, and the event was anything but austere. The central feature was a Mass in the cathedral conducted by a major cathedral canon assisted by seven other major canons (the full complement was thirty major canons) and all twelve minor canons together with a goodly portion of the entire staff of the cathedral. At the Savoy, his London house, John of Gaunt provided a supper for the celebrants after vespers for the dead on the eve of the anniversary as well as refreshments (at the cathedral) after the anniversary service. The clergy were of course paid fees for participating. The cathedral was draped for the anniversary service with black cloths, and the forty wax candles kept burning at Mass times around Blanche's tomb were replaced and eight additional mortar-lights were placed on the tomb. Twenty-four poor men acted as torch bearers around the tomb, and were dressed in the white and blue livery of the Duke of Lancaster. As well as the High Mass celebrated at St Paul's, Masses were said by the orders of friars in London, and alms were distributed to the poor and to prisoners. The total cost was over £45. The anniversary service for Blanche of Lancaster in 1374 seems to have been the norm for one of her position in society, and was not an unusual sort of event.

When John of Gaunt himself died on 3 February 1399, his passing was marked by ceremonies on a princely scale. He died at his castle at Leicester, and there was no hurry to organize a dignified procession to convey the body from Leicester through Dunstable, St Albans, and Barnet to St Paul's for burial. For reasons not entirely clear, the duke wished his unembalmed body not to be buried for forty days, perhaps in imitation of Jacob as recorded in Genesis (50:3), or conspicuously to underscore religious teachings on the corruptibility of the flesh and the need to focus upon things spiritual. Interment took place on 16 March. Reports indicate that the funeral was conducted on a magnificent scale. Gaunt's heir, Henry Bolingbroke, had been exiled in 1398 by Richard II, but some slight circumstantial evidence suggests that he was in London for the funeral. Richard himself was present for the funeral, and Bolingbroke would be back in the kingdom before the year was out to supplant his first cousin on the throne and become King Henry IV.

Pageantry was sometimes meant to convey a message more sophisticated than position, wealth, and power. In October 1390 Richard II held a tournament at Smithfield, London's recreational suburb. In May 1389 Richard had, quite correctly, declared himself to be of age and taken over the personal rule of his kingdom. He wished to put behind him the tutelage of his minority and to erase in so far as he could the power which had been exercised since late 1387 by five powerful nobles known as the Lords Appellant, especially as that power had been displayed in the Merciless Parliament of 1388 in which Richard had been humiliated and five of his supporters destroyed. Thus Richard wished to assert himself as a leader, encourage harmony among political factions, and to cultivate concord between his government and the London establishment and, more broadly, between his courtiers and the Londoners.

The tournament of 1390 was in many ways a pageant of harmony in the guise of a martial game. The king's tournament team of sometime rival lords – twenty men led by the king – displayed unity by being arrayed in identical livery displaying the king's white hart emblem; the visiting team of foreign knights would display no such uniformity. The Smithfield tournament was in fact the first time Richard II had given the white hart to his followers as a personal badge. Spectator participation was another ingredient in the promotion of harmony, and at least some of the scaffolding for the tournament observers was provided by the king's clerk of the works, Geoffrey Chaucer. The king, his queen, Anne of Bohemia, Mayor William Venour and the aldermen of London and their wives, were among the spectators. The tournament involved socializing and banqueting, and the three

A manuscript of the romance of Lancelot showing a tournament in progress (The Pierpont Morgan Library, New York, M. 806, f. 262)

days of jousting were restricted to individual *joustes à plaisance* employing blunted weapons. The active participants in the tournament were the knights, an élite group. Everyone else was there for the most part in the passive role of spectator. The notion of concord underlying the Smithfield tournament of 1390 must not be pressed too far, then, because the tournament became a chapter in the history of international chivalry, and the remaining years of Richard's reign were a rotten failure as regards political harmony.

Another highly symbolic episode of pageantry was the entry of Richard II's third cousin, the eight-year-old Henry VI, into London in 1432 on his return from his coronation in Paris as King of France. This was part of the effort of the Lancastrian government to complete the programme started by his father, Henry V, to create a dual monarchy of England and France under a single king. As Henry VI made his way into the capital he was greeted by seven pageants at seven stations, each pageant a dramatic scene with different characters. The first pageant, for instance, was on the gate of London Bridge, and consisted of a giant figure holding a sword (probably the same giant, now reconditioned, that had greeted Henry V on his return from the Agincourt campaign), suggesting that young Henry VI would become mighty through virtuous living. As a show, the series of stations would have been impressively dramatic, but for the subtly analytic mind the cumulative effect of the sequence of pageants would have been the suggestion that in King Henry was to be seen the joining of two dynasties, each of which had been enhanced by a royal saint (St Edward the Confessor of England and St Louis IX of France), and that, *imitatio Christi*, this new messianic king, this embodiment of justice, would bring peace and reconciliation to the warring kingdoms of England and France, and usher in a glorious age of order and prosperity. This was not to be, but it was the message behind the pageantry of 1432, and the royal entry into London was long remembered because it was so spectacular and because its sequence was detailed in a poem by the renowned poet-monk of Bury St Edmunds, John Lydgate.

Heraldry

The science and art of heraldry probably began in the era of the crusades when men who were strangers to one another and speaking different languages found themselves in need of individual insignia of some sort so that they would know who was who. Heralds and

Heraldic devices are clearly displayed on these knights in combat, from Sir Thomas Holme's Book, *c.* 1443 (British Library, Harley Ms. 4205, ff. 19v–20)

judges already existed as a result of the development of tournaments. Heraldic devices to identify individual owners on the field of battle or in tournaments appeared in the twelfth century, and heraldry gradually became a part of everyday life. Conventions soon developed to regulate the forms and usages of heraldry, and turn it into an exact and precise system of identification. Each device was used by one individual, but the device was hereditary. The devices needed to be seen at a distance, so bold and simple designs were most effective. The obvious place to paint a device was the shield, and the heater shield – in essence a triangle with a straight line top and sides slightly curving to a point at the bottom – has continued to influence heraldic design. Another obvious place to paint a device was on the front and back of the linen surcoat which knights wore over their armour as protection from the direct rays of the sun, hence the term 'cote armure', or coat-of-arms.

Heraldic devices soon came to be employed beyond just the military environs of their origin. They were engraved upon seals used to authenticate documents. The heraldry of donors appeared on vestments and liturgical vessels used in churches, on funerary monuments, and as architectural decoration for ecclesiastical and secular buildings. Gateways, roof bosses, wall paintings, stained-glass windows, illuminated manuscripts, and household objects like furniture and plate were decorated with heraldic devices. The use of heraldry also expanded beyond the knights to include gentry, merchants, women, and corporations. Heralds took on the responsibility of keeping track of the devices of heraldry, employing such methods as compiling collections of drawings with identifying descriptions and information, which are known as rolls of arms. Richard III ultimately gave corporate status to the College of Heralds in 1484. The enjoyment of the decorative qualities of heraldry and the game of identification would have been available even to persons who were not themselves armigerous, for heraldry was both an individual and private matter, and a public art of display and prestige.

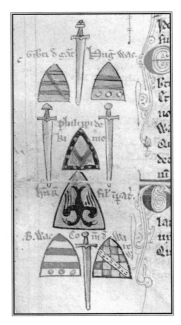

The chronicle of Matthew Paris is an important source for early thirteenth-century heraldry. In this case he has painted the shields of deceased knights upside down in the margin close to where their deaths are recorded in the text (The Master and Fellows of Corpus Christi College, Cambridge, Ms. 16, f. 144v)

FIVE

Sport, Hunting and Tournaments

As with games in the previous chapter, many outdoor sports have changed little since the thirteenth century. Quoits, football, tennis and golf all found their origins in the Middle Ages, while the practice of archery went back even further. If we use the convenient concept of an outdoor physical game being a sport, then there existed numerous activities pursued in late medieval England that must be thought of as sports.

Throwing Games

Throwing stones for sport was a straightforward activity, and the essential equipment was abundantly available. It could be attempted over considerable distance with a modest stone, or a shorter distance with a heavier stone, like putting the shot. The story was recorded in the 'Histoire de Guillaume L'Marechal', composed around 1225, that the athlete famed for his prowess in tournaments, William Marshal (died 1219), Earl of Pembroke, endeavoured before an audience of knights to throw a stone further than the accepted record, and set a new record by a foot and a half. An awareness on the part of the knights of the best ever throw emphasizes the competitive nature of the activity. Throwing a stone with a sling could be done for pleasure or in fowling, and had a worthy reputation as an ancient activity due to the story of David and Goliath.

Quoits was a throwing game with wide familiarity, and could take various forms. A medieval quoit could be a horseshoe, a disc-shaped stone, or something similar, and the target, which seems not to have been absolutely necessary, could have been almost anything. Bowls was another similar game. The player used a

turdicens. partiti sunt uestimeta
mea sibi & in uestem meam mise
runt sortem & milites quide hec
fecerunt. Stabant aute iuxta cru
cem iesu mater eius & soror ma

Left: A bowler aims for a feather target, while two others await their turns (Bodleian Library, Oxford, Ms. Douce. 276, f. 12r) Below: Playing kayles outside a tavern (British Library, Additional Ms. 22494, f. 42)

round, usually stone, bowl which was rolled across a stretch of flat ground towards targets, often small conical jacks, which the player was attempting to knock over. Bowling could be done on any piece of flat land, and the equipment could be elaborate or simple, according to the resources of the men and women playing. In the later Middle Ages, several variants on bowls appeared. The children's game of marbles was probably in origin a miniature form of bowls. The game of half-bowl used a hemisphere (half a bowl) which was slid on its flat side towards target pins. The game of closh used an implement like a stick to move the bowl through a hoop or ring, as in croquet. Kayles used a stick, rather than a bowl, to bring down the target pins, and might best be thought of as a form of the game of ninepins or skittles. In 1477 Edward IV issued an edict against the playing of several new games, including closh, kayles and hand-in and hand-out, both of which were apparently ball games, and neither of which can now be defined.

Outdoor Ball Games

Ball games figure prominently in the list of sports. In Old English the word 'camp' meant a martial contest, a fight, or a battle, and an old form of football, with large numbers engaged on opposing sides, was called camp-ball. The game was not too tightly organized. There were two sides, and two goals on each side. The goals could be any distance apart, from a few dozen yards to miles if, for example, the game was being played between men of two villages with a pair of goals in each village. The field of play, the camping-close, could thus be defined as desired. Initially the ball was made of leather and was about the size of a modern cricket ball; later in the Middle Ages the ball was made of a pig's bladder filled with dried peas, which could be kicked as well as thrown. There was no specified number of participants on each side, and the number of players could range into the hundreds. To start the game, the ball was thrown up between the two sides, and whoever gained control sped off for the opposing side's goals. Getting the ball there and trapping opponents with the ball gained points, and little imagination is needed to realize the potential for mayhem in camp-ball. The activity seems, in fact, to have been as much fighting as playing. When the ball and the game permitted kicking as well as throwing it took on a different quality, and if only kicking of the ball was permitted the contest was known as kicking-camp. The term football came to be used for kicking-camp in the fifteenth century.

The potential for injury or worse while playing ball games is illustrated by an incident from Newcastle-upon-Tyne in 1280 when some fellows were playing at ball (*ludens ad pilum*), although the form of the game is not made clear, when Henry de Ellington ran into David le Keu, who was wearing a knife hanging from his belt. The knife cut through the sheath and stabbed Henry in the belly, and Henry died from the misadventure. A similar incident occurred several decades later when a Gilbertine canon of the priory at Shouldham in Norfolk named William de Spalding was kicking a ball during a game when one of his friends ran against him and was wounded so severely by the sheathed knife carried by the canon that the man died some days later. The canon, feeling deeply remorseful about the accident, obtained a papal dispensation in 1321. Not all accidents were fatal, and John Hendyman merely broke his leg while playing football to celebrate a baptism in Sussex in 1403. It is no wonder that responsible authorities, such as the London Mayor Nicholas Farndon in around 1320, issued a long sequence of totally ineffectual prohibitions against playing football.

Various ball sports, using different equipment, evolved out of camp-ball, such as golf, hockey, handball, different forms of bowling, and ball games using rackets. Stoolball was played with women perched on milking stools, who tried to avoid being struck by balls bowled by men, and this social sport was played for prizes of cakes or kisses. Handball, which set the ball in motion with a strike of the hand, was a simple and basic game that could be played in the open between participants or against a wall by one or more players. The parish church might well offer the only solid and flat wall-surface against which a ball could be thrown in a village, and it is hardly a wonder that 'pleying at the balle' was reported in the churchyard. Handball altered with the addition of a court and rackets to become tennis, a more aristocratic game. Tennis played with rackets was present in England by the last third of the fourteenth century, and was familiar enough for Chaucer to mention it in his *Troilus and Criseyde* as 'pleyen racket to and fro'.

Adding a bat to a ball game opened up other possibilities. A curved stick was called a bandy, and bandy-ball was a basic bat-and-ball game whose rules could be determined for the occasion. A straight stick was called a crick in Old English, and is the basis of the word cricket. No game called cricket was played in the Middle

Tennis played with bound hands, in a walled court (British Library, Harley Ms. 4375, f. 151v)

n mozt abatu lame li eftuet rendze
vaches garder ne pozra mes entendze

Monks and nuns play a bat-and-ball game (Bodleian Library, Oxford, Ms. Bodl. 264, f. 22)

Ages, but there were many ball games described that are similar to cricket. Cricket could be an amalgam of stoolball and crick-ball. The story of the origins of cricket may be murky, but that of golf has greater clarity. A stick with a head attached was called a bittle stick, or a camboc or cambuc, and a sport with the name bittle-battle appears in 'Domesday Book' (1086). This game was gradually refined into golf, formerly pronounced 'goff', and was called by that name in Scotland in 1457.

Winter Games

When cold weather produced ice, ball games were moved on to the ice. Ice camping, and ice bandy-ball are mentioned, and curling, which probably resembled quoits in its earliest form, could be played. Skating on ice was not unusual, and skates made from the bones of cattle and horses have been recovered from archaeological sites, many from London and York. The bone skates were sometimes strapped on to the feet, but not always, because the skating technique used was to keep the skates flat on the ice and move by pushing against the ice with a stick or pole. William fitz Stephen, in his 'Life of Thomas Becket' (written between 1170 and 1183), described skating on the Moorfields outside London, indicating that the skaters used poles to propel themselves along, had their skates made of animal shin-bones bound to their feet, and that sometimes reckless youths deliberately raced at each other from a distance and crashed together using their poles as if tilting. Bodily injury was not at all unknown. All ages engaged in skating, and a poignant archaeological find of 1899 was at College Street, Ipswich, where a female skeleton was found with bone skates, embedded in the mud of what had been the bed of the river. Another obvious activity for frosty weather was throwing snowballs. Smacking one's target with a packed sphere of snow is a sensation to be relished. No rules would be needed for a spontaneous snowball fight among a group of people willing to laugh through a spell of cold. In a more serious context, the 'Brut' chronicle recorded that when Earl Thomas of Lancaster was being drawn to his place of execution in 1322 the onlookers pelted him with snowballs.

Swimming

Swimming ranked among the minor recreations in late medieval England. The Romans had valued swimming as a military skill, and Julius Caesar, who led reconnaissance missions into Britain in 55 and 54 BC, was an accomplished swimmer. In Anglo-Saxon England, if the three references to swimming by the hero in the singular epic, *Beowulf*, are any indication, swimming continued to be a respected skill. The seafaring Vikings certainly did not disparage swimming. The Norman conquerors, the evidence suggests, were little inclined towards swimming in spite of its recommendation in Roman military manuals of continuing popularity such as Flavius Vegetius Renatus' 'De Re Militari' (fourth century AD). The Norman warriors were knights, and swimming and knightly armour lack compatibility. References to swimming on the part of knightly heroes are few in romances and *chansons de geste*. Edward II may have been a swimmer, but he had

Naked boys being taught to swim (British Library, Additional Ms. 38126, f. 7)

no great reputation for dignity. The poem 'Piers Plowman', however, written in the fourteenth century sometime after Edward II's reign, speaks appreciatively of swimming. Not just men, but women as well, participated in swimming. Records state that in 1244 a woman in London drowned while swimming alone, and there were other women who suffered the same fate in London and in Wiltshire in 1276.

Nothing can be said with confidence about the techniques of medieval swimming, because the first English treatise on swimming was not composed until the late sixteenth century when Everard Digby composed his 'De Arte Natandi' ('Art of Swimming').

Mimic Combat Games

Wrestling, which seems to have been highly popular especially with humble audiences, was a sport high on the virility scale, and offered an opportunity for wagering on the outcome. It was a common sport, required no special equipment, and was a display of strength and agility. The participants might number two at a time,

Two wrestlers on a misericord at Gloucester Cathedral (Jack Farley)

but the spectators could be many. On the festival of James the Apostle (25 July) outside the walls of London wrestlers competed for the prize of a ram, an obvious symbol of virility, before crowds of observers. Not everyone found wrestling attractive, and the fourteenth-century Dominican preacher John Bromyard denounced it as 'a foul and unthrifty occupation'. Bishop Thomas Brinton of Rochester (died 1389) is recorded as disapproving of vain recreations of the body, such as tasty dinners, markets, shows, and wrestling matches, that men found more attractive than sermons. In the same era, Robert Rypon, sub-prior of Durham, commented disparagingly in a homily on empty displays of bodily strength like wrestling, lifting weights, and hurling stones.

In this style of wrestling each opponent grabs the scarf of the other as the starting position (British Library, Royal Ms. 2 B VIII, f. 160v)

Various styles were employed in wrestling. One form required that an opponent be thrown so that he would make a solid 'three-point' landing on the ground; in another each opponent grasped the tunic, scarf, or body of the other as the starting position, and then tried to pull the opponent to the ground; and another style was to wrestle in pairs with one contestant riding on the shoulders of his partner and struggling against a similarly mounted pair.

Sword and buckler play was a youthful game in imitation of knightly combat. The short swords and small round shields were made of wood, and the fun would have been analogous to a modern game of soldiers. Evidence suggests that some medieval aristocrats thought sword and buckler play compromised the dignity of chivalry. A far more serious game with swords is found in the Yorkshire judicial eyre of 1218–19, which contains a note that Adam de Monceaux was killed with a sword by William Aguillun as they played (*ludebant*) in the house of Robert de Percy of Bolton Percy. The cryptic reference says nothing about the nature of the play, but it could have been martial for all three men mentioned were members of knightly families.

Tilting at the quintain was a sport designed to help males train for war and for tournaments. The essential equipment for the game was a pole fixed into the ground upon which was mounted a cross-piece that would pivot easily. A tilter would ride swiftly with couched lance at this quintain device, attempting to strike a target

Training in knightly skills began at an early age. A fourteenth-century manuscript shows the initial stages in the development of the necessary techniques. On the left a youth is approaching the quintain on foot. On the right, a youth with a lance is being pulled towards a target while riding on a mock horse (Bodleian Library, Oxford, Ms. 264, f. 82v)

.y.   o jō. ꝟ aint lilt.
     c jō. ꝟ aint auuen
.x.   f jō. ꝟ aint landn.
     g jō. ꝟ aint bertin

Spectators on the river banks enjoy scenes of water-tilting. The fellow liable to fall into the water is easily identified (Giraudon)

on one end of the pivoting bar, so that it would move out of the way and prevent a collision. Speed and agility were vital to prevent the pivoting bar from whizzing around and striking the tilter from behind. A variant on this sport was to make the target an object suspended from above, for example between two posts, and the tilter then developed skill with the lance by aiming at the target. William fitz Stephen mentioned London youths armed with lances floating in boats down the Thames toward fixed targets in the water. If the lance did not break when the target was struck in this 'water quintain', the tilter went in the water (which was doubtless part of the fun), and companions in boats needed to be on hand to effect a rescue.

Archery

Another sport with obvious military overtones was archery, which might be called the national sport of late medieval England. The weapon of choice was the longbow, the war bow of the medieval English, being simpler and having a greater rapidity of fire than the crossbow. The stave of the longbow ran to about 6 ft, and might be made of ash, hazel or, better, of wych-elm or, best, of the mountain yew. The most suitable yew would be the trees grown in the shade so as to produce year-rings lying close together. If properly cut from the tree, a yew log would by its very nature be

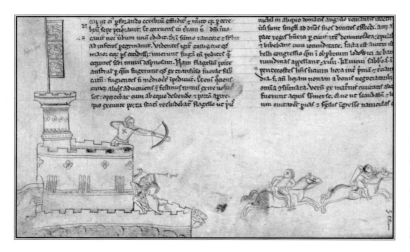

Longbows were used in the siege of a city – in this case Lincoln in 1141 (The Master and Fellows of Corpus Christi College, Cambridge, Ms. 16, f. 55v; photograph: Conway Library, Courtauld Institute of Art)

suitable for making a composite bow: the heartwood had a natural resistance to compression and would become the belly of the bow, while the sapwood under the bark had a natural resistance to tension, so would form the back of the bow. Once cut, the yew logs were split and seasoned, perhaps for three or four years, before the bowyer would begin the final shaping of the log into a slender stave.

Much has been learned about longbows as a result of the archaeological work on the royal ship, *Mary Rose*, which went down in the Solent during a battle with an invading French fleet in 1545. A hundred and thirty-eight yew bows were recovered from the *Mary Rose* in the course of two years. One wooden chest held forty-eight, and another thirty-six, while the remaining bows were found scattered about the ship. Each of these had been made from a single stave of yew; there were no jointed bows. It is believed that the *Mary Rose* bows were fitted with horn nocks but, if so, the nocks did not survive the conditions of immersion for over four centuries. Nocks were the slots on each end of the bow that held the string in place. They could be cut into the wood of the bow or horn nocks could be fitted on and held with glue. The *Mary Rose* bows ranged in their draw weight from about 100 lb to about 170 lb at 30 in. It would have required a hefty fellow to use such a bow. The technique apparently used by medieval archers to draw a bow was to begin with the arms lowered holding the bow, and then, while pushing the stave and pulling the string, to raise the bow into a position of full draw. The string would be near the ear, and the archer would appear as if framed by the bow and string, which is why it is still customary to speak of shooting *in* a longbow. The *Mary Rose* bows do not have a thicker portion remaining at the centre to serve as a handle. In medieval drawings of archers with drawn bows, the bow seems to be a true arc, and this must be a portrayal from life: even the part of the bow in the archer's hand would, therefore, have been working to launch the arrow, which speaks of the skill and strength required.

The strings fitted to longbows were made of beeswax-impregnated hemp or flax. Arrows were made of various kinds of wood. Thousands of arrowshafts were found on the *Mary Rose*, but they were in a poor state of preservation because the wood, such as poplar and alder, was not as durable under water as the yew from which the bows were made. Ash had a good reputation as a wood for arrows. Goose feathers were highly regarded for fletching the arrows to give them stability in flight, but feathers from cranes, swans, or the wings of peacocks were also used. Three quills were glued in place on each arrowshaft and then, for insurance in the event that the fletching glue failed, a thread would be wound in a spiral through the flights of feathers.

Crossbows were used in war and for sport in England, but they did not capture the devotion of the English as did the longbow. Crossbows were slower to use than longbows and more complicated. They probably also did not have the reputation for being a weapon of skill.

Practice and competition at archery were commonly undertaken at butts, which were often established in churchyards, but archery play could be very informal, and the tight smack of an arrow impacting would have been a common sound. A popular form of competition was to shoot from a distance, even as much as 200 yd,

Longbowmen practising at the butts (British Library, Additional Ms. 42130, f. 147v)

at a wooden stick fixed in a target or staked vertically in the ground, with the objective of splitting the peg with an arrow. Another popular form of archery practice and competition was roving, where groups of people traipsed through the countryside shooting at random targets, sometimes to the considerable dismay of landowners.

Animal Sports

In some sports humans and animals competed together toward the goals of a contest, while in others animals were the centre of the action as humans observed. In hunting, animals were often used to assist the hunters, but hunting was so distinctive that it requires more intense individual treatment.

Among the sports where animal and human functioned as a team, an obvious one is horse-racing. The desire to race horses probably dates from the domestication of the animal, and was certainly not the invention of late medieval England. Horse-racing was for the most part, it seems, informal. It was a matter of seeing which horse could run most quickly from one point to another. A famous reference to horse-racing was made during the reign of Henry II by William fitz Stephen who spoke of the horse market held at Smithfield outside the walls of London every Saturday, and how horses ridden by teenage boys would be raced in competition with one another over a flat distance to show the speed and power of the horses as well as to entertain those who watched. Fitz Stephen has nothing to say about starting procedures or rules for racing, and the sport was probably fairly unruly. Henry II's sons, Richard the Lionheart and King John, were both patrons of horse-racing and appreciators of fine horses, as for the most part were their successors to the throne.

Gambling was an integral part of horse-racing just as it was with many other sports. It seems most easily associated with cock-fighting. Cock-fighting was a sport mentioned by fitz Stephen, who noted that on Shrove Tuesday boys had a holiday from school, and in the morning brought their fighting-cocks to their masters, who presumably would supervise the contests, and then the boys spent their time watching the battling cocks. Fitz Stephen associated cock-fighting with the games of boys, although many modern parents would think it far too savage. Variants on cock-fighting were no less cruel. Cock-throwing involved chasing a cock while throwing objects to strike and stun it, and the objective was to get in the first good hit. Then the bird was propped up in some

Children mock-jousting (left) and cock-fighting (Bodleian Library, Oxford, Ms. Bodl. 264, f. 50)

fashion, and projectiles were thrown at it until it was killed. Although anthropologists argue about the relationship of such games to the ancient association of cocks with fertility and virility, medievals thought of cock-fighting and throwing at cocks as children's games, along with spinning tops, catching butterflies, blind man's buff, and other more gentle activities.

The acquisition of cocks for sporting use was possible for most ranks in society, but to come up with a bear for bear-baiting was another matter. There were no longer any native bears in England, and they had, therefore, to be imported. In one form of bear-baiting a gang of five or six dogs would be set upon a bear, and the entertainment was to watch the fight and the increasing agitation of the bear, and bet on the survival of the animals involved. A fifteenth-century grammar master at Magdalen School, Oxford, made bear-baiting sound like good fun when he prepared the following prose passage for his students to translate into Latin:

> All the yonge folkes almoste of this towne dyde rune yesterday to the castell to se a bere batyde with fers dogges within the wallys. It was greatly to be wondrede, for he dyde defende hymselfe so with hys craftynes and his wyllynes from the cruell doggys methought he sett not a whitt be their woodenes [madness] nor by their fersnes.

In another form, bear-baiting involved a human prodding a bear as the spectators delighted in its growing frenzy. There is a scene of bear-baiting in the Bayeux Tapestry. Bull-baiting was similar to bear-baiting, and it was a pleasant diversion prior to the butchering of the bull. For this reason the bull-ring in Coventry in the late Middle Ages was adjacent to the butchers' workplace. Bull-running was a sport said to have begun in the days of King John in Stamford, Lincolnshire, and it caught on in some other locations, with a mad bull being turned loose to be chased by dogs

Bear-baiting, as depicted on a fourteenth-century misericord in Gloucester Cathedral. A chained bear, on the left, is being attacked by a ferocious dog, while the bear's keeper, with stick in hand, stands near (Jack Farley)

and people alike. William fitz Stephen mentioned boar-baiting as well as bear- and bull-baiting, but this seems to have been rare.

Many people spent time in the company of horses, which engendered affection as well as respect for the work they could do. Names came into use for the various kinds of horses encountered. Carrying Chaucer's imagined pilgrims on their journey to Canterbury, the Nun's Priest rode a jade (an inferior horse, even a draught-horse as opposed to a riding horse), and the Canon rode a hackney (a middle sized horse used for ordinary riding). Neither the jade nor the hackney was thought to be especially impressive. Chaucer's Cook and Ploughman rode upon mares, which were given no further description as to quality or colour, suggesting that they were undistinguished. Chaucer's Reeve rode a stot (another inferior sort of horse, and a word also used contemptuously for a woman), but it was elevated in quality as 'full good' and 'pomely grey', while the Shipman had a rouncy (a decent horse for ordinary riding). In the fifteenth century a breed of rouncy called the trotter became fashionable. A horse called an ambler, such as was ridden by Chaucer's Wife of Bath, was clearly more comfortable moving at a slower pace than a trotter. The best of amblers were highly

A performing horse (Bodleian Library, Oxford, Ms. Bod. 264, f. 96v)

desirable horses, but the very best of riding horses were classed as palfreys, and they had style, beauty, and swiftness. The status of Chaucer's Monk was elevated by his riding upon a palfrey.

A gem of medieval wisdom about horses was printed in the 'Boke of St Albans' towards the end of the fifteenth century:

A goode hors shulde have xv propertees and condicions.
It is to wit, iii of a man, iii of a woman, iii of a fox, iii of an haare and iii of an asse.
Off a man, boolde, prowde, and hardy.
Off a woman, fayre brestid, faire of here, and esy to lip uppon.
Off a fox, a faire tayle, short eris with a good trot.
Off an hare a grete eyghe, a dry hede and well rennyng.
Off an asse a bigge chyne, a flatte leg and a good houe.

Hunting

Hunting was a physical activity that brought delight as well as sustenance to participants, and it had many shades of aristocratic and virile association. Many members of the upper ranks of society kept horses and hounds strictly for the purpose of hunting, from which it is clearly to be observed that the aristocracy of medieval England was a warrior class. Among the leading pastimes employed as preparation and rehearsal for war was hunting. If there was no immediate opportunity for war, hunting served as an identifying marker for society's military élite. As to the establishment of hunting preserves, it was William the Conqueror who introduced the institution of the forest into England, which was not necessarily a place where trees grew, but a hunting preserve, like the Conqueror's New Forest. Hunting in a royal forest was restricted to the king and those whom he designated as eligible to participate. Forest hunting was to be a royal monopoly and an aristocratic privilege, and within the forest the beasts of the chase were protected: red deer, fallow deer, roe deer, wild boars

Searching out a stag (Bodleian Library, Oxford, Ms. Douce. 335, f. 57)

and, in some cases, hares. Royal foresters, forest justices, and other officers maintained and protected the forests and enforced special laws. The nobility could not, however, endure forest hunting as a royal monopoly, and when Magna Carta was reissued in 1217 in the minority of Henry III, a separate Forest Charter was issued which extended the forest hunting rights of the nobility, ended the royal monopoly, and reduced the amount of land designated as royal forest. The trend towards relaxing the forest laws continued over time.

Terms other than forest were employed to designate places for hunting, although the terms were not always carefully used. Some privileged persons were given a royal grant of warren for lands not included in royal forests. The right of warren on specified lands did not extend to hunting the royal beasts of the forest, but meant that the holder could keep dogs and hunt hares and foxes. The right of a chace (or chase) was also obtained by royal grant, and it involved the transfer of forest law into the hands of a private individual, thus creating essentially a private forest. A park was another designation for a hunting preserve, properly established only with a royal licence. A park was an enclosed piece of land which contained deer for hunting. One way of enclosing a park was with a pale of stakes set in an earthen bank created by digging an internal ditch. The idea was to keep the deer contained by means of a barrier of some sort, and a park was expensive to establish and maintain.

Should we seek an authoritative guide to hunting in the late Middle Ages, one is ready to hand. Edward, Duke of York, who was killed in the battle of Agincourt in 1415, was passionately devoted to hunting. Between 1406 and 1413 he developed his hunting treatise, 'The Master of Game', which was a translation, with additions based upon the duke's experience, of 'Le Livre de Chasse', written some two decades earlier by Gaston III, Count of Foix (known as Gaston Phoebus because of his blond hair). Edward desired from the outset that those who read his book would understand that the life of a skilful hunter was pleasing to God. The argument of his prologue might be slightly lacking in logic, but his conviction is not to be doubted. The work's basic premise is that idleness is the enemy of the soul. A man who is idle is prone to turn his imagination to evil, and be captured by those great enemies: the Devil, the world, and the flesh. A busy man will not be drawn to evil imagination. A hunter, he asserts, as a busy man, will not be drawn in by the seven deadly sins. The hunter, engaged with respectable activity, will eschew pride, avarice, wrath, sloth, gluttony, lechery, and envy. We are told as well that hunting requires so much concentration that there is simply no time for evil thoughts, and therefore no resulting evil works. Living without idleness, evil thoughts, or evil deeds, the dedicated hunter is assuredly destined for heaven. Moreover, the active hunter is out and about in the world, alert to his surroundings, and this makes him knowledgeable of places, customs, and manners, and altogether more understanding and just. If this were not enough, the duke was convinced that a hunter lived more joyfully in the world because of his experiences with nature, from a bright and clear morning to the songs of the birds to the dew on the grass. Because hunters lead a vigorous life, sleep well, mind what they eat, avoid sin, and have joy in their hearts, they are not beset by evil humours, and live longer than non-hunters before going straight to paradise. Some would also have added to the overwhelming aristocratic approval of hunting the notion that for noble youths destined for military training, hunting had an educational aspect. In the middle of the fifteenth century, the chronicler John Hardyng wrote that hunting could teach hardiness, courage, strategy, and mental quickness to the young. If hunting was seen as a useful part of the education of a young man born to privilege, it could serve as well as an adolescent rite of passage, in part because hunting was a situation in which individual prowess, a sort of chivalric single combat, could be displayed. Edward maintained that boys should start learning to be hunters around the age of seven or eight, and should start out by learning about different sorts of dogs and how to maintain a clean kennel.

Edward of York was of the opinion that the hare was the best game for hunting. These he liked hunting because it could be done year round, morning or evening, and he respected the hare as a watchful, swift, and clever quarry. The hare, though common enough, required skill to seek out and could give the hounds a long and cunning chase, and therefore a satisfying kill. Edward had a very different opinion of the coney, in medieval usage a mature rabbit. He remarked that conies were sought only by fur hunters using long-handled nets and ferrets, from which it may be guessed that he held in contempt hunting without dogs. It should be noted that some people, lacking the resources or pretensions of Edward of York, enjoyed ferreting as a sport.

Edward of York was devoted to hounds, and we may sample his commentary on dogs before returning to his discussion of the various types of game pursued by hunters. Firstly he thought them to be among God's finer works of creation, being wise, kind, understanding, strong, obedient, hardy, loyal unto death, persistent, and blessed also with a fine memory and sense of smell. The plaudits for hounds roll on in 'The Master of Game'. A proper hunting pack, we are informed, would consist of assorted types of

Medieval hunting greyhounds, wearing ornamental hunting collars (British Library, Additional Ms. 27699, f. 34)

hounds, which is not to say assorted breeds. One type was the running-hound, known as harriers, crachets, or raches, and they hunted by their sense of smell. This was the duke's favourite kind, and he liked the brown tan colour best. He described the characteristics of raches as including large open nostrils and a long nose, large lips hanging down, and great eyes beneath a substantial forehead. Long ears, powerful chest, shoulders, and legs, together with a tail carried straight or turning slightly upward were other desired characteristics. In the hunt, these dogs were the responsibility of servants called berners.

Another type of hunting hound was the miscellaneous breed known collectively as greyhounds, of which the duke liked best those of a red fallow colour with a black muzzle. Greyhounds hunted by sight, and it was necessary that they be swift enough to overtake game, fierce enough to seize it and bring it down, and possessed the large mouth, strong teeth, and jaws essential to the task. The duke liked greyhounds to be of middle size, and he described them with various beast analogies (borrowed from Gaston Phoebus): eyes like a sparrowhawk's, neck like a swan's, chin hair like a lion's, head shaped like a pike's with the ears high, and shoulders like a roebuck's. Greyhounds were in fact so various in size that they were used for hunting all manner of game, and were so constantly with their masters that they were as much companions as working dogs. When hunting, the greyhounds were managed and let loose by servants known as fewterers. Edward also discussed the alaunt, or alant, which was used like the greyhound to bring down running game. These he categorized as alaunts gentle, alaunts veutreres, and alaunts of the butcheries. Aside from the head, which should be broad and short with the ears short and erect, the alaunt gentle resembled the greyhound in general shape, but it was more husky of build and able to hold game more tenaciously than a greyhound. Alaunts were used to hunt ferocious game, but their personalities made them difficult to handle, and Edward of York thought it difficult to find a satisfactory one. The colour favoured for the alaunt gentle was white with black spots around the ears. The alaunt veutrere, as the duke distinguished it, was shaped like a large greyhound, with large lips and ears, and so ugly that if one were killed while hunting it would be no great loss. These heavy hounds were used for such things as bull-baiting and hunting wild boars. Alaunts of the butcheries were also used for bull-baiting and hunting boars, and Edward noted that they were to be seen assisting butchers to control animals and were good for guarding a household. The mastiff was another hound useful for protecting its master's household, but Edward thought the nose of the mastiff to be inadequate for sophisticated hunting.

The duke also differentiated a type of hound he called hounds of the hawk or spaniels (on the understanding that they came from Spain). Such hounds should be large of body and head, and preferably white or tawny in colour. They were especially good for raising partridges and quail, and would run along before their masters. They could also be taught to be 'couchers', or setters, and would call attention to game. A final type of hound must be mentioned because it had a place in a hunting pack. This was the lymer, or scenting-hound, used to locate the game before the hunt. In the course of the hunt lymers could be used as needed, but their main task was to use their noses to discover quarry, and they were trained to run silently. In their work, lymers were handled by huntsmen called lymerers.

'The Master of Game' offers assorted comments on other hunting matters. Sicknesses of hounds are mentioned, such as furious madness (rabies) or flank madness (where the flanks are drawn in), and it is suggested that mange is caused by melancholy. Tracking and trailing are discussed, as is the importance of learning about the *fumes* (excrements) of the hart, which served to suggest the qualities of the animal. The cries of the hunter at different stages of the hunt and the language employed when speaking to the hounds, most of which was Norman-French in origin, are remarked upon. Importance is also placed upon the use of the huntsman's horn. Hunting music from the horn, using notes of different length and with varying intervals between notes, would signal to hearers the progress of the hunt. Also discussed is the *curée*, the ceremonial rewarding of the hounds at the end of a successful hunt. The form taken by the *curée* (the source of our word quarry) varied from place to place and with different game. The *curée* followed the field dressing or breaking up of the slain animal, and this was itself done artfully, for it was a point of pride for a huntsman to be able, say, to break up and skin a hart without covering himself or his clothing with blood and without even rolling up his sleeves. The manner of performing the *curée* for a hart, as described by Edward, was to find a grassy spot to place bread soaked in the carefully saved blood of the hart among which was mixed the cleaned and chopped intestines. The hide of the hart, with head still attached, was spread over the mixture, hair-side up. The hunting pack meanwhile was leashed and resting close by. When all was ready, the berners would bring the running-hounds up to face the antlered stag head being held by the lord of the hunt and the master of game. A hunting cry of death was called; hunters with horns blew the death; other hunters bellowed; the hounds bayed. The stag head and hide were then drawn away as all the hounds were allowed to rush in and devour their reward, and throughout the horns continued to sound. It was very exciting, and it had the practical effect of associating for the hounds the reward, the stag, and the sounds of the hunt.

The deer sought by hunters in England were, as a rule, either the native red deer or the smaller fallow deer, which had been introduced by the Normans. It was the red deer that are referred to by Edward of York as the harts, respected as swift, strong, and clever animals. He especially admired the hart in the season of the rut for two months following Holy Rood (14 September), when, he remarked, they were bold and wild enough to attack and slay not only each other, but also hounds, horses, and men. The duke detailed certain lores of the hart, such as the fact that a hart could live for a hundred years growing ever fairer of body and head while becoming increasingly lecherous, that within the heart of the hart is a bone which is good medicine for the human heart, and that the hart surpasses other animals and man in wit and cunning and in the ability to select plants for eating that were salutary to himself. The fallow deer, which breeds prolifically and rates high for sport as well as for its venison and hide, was the species most often hunted in the later Middle Ages. Edward used the term buck for the fallow deer, which he described as being smaller than the hart but larger than the roebuck, and as having palmed antlers. The duke says that he finds the flesh of the buck more savoury than that of the hart or the roebuck, but he takes special delight in the fact that the roebuck can be hunted all year and that to hunt the roebuck requires great skill. He believes the flesh of the roebuck to be very wholesome because the roebuck feeds on good herbs and beneficial vegetation.

Edward of York is not thinking of food but of a hunter's challenge when he speaks of the wild boar, which he classes as the most strongly armed of beasts, able to slit a man from knee to breast with one stroke of the tusk. He has obvious respect for the powerful and dangerous boar, as he does for the wolf, regarded in the Middle Ages as vermin, which needed to be slain to protect livestock. Edward believed their bite to be venomous because of the animal's foul diet, and he says that as many as four relays of hounds could be needed, together with mastiffs, to hunt the swift, wily, and long-running wolf. He remarks ominously that wolves when old or injured or living near a field of battle or a gallows

Deer-stalking: a misericord in Gloucester Cathedral shows a man with a long-bow (partly broken away) shooting at a stag in full flight; spare arrows are attached to his belt (Jack Farley)

develop a taste for human flesh, and these 'wer-wolves' are an especial danger. The sporting duke so disliked wolves that he suggests killing them with snares, pits, and poisons, but he does concede the possibility that the right forefoot of the wolf is useful medicine for 'evil of the breast' and that the dried liver of the wolf just might be beneficial for a man's liver. The fox is not so threatening as the wolf, but it is nonetheless vermin with a similarly venomous bite. The fox may be a threat to domestic fowls, but it is somewhat redeemed because it provides cunning quarry for hunting and makes the hounds bay marvellously. The fur of the fox, moreover, is warm and more attractive than that of the wolf. Also mentioned is the badger, which is called the 'grey', but without enthusiasm because the badger is not much sport to hunt and the flesh is not for eating. The duke is dismissive, too, of wild cats as quarry, although he acknowledges that they (and their tame kindred) have in them the devil's spirit. He thinks of otters, which destroy fish supplies, as vermin to be hunted as a matter of pest control, and the same is true of martens and polecats. Edward of York may have hunted such animals, but it gave him no particular pleasure and was therefore not mentioned.

Edward of York is an informative guide to hunting in late

medieval England, but his was not the only voice. Nearly a century before, William Twici or Twiti, a huntsman to Edward II, wrote a treatise on hunting called 'Le Art de Venerie'. Hunting was a highly refined and ritualized activity, and it is an aspect of medieval life that merits careful attention from those who wish to understand noble recreation.

Hawking

One highly specialized and aristocratic form of hunting was hawking or falconry. The two terms were used as synonyms, although hawks and falcons are different types of birds of prey. Not everyone was able to participate in the costly sport of hawking: the birds were a substantial investment, and their care and feeding, to

Falconry, fourteenth century (Bodleian Library, Oxford, Ms. Rawlinson D939, section 2, May)

say nothing of the lengthy and specialized training they received, could be very expensive. For instance, in the 1270s Edward I had a chamber built at Charing Cross for his falconers, which backed on to an enclosed garden in which was built a bath for the king's birds. An aqueduct carried water to the bath, so it would be fresh as it issued from the four brass, leopard-head spouts. The birds resided in cages, were fed doves raised in the dovecots on site, and cranes were brought in for the raptors to practice on. This was not a modest operation, and Edward I was devoted to falconry. Nearly two centuries later John Paston revealed his passion for hawking by writing to his brother: 'I axe no more goods of you for all the servyse that I shall do yow whyll the world standyth, but a gosshawke.'

It was common to have fixed or swivelling perches for the hunting birds to rest upon, and these were placed wherever the bird's owner might wish, even in private rooms. The birds were attached to their perches by leather or silk strings called jesses, tied at one end to the foot of the bird and at the other to a ring on the perch called a terret. A person could put the terret around a finger when carrying the bird, an activity that required a heavy leather glove. The glove was worn on the left hand. To keep resting birds calm, it was usual to cover their heads with hoods, which prevented the bird from seeing its surroundings. Hoods could be decorated with embroidery or heraldic colours, and jesses could have jewels attached or bells, which could be tuned for a musical effect. The opportunity to spend lavishly upon the sport of falconry was seemingly limited only by the monies available. If a person found a hawk, they were obliged to turn it over to the sheriff of the county, who then made proclamation of the find so that the owner could recover the valuable bird; an unclaimed bird might be kept by the sheriff or the finder, as they made agreement, provided the finder were of an appropriate social rank. Owners could become very attached to their birds, as Nicholas de Litlington, Abbot of Westminster, must have been when, in 1368, he bought a waxen image of a falcon to offer at the church altar for the benefit of a sick falcon.

A hawker, wearing a large and handsome leather glove upon which a bird was perched, or 'on the creep', was a striking and noble sight. Hunting on the creep was one way to use the birds. Raptors were also trained to remain in place while the hunter flushed the game, at which moment the hunter would command the bird to attack. Birds could be trained to catch prey, such as hares, on the ground, or to take other birds in the air, and this was the most dramatic and popular form of hawking. The larger the prey (and the larger the raptor used), the more spectacular the falconry. Whether on foot or from horseback, hawking was a delightful and ever-popular diversion.

A body of literature was developed on falconry, just as with hunting, and a culminating contribution to the literature on falconry is known commonly as the 'Boke of St Albans'. This compilation of information on hawking, hunting, heraldry, and other matters is attributed on most challengeable authority to one Dame Juliana Bernes or Barnes, and was printed at St Albans in 1486. In the section on falconry information is to be found on different types of birds, their training, their illnesses and the cures thereof, their feeding and maintenance, and their use in hunting. At the end of this section there is an appended list, arranged hierarchically, of different social ranks and the trained hunting birds appropriate to them. The list is thus both a human and an avian hierarchy. It commences with an emperor, a rank which did not exist in England, whose hawks are an eagle, a bawtere (probably a vulture), and a melowne (probably a kite). The king's hawks are the gyrfalcon and her tercel (the male of any kind of

Hawking, as depicted on a misericord in Gloucester Cathedral. A rider on horseback, holding a long whip, is following a hawk which is striking a large duck on the wing. An attendant on foot is beating a tabor to frighten the duck into flight (Jack Farley)

hawk is a tercel). The powerful gyrfalcon was especially admired if it were white. The hawks of the prince are the 'fawcon gentill' and 'tercel gentill' (that is, the peregrine falcon and her tercel). The adjective 'gentil' conveyed the notion both of superior innate quality and excellence as a hunter. To the duke is assigned the falcon of the rock, the peregrine falcon by another name, and for an earl 'a fawken peregryne' is also appropriate. A baron is to have a bastard (seemingly a sub-species of the peregrine). A knight has a sacret; a squire a lanare; a lady a merlin; and a young man a hobby. The list continues its descent through four more ranks: for the yeoman a goshawk; for a poor man a goshawk's tercel; for a priest a sparrowhawk; and for the holywater clerk a musket (that is, a male sparrowhawk).

The sparrowhawk calls to mind the fact that clerics were prohibited by canon law from engaging in military activity and, because of the weaponry used and the methods employed, the prohibition was extended to hunting and hawking. It is clear, however, that the prohibition was not rigorously respected. It might be suggested that in courtly culture the qualities and characteristics of the avian hierarchy and of the aristocratic human hierarchy sometimes merged in thought and literature, as with a peregrine falcon, a courageous hunter, evoking the image of a valiant chivalric warrior. Against the hierarchy of avian raptors and falconry might be set the more humble sport of fowling, which involved the catching of birds with snares and traps of one sort or another. Fowling and ferreting fell at the lower end of falconry and hunting.

Angling

Another less costly sport, like fowling or ferreting, though more contemplative, was angling. When the 'Boke of St Albans' was printed for the second time in 1496, the printer, Wynkyn de Worde, included 'The Treatyse of fysshynge wyth an Angle'. This is an anonymous work, probably dating from the early fifteenth century and sometimes attributed, like the 'Boke', to that otherwise unknown and perhaps legendary Dame Juliana Bernes. The author of the 'Treatyse' discussed hunting, hawking, fowling, and fishing, and then concluded that fishing is the most conducive to a long and satisfying life. Information is provided on tackle and how to handle it, how to be more successful at angling, and how to select baits for different sorts of freshwater fish. The best rods were made of hazel, willow, or ash, and were formed from two wands,

The angler. Book of Hours, early fifteenth century (British Library, Additional Ms. 29433, f. 2)

the sharpened end of one fitting into the hollowed end of the other to give length and flexibility. Line was made by twisting together the hairs from horses' tails, and the number of hairs was varied according to the weight and strength of the fish being sought. Hooks were made of bent wire or needles, and the depth of the hook in the water was regulated by floats and weights. Live bait might be caterpillars, minnows, or worms, and artificial flies were made of coloured bits of wool, feathers, and insect wings. It is noteworthy that when Izaak Walton wrote *The Complete Angler* in the seventeenth century he drew extensively on the 'Treatyse' printed in the 'Boke of St Albans' of 1496.

Two other fifteenth-century literary works which treat fishing as a leisure activity are the anonymous poem 'Piers of Fulham' and the quasi-historical Scots epic 'Wallace', attributed to Blind Hary the Minstrel and written in the 1470s. In 'Piers of Fulham', thought to date from mid-century, both fishing and fowling are used as metaphors for the pursuit of love's pleasures. The reader is given such advice as to be honest, to use self-control, not to take underage fish, and not to poach the fish of another. The main figure in 'Wallace' is William Wallace (died 1305), the hero of Scottish resistance to the aggression of Edward I of England. In the literary work, William Wallace is in one episode portrayed as a fisherman thoroughly enjoying his sport in all innocence until he is interrupted and mistreated by five men, representing King Edward's authority, whom Wallace ends up successfully fighting, killing three of his tormenters in the process. How deep into the English past fishing as a leisure activity went, as opposed to fishing as a means to survive, is not certain. There is no sound reason to say that fishing for sport did not begin in England until we have such literary evidence as Chaucer's *Complaint of Mars*; the activity itself could have begun long before. In fact, the financial accounts of Queen Philippa for 1351 record a gift of *4d* to two small children 'who fished in front of my Lady' ('qui pescherunt devaunt ma dame'), presumably for her entertainment. At any rate, angling was not as popular as hunting and hawking, and it seems to have been thought more appropriate for children and theoretically less vigorous adults like monks and nuns. The Oxford grammar master who offered his students lines on bear-baiting to be translated into Latin, wrote the following on angling: 'I trow ther be never onn here that hath more delyte in fyshynge than I. For after I am gotyn onys oute of the dorys, all my diligence is to make me redy to the water side.'

Tournaments

Tournament is a word familiarly used in a general way for games of knightly skill, but the word also had the more restricted meaning of a meeting of two teams of knights on a designated field of combat – often miles of varying terrain – in a free-for-all or mêlée. It was rather like scheduling a small war for sport, and was highly dangerous. The excitement of an early tournament would come from booty in the form of armour, horses, or captured rivals who could be held for ransom. The victors were those who held the field or the most booty at the end of the day. William Marshal, Earl of Pembroke (died 1219), is famed as a successful and ferocious opportunist in tournaments; those whom he vanquished have been forgotten.

The early form of tournament was so hazardous, in fact, that it gradually diminished in popularity, but as it passed from the scene, the word 'tournament' came to be used for all sorts of knightly combat. Writers in England and France commonly used the Latin term *hastiludium*, which is brought into English as 'hastilude' (meaning a game fought with spears), for contests of mounted combat. It could be argued that it would be more correct to use 'hastilude' than 'tournament' as a collective term for knightly combats in England, but 'tournament' is too familiar a term to discard casually for lack of precision. Single combats of one knight against another were called 'jousts', to clarify another term. Early

Training for war: knights jousting with tournament lances, as depicted on a fourteenth-century ivory tabernacle (Alinari: The Mansell Collection)

tournaments were fought in a broad area with the occasional sanctuary for resting and rearming, and are often described as being fought between villages. When an enclosed area was established for a tournament or joust, it was called the 'lists'. In about the 1420s it became customary to erect a wooden barrier (originally a rope strung a few feet off the ground with a cloth draped over it), or tilt, down the centre of the hastilude ground, the lists, to keep charging horses from crashing into one another. The lance-rest attached to the breast plate and looking like a prong steadied and supported the lance. This essential piece of equipment appeared in the second half of the fourteenth century, and made possible the use of longer and heavier lances. It made mounted combat potentially even more dangerous and, in turn, prompted the introduction of the tilt barrier in tournaments. A joust where a tilt was used often came to be called a tilt itself. The mounted combatant rode with the tilt on his left side and his lance couched under his right arm and pointed across the barrier as his opponent charged from the opposite direction on the other side. If the tilt was available but not employed in a joust, such mounted combat was called 'at random' or 'at large'.

The knightly outdoor sport of the tournament evolved over time. It is not possible to say when the first tournament took place, when it became a spectator sport, or when the sport arrived in England. It seems safe to say that the long tradition of military

ien set se il lataignent/ que de lamort est fis
e prison a lessie mes ce su aenius

Que li escuier ont/ depar crates contre
es batailles groie sa gent a ozteree

Knights jousting, fourteenth century (Bodleian Library, Oxford, Ms. 264, f. 92r)

exercise had produced the martial game we call the tournament in northern France towards the end of the eleventh century, and that it was related to the development of the tactic whereby a co-ordinated group of knights fought as a unit using lances couched tightly under their arms. The English tradition was that the tournament came from France, and Matthew Paris (died 1259), a monk at St Albans, referred to the tournament in his 'Chronica Majora' as '*conflictus Gallicus*'. It cannot have been long before the sport came to England, because many English lords had lands in France as well. Also, it was because the tournament became popular so quickly that its violence prompted a prohibition from Pope Innocent II in 1130, and the papal ban was repeated at intervals until it was revoked by Pope John XXII in 1316. Despite uncompromising papal disapproval, the tournament flourished.

The tournament was a sport with international appeal, and was essentially the same wherever it appeared. However, in England it did have the distinction of being the subject of regulation by two kings: Richard I and Edward I, both of whom were participants. Richard's ordinance of 1194 set forth that any tournaments held in England must be licensed by the king; that combatants must pay entrance fees graduated in amount according to rank (and pay them in advance); that tournaments be held only at one or another of the five designated places; that no foreigner could participate, and that the king's peace be maintained by anyone going to or from a tournament. Richard therefore recognized the popularity of tournaments and their utility for military training. He saw them also as a potential source of revenue, and it appears that he was trying to confine the assembly of armed men to certain locations and, as it happened, the five recognized tournament grounds were located in areas amenable to royal control. The gathering of armed men could have potent political implications, as in the instances when barons and their armed followers gathered under the guise of holding tournaments in the period when King John was forced to

Plate 1: Chaucer reading *Troilus and Criseyde* to the Court (The Master and Fellows of Corpus Christi College, Cambridge, Ms. 61, frontispiece)

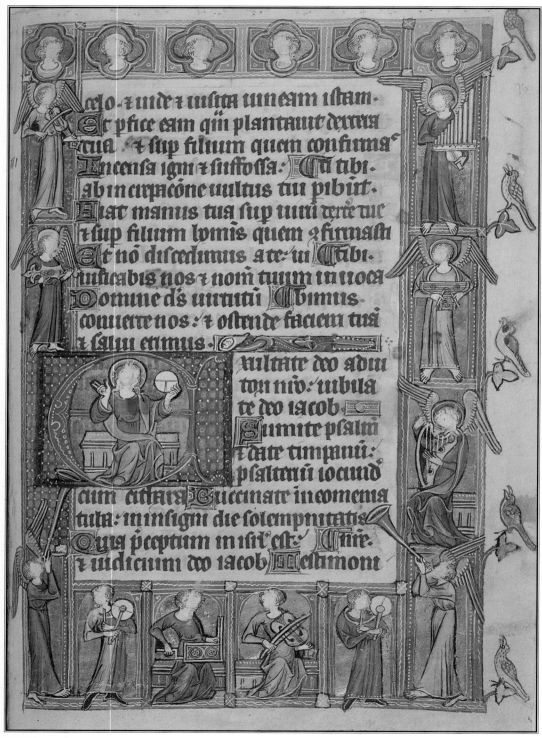

Plate 2: Musicians from a psalter copied in England in the mid-fourteenth century (By Permission of the Master and Fellows of Sidney Sussex College, Cambridge, Ms. 76, f. 76r)

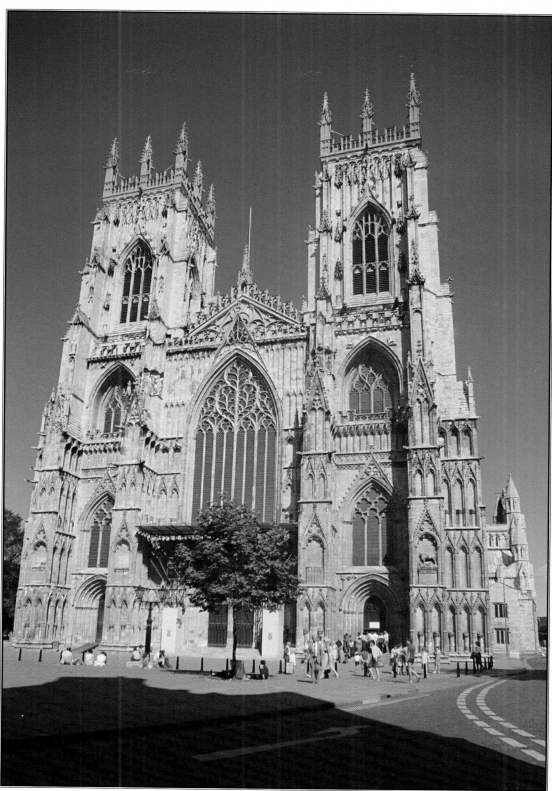

Plate 3: The west front of York Minster (Tim Hawkins)

Plate 4: Rustics, with may-branches in their headgear, celebrate May Day by dancing to the music of the bagpipes (Bibliothèque Nationale, Paris, Ms. Latin 873, f. 21r)

Plate 5: A medieval game of blind-man's bluff in a garden (British Library, Stowe Ms. 955, f. 7)

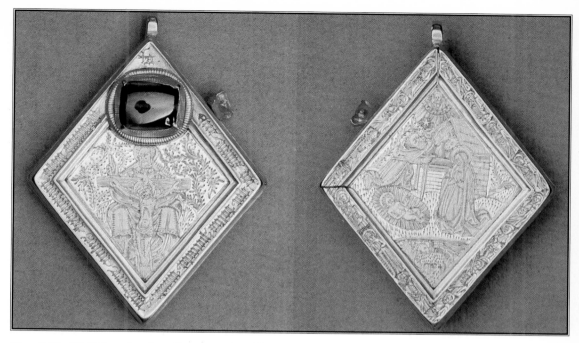

Plate 6: The Middleham Jewel, a reliquary pendant 64 mm high and 48 mm wide (Reproduced by permission of the Trustees of The British Museum)

Plate 7: Mummers wearing animal masks dance to music provided by a boy playing a cittern (Bodleian Library, Oxford, Bodleian Ms. 264, f. 21v)

solennitate beatorum martyrum
dyonisii rustici & eleutherii passio
ne decorasti concede nobis famuli
tuis digna veneratione eorum me
moriam celebrare vt quorum do
ctrina exeplo tibi gallorum sub
didisti colla fauertica ipsorum i
teruentione assidua mereamur
adipisti gaudia sempiterna. Per.
De Sancto Martino. Antipho.
Bea
tu
virum cu
ius anima
paradisu
possidet
vnde ex
ultant angeli letantur archangeli
chorus sanctorum proclamat turba
virginum inuitat mane nobiscum
ineternum. ℣s⁹ Amauit eum dns

Plate 8: Boys riding hobby-horses (Bodleian Library, Oxford, Oxford Ms. Douce. 276, f. 124v)

Plate 9: Catching small birds (Bodleian Library, Oxford, Bodleian Ms. 264, f. 21v)

Plate 10: The golfer: a fourteenth-century roundel in the Great East window, known as the Crecy window, in Gloucester Cathedral (Sonia Halliday Photographs)

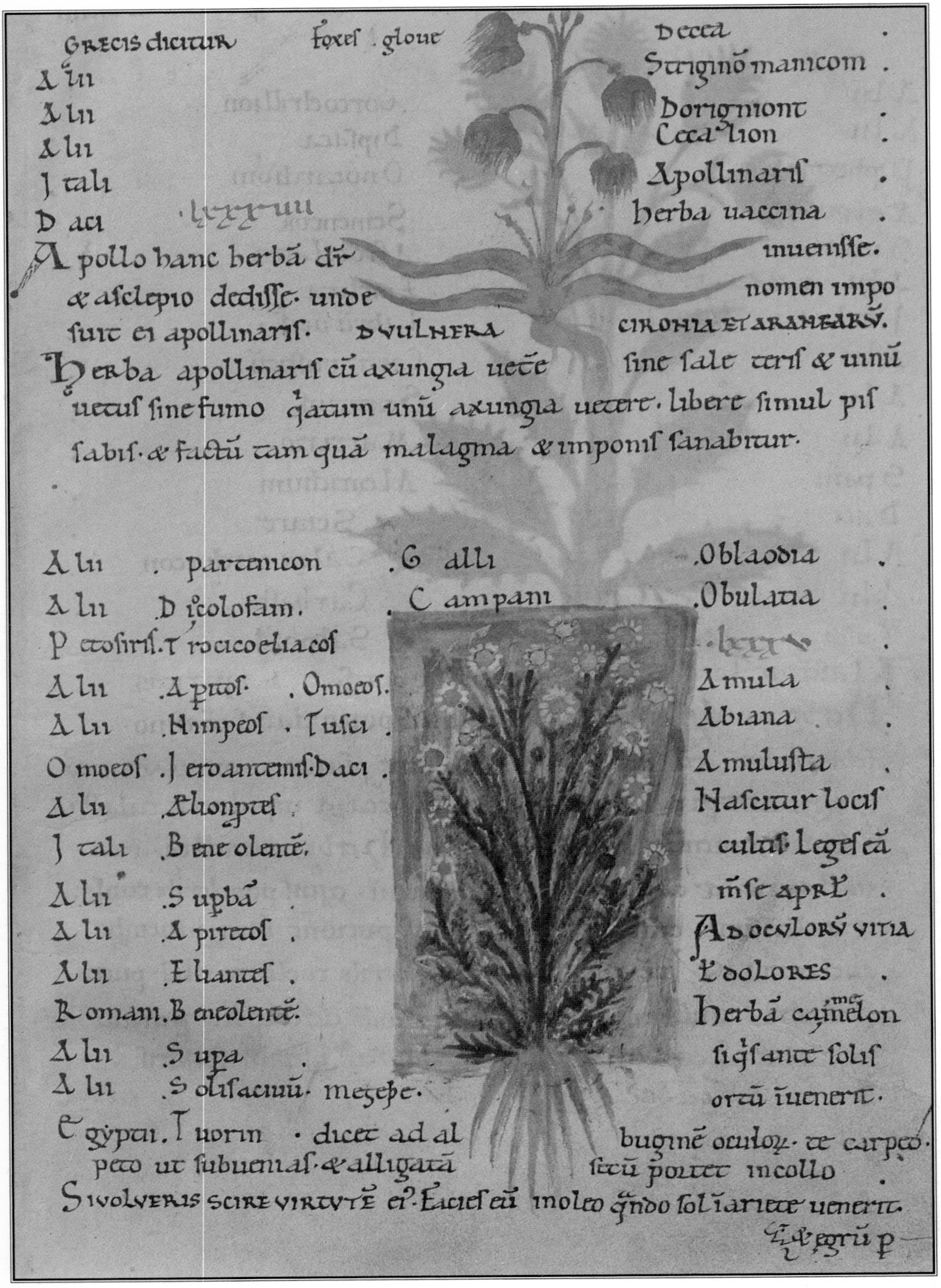

Plate 11: Illustrations of the great herbal from the abbey of Bury St Edmunds: the unrecognizable foxglove above, and an exquisite study of chamomile below (Bodleian Library, Oxford, Bodley Ms. 130, f. 44r)

concede Magna Carta, or in the times of troubles between some of the barons and Henry III.

Edward I's contribution to the regulating of tournaments came with the 'Statuta Armorum' of 1292, and it was the team-game that he had in mind. In this statute Edward focused upon keeping the king's peace at a tournament. A committee of five members was established to enforce rules of the tourney, which included one that said no participant could bring with him to a tournament more than three armed knights or squires, who were to wear a cap bearing the badge of their lord so that their affiliation could be readily identified, and who were not to carry such offensive weapons as clubs, knives, or pointed swords, but only a defensive 'broadsword for tourneying'. A fallen knight could be assisted only by his own squires, and spectators were to be without weapons or armour. Heralds were to carry no weapons and were to wear their tabards for clear identification. At any banquet, only tourneyers were to be admitted, together with the squires serving them personally. Stiff punishments of monetary fines and imprisonment were threatened to any who violated these and similar provisions laid down in the 'Statuta Armorum'. Neither Edward I nor Richard I before him attempted to outlaw tournaments, but they did seek royal control and the imposition of order.

It becomes clear that the noble sport of tourneying had not only social and military dimensions, but political ones also. Where the evidence survives to provide an understanding of the connections of the participants in tournaments during the developmental stages of the sport, it appears that it was far from unusual that what on one occasion would be a lord and his military retinue would on another occasion be a lord and his tournament team. A listing in the form of a roll recording the heraldry of the participants in a tournament at Dunstable in 1309 is a noteworthy piece of such evidence. If we were to imagine two lords who were rivals in the political arena appearing in a tournament with their military/tourneying retinues, what ensued might be more than military and sporting competition. It could also be seen as private political warfare under cover of noble athleticism. At the same time, a king could use such trained knightly companies in his armies, and it was therefore more important for him to control tournaments than to abolish them.

Building upon the work of certain of his predecessors, like Richard I and Edward I, and owing to the cast of circumstances, it was Edward III with his lengthy wars in Scotland and France who finally got tournaments and royal policy in close alignment.

De la maniere et ordonnance de la grant feste et Joustee que le noble Roy

A joust at large being fought as King Edward III holds a tournament in honour of the Countess of Salisbury (Bodleian Library, Oxford, Ms. Laud Misc 653, f. 5)

Edward III loved tournaments and he loved war, and when he founded the Order of the Garter in the late 1340s he selected as founding members the men (twenty-five in addition to himself) who had distinguished themselves as commanders. It is possible that the device Edward selected for the Order, *Honi soit qui mal y pense* (Shame to him who thinks ill of it), was to defend his French campaign of 1346. It is no accident that St George's Chapel at Windsor, built for the Order, has equal rows of stalls for the seating of the members running along both sides of the length of the chapel, facing one another. It may be thought of as a metaphor for the tournament team of King Edward on one side, and on the other that of his already distinguished eldest son, Edward the Black Prince. By this time jousting had become more popular than the team engagement of the early days of the tournament, and Edward III was popular with his nobility, who found no reason to use tournaments as a cover for plotting treason.

Tournaments had changed markedly from their beginnings as a mêlée with virtually no rules to the more orderly and confined contest of Edward III's time. Armour had changed from mostly chain mail to predominantly plate, which provided more protection for the participants, but did not eliminate the possibility of serious or mortal injury. The safety of noble warriors was important to kings, who needed such men for real wars. From about the middle of the thirteenth century distinctions were made between jousts of war (*joust à outrance*), in which the weapons of war were used, and jousts of peace (*joust à plaisance*), in which blunted, or rebated, weapons were used. Details of a royal tournament of peace held at Windsor Park in July 1278 survive in the form of financial accounts. These reveal that the tourneyers were provided with leather armour (likely *cuir-bouilli* – the boiling would have made it hard yet lighter than metal) and swords made of whalebone. By around 1300 it was common format for a joust to go three courses with lances, three with swords, and three with axes – if the participants endured. About a century later, special armour started to be designed for tourneying, beginning with the 'frog-mouthed' helm, which was heavier and offered more protection but less mobility than the armour used in war.

The increasing refinement, ostentation, and spectator enjoyment of tournaments can be illustrated with the following fifteenth-century example. Anthony Woodville, Lord Scales, brother of Elizabeth, the wife of King Edward IV, and Anthony, Count de la Roche, known as the 'Bastard of Burgundy', had been planning to test their martial skills against one another for more than two years before their contest took place at Smithfield in June 1467. As it happened, the tournament proved to be more show than substance. Great display had characterized the enterprise, from the arrival of more than 400 Burgundians in England, to the opening of the tournament proper before a large audience that included Edward IV. Contemporary accounts of the tournament differ, but a plausible sequence of events would be that in riding at one another in the first course in the lists, Lord Scales and the count each missed the other with their lances. They then discarded lances, and assaulted one another with swords. In the swirl of action the count's horse collided with that of Scales, and collapsed (perhaps dead), pinning its rider to the ground. The use of spiked armour had been forbidden by the rules of the tourney, and suspicion was rife that Lord Scales had engaged in skulduggery. Lord Scales cleared his reputation soon afterwards. In the meantime the Bastard of Burgundy's servants extricated their master from beneath his horse, and he declined the king's offer of a replacement horse, preferring to bring the day's action to an end. The following day the combatants met again, this time fighting on foot with axes. They flailed away at one another until Scales struck a smashing blow against the visor of the count's helmet, whereupon the king halted the combat, with Lord Scales gaining the honour of victory. The main event of the tournament was over, and subsequent contests between English and Burgundian knights seemed anticlimactic.

The Scales–de la Roche contest might suggest that English tournaments by the fifteenth century tended more toward ritualized athletic entertainment than martial mayhem, but tournaments could be highly dangerous and they were still taken very seriously as training for war. This sort of education was literally that of the *Collegium Pulsationum Durarum* (School of Hard Knocks). To dismiss late medieval tournaments as mere chivalric display would be to miss the point. Even if that were their only purpose, which would be a distortion, they were also significant as manifestations of aristocratic wealth and prestige.

Another noble pastime akin to the tournament was the round table, an expression of the growing popularity of the King Arthur legends among the nobility. The round table was a social occasion including various games, of which jousting with rebated weapons was one. The earliest mention of a round table in England is the royal prohibition of 1232 to hold one. The chronicler Matthew Paris mentions a round table held at Walden in 1252 where only blunted weapons were used in the jousting. Very few of these sessions of knights are mentioned in the records, and little is known about them. The appeal of Arthurian round tables would have diminished as tournaments became more disciplined, social events.

SIX

Nature, Pets and Gardening

For some people the natural world was full of pleasurable wonders as opposed to being a source of food and sport. The poet Geoffrey Chaucer was an accomplished birdwatcher. That some of Chaucer's birds are figurative representations of stars and other heavenly bodies does not detract from his knowledge. There are well over five hundred references to birds in Chaucer's writings, with some fifty species being mentioned. That Chaucer would write a dream-vision called *The Parlement of Foules* was in accordance with this interest. In The Prologue to *The Canterbury Tales* he mentions, among other bird references, the dashing Squire who sleeps as little as a nightingale, the Monk who loved roasted swan, the Franklin who salivates over a fat partridge, the unsavoury Summoner who is compared with a lecherous sparrow, and the foppish Yeoman whose arrows are fletched with colourful peacock feathers, when even the proverbial English schoolboy knows that peacock feathers are no match for goose feathers for fletching arrows.

Five times in his works Chaucer mentions the kite, today a respected and rare bird, but in Chaucer's time considered to be a coward – its indulgence in carrion made it a useful and familiar but dishonourable bird. It was an insufferable affront to the peregrine falcon in *The Squire's Tale* when her lover went off with an ignoble kite. The peregrine was Chaucer's second most frequently mentioned bird. He usually simply called her a falcon, while the smaller and less powerful male of the species he called a tercel or tercelet. Chaucer was certainly not alone in admiring the aristocratic demeanour and hunting prowess of the peregrine. A less imposing bird was the rowdy cuckoo, and the female's habit of laying her eggs in other birds' nests to avoid the struggle of raising her own young was as familiar to the poet as the lore that the cuckoo knows which nest to invade and correspondingly that men who do not take care of their wives can find themselves cuckolded (cuckoo'd). Chaucer revealed in *The Parlement of Foules* that he was also familiar with the, in this case, unfounded lore which held that the barn swallow kills honey bees. The poet seemed nevertheless well disposed toward swallows, and used the comparison in *The Miller's Tale* that the singing of the miller's wife was as lively and loud as that of a swallow. Like other writers, including the author of the biblical 'Song of Solomon', Chaucer used the turtledove as a symbol of integrity and consistency in love; it is mentioned eight times. The bird most frequently mentioned by Chaucer is the golden eagle, the sovereign among birds, the queen of all birds of prey. In contrast to the twenty-two references to the noble eagle, Chaucer only once, in the *Book of the Duchess*, mentions the phoenix, a female bird found in myth but not in the English sky.

A sense of wonder about the natural world was caught by the anonymous grammar master of Magdalen School, Oxford, when in the last years of the fifteenth century he wrote as a lesson for his students to translate into Latin: 'It is a mervelous thynge that of the hete of the dame the stream of bloode beynge within the Egge sholde growe to a thynge of lyffe, but it sholde not be marvelide of the crafty werke of nature.'

Domestic Pets

The most casual observer of English society today cannot help but notice a genuine penchant for the company of domestic pets. This is not a recent social development, for our medieval ancestors also enjoyed pet animals. Evidence suggests that at least some medievals liked having pets about even if the creatures did no useful work. A late medieval grammar master prepared as an exercise to be translated by his students into Latin the passage: 'Wolde it not angre a mann to be lyde upon of this fascyon? Thei say that I kepe a dawe [jackdaw] in my chambre, but iwys [surely] thei lye falsly upon me for it is but a pore Conye.' As Geoffrey Chaucer pictured the Prioress for his readers in *The Canterbury Tales*, he said:

> Of smale houndes had she, that she fedde
> With rosted flesh, or milk and wastelbreed.
> But sore weep she if oon of hem were deed,
> Or if men smoot it with a yerde smerte:
> And al was conscience and tendre herte.

Eileen Power, who did impressive research on English medieval nunneries, remarked that in spite of ongoing efforts by ecclesiastical authorities to banish such worldly customs, the nuns persisted in keeping pets and that the favourite pets were dogs. Cats are mentioned, as are monkeys, birds, rabbits, and squirrels, but dogs were the most popular with nuns as pets. Power discovered that John Pecham, who was Archbishop of Canterbury between 1279 and 1292, had on one occasion to order the abbess of the Benedictine nunnery of Romsey not to keep dogs or monkeys in her chambers, and the abbess was at the same time accused of not providing adequate food for her nuns. William of Wykeham, Bishop of Winchester, wrote in 1387 to a later abbess of Romsey:

Item, because we have convinced ourselves by clear proofs that some of the nuns of your house bring with them to church birds, rabbits, hounds and such like frivolous things, whereunto they give more heed than to the offices of the church, with frequent hindrance to their own psalmody and that of their fellow nuns and to the grievous peril of their souls; therefore we strictly forbid you, all and several, in virtue of the obedience due unto us, that you presume henceforward to bring to church no birds, hounds, rabbits or other frivolous things that promote indiscipline; and any nun who does to the contrary, after three warnings shall fast on bread and water on one Saturday for each offence, notwithstanding one discipline to be received publicly in chapter on the same day . . . . Item, whereas through the hunting-dogs and other hounds abiding within your monastic precincts, the alms that should be given to the poor are devoured and the church and cloister and other places set apart for divine and secular services are foully defiled, contrary to all honesty, and whereas, through their inordinate noise, divine service is frequently troubled, therefore we strictly command and enjoin you, Lady Abbess, in virtue of obedience, that you remove these dogs altogether and that you suffer them never henceforth, nor any other such hounds, to abide within the precincts of your nunnery.

Here, indeed, is an extreme instance of pets being allowed to distort the prescribed pattern of spiritual life and obligations. At the other extreme one can readily imagine those individuals who cared nothing for the company of pets. Eileen Power became convinced, however, that the keeping of pets was commonplace among the nuns of medieval England.

Nuns were drawn from the upper reaches of society, and women in general of higher society were often portrayed with pets. One of the pictures in the famous Luttrell Psalter shows a group of elegant women being conveyed down a road in a sumptuous wagon with a painted top. A lapdog is being handed between a woman in the back of the wagon and a servant on a horse, while a woman at the front of the wagon has a pet squirrel on her right shoulder. The pets, it should be remembered, added to the message being conveyed that these were women of means well beyond what was required for mere survival. Another drawing in the Luttrell Psalter shows a woman playing with a pet squirrel wearing a collar to which a bell is attached. The tomb effigies and monumental brasses of people of position not infrequently include foot supports. Sometimes these are heraldic or play on the name of the deceased or are merely decorative, but at least some represent pets. At the feet of the image of Alice Cassy on her monumental brass at Deerhurst, Gloucestershire, is a dog identified as Terri, while there was formerly a dog by the name of Jakke at the feet of the monumental brass image of Sir Brian de Stapilton at Ingham in Norfolk. Unnamed dogs are shown commonly in the folds of women's dresses on monumental brasses, such as that of Margarete Lady Camoys at Trotton, Sussex, dated *c.* 1310, or that of the wife of Sir John Harsick at Southacre, Norfolk, dated 1384, or that of the wife of Sir Thomas de Cruwe at Wixford, Warwickshire, dated 1411. In another artistic medium, there is a charming small dog wearing a collar decorated with bells at the feet of Lady Margaret Roos (died 1438) shown in the St William window in the north choir transept of York Minster. This dog, with its happy face, was surely a pet.

In some households birds were kept in cages as pets. Jays were among the more common birds kept, as were magpies, which were often called simply pies. These could be especially entertaining because they could be taught to imitate human speech, which could make the time spent in their training highly rewarding. Parrots, which were called popinjays, were available only at a very high price. They were exotic, colourful, and entertaining, but being imports from the Middle East were not easily obtained. Geoffrey Chaucer mentions the popinjay six times in his works, in every case humorously. Elizabeth of York, wife of Henry VII, paid 13*s* 4*d* just to have a servant bring one to her at Windsor in 1502, whereas just a few days before she had bestowed, by way of

A woman with a pet squirrel (British Library, Additional Ms. 42130, f. 33)

While the majority of animals in medieval glass are of the working variety, there are occasional glimpses of those creatures kept as pets and companions. One such is this little lap dog at the feet of Lady Margaret Roos, depicted with great warmth and affection, in the St William window at York Minster (© RCHME Crown Copyright)

comparison, a reward of 4s for the delivery of two bucks. An earlier queen, Joan of Navarre, also had a popinjay to give her pleasure during a period of captivity, as is revealed by a financial account for her household covering the period 1419–21. For those who could not afford popinjays or who preferred singing birds to talkers, the birds of preference were nightingales and larks.

One of the most curious instances of a pet bird in medieval England is that of St Hugh's swan. Hugh of Avalon (in Burgundy) came to England in 1180 to lead in the foundation of a house of the rigorous monastic order to which he belonged, the Carthusians. Henry II was still trying to atone for the murder in 1170 of

Thomas Becket, Archbishop of Canterbury, and the foundation of a Carthusian house at Witham in Somerset was part of the programme. Hugh's talents led in 1186 to his departure from the priorate of Witham to occupy the office of Bishop of Lincoln, in which he served admirably until his death in 1200. On one occasion, while residing at the manor of Stow near Lincoln, a swan attached itself to him as pet and guardian. Hugh had developed a reputation for his charity toward the less fortunate members of society and for his love of animals and birds, but the swan was a singular pet. It was an obstreperous bird, as swans generally are and, according to eye-witness accounts, it noisily discouraged any man or beast from coming near the bishop. Toward Hugh, on the other hand, the swan was gentle and affectionate. Obviously a special man to others as well, he was the only Carthusian to be an English bishop and the first Carthusian to be canonized (by Pope Honorius III in 1220).

A domestic cat playing with a mouse (British Library, Additional Ms. 42130, f. 190)

If cats were not such common pets as dogs, they must have been more usual pets than swans. It would seem that cats were viewed in more practical terms as mousers and ratters, and there is a drawing in the Luttrell Psalter of a tabby cat toying with a mouse. There is also a carving of a cat with a rat in its mouth, by a craftsman who appreciated everyday scenes, on the fifteenth-century timber watching gallery beside the shrine of St Alban in St Alban's Abbey (now the cathedral). On a further practical note, William Langland wrote in 'Piers Plowman' of a pedlar who was disposed to kill cats for their skins if he could manage to catch them. Archaeologists have found cat bones with cut marks suggesting that the fur had been removed. Such a use of the animal signifies the keeping of cats as livestock, not as pets. Eleanor de Montfort, Countess of Leicester and sister of Henry III, appreciated cats, although whether for practical or affectionate reasons is not clear, for in 1265 one was purchased for her household on arrival at Odiham and another was purchased when the household moved to Dover.

Bartholomew de Glanville, who is better known as Bartholomew the Englishman, completed a widely used encyclopaedia in about 1240. In this he wrote some observant lines about cats, which were translated from Latin into English late in the fourteenth century by John Trevisa:

> . . . a beste of uncerteyn heare [hair] and colour. For some catte is whyte, some reed, and som black, som scowed [piebald or calico] and spenked in the feet and the face and in the eeren . . . And hath a gret mough and sawe teeth and

scharpe and longe tonge and pliaunt, thynne, and sotile. And lapeth therwith whanne he drynketh . . . And he is a ful leccherous beste in youthe, swyfte, plyaunt, and mery. And lepeth and reseth [rusheth] on alle thyng that is tofore him and is yladde by a strawe and pleyeth therwith. And is a wel heuy beste in eelde [old age] and ful slepy. And lith sliliche in awayte for mys and is ware where they ben more by smelle than by sight. And hunteth and reseth on hem in priuey place. And whanne he taketh a mous he pleyeth therwith, and eteth him after the pleye. And is as it were wylde, and goth aboute in tyme of generacioun. Among cattes in tyme of loue is hard fightynge for wyues, and oon craccheth and rendeth the other greuousliche with bytyng and with clawes. And he maketh a reweliche noyse and horrible whan oon profreth to fighte with another. And is a cruel beste whanne he is wilde and wonyeth in wodes and hunteth thanne smale wilde bestes, as conynges and hares. And falleth on his owne feet whanne he falleth out of highe place . . .

The words of the Franciscan friar Bartholomew reach with clarity from the thirteenth century any observer of cats today, and urge us to believe that some medievals took pleasure in cats as pets. We must note, however, that Bartholomew concluded his remarks on cats by saying that the animal 'is ofte for his fayre skynne ytake of the skynnere and yslayne . . .'.

Notice is due here of the succession of official cats of Exeter Cathedral. The obit accounts for the cathedral from 1305 through 1467 contain the entry *custoribus et cato*, (to the custors (keepers) and the cat) or, on one occasion *pro cato*, (for the cat) amounting to a penny per week. This sum was apparently to supplement the diet of the official cat, who was expected to control the pest population of the cathedral. A cat-hole is still to be found in the door in the north transept wall beneath the clock, through which the salaried feline could enter and egress while going about its task of hunting rats, mice, birds, and other threats to the cathedral. One wonders if John Catterick during his brief tenure in 1419 as Bishop of Exeter was ever informed by someone with a whimsical sense of humour of the existence of the official cat.

Gardening

The observer of English society today who would note an interest in pets would also be likely to notice the cultivation of gardens, another activity for which the medieval tradition is clearly evident. With gardening, as with keeping animals, it is not always easy or especially useful to distinguish between pleasure and utility. Any space in which people were deliberately cultivating plants we can call a garden, and we might go on to categorize the kitchen garden, where some vegetables and herbs might be grown; the orchard, where nut and fruit trees of many sorts could be grown for

Pleasure gardens of the fifteenth century, with trellised fences, raised beds, turfed benches and an ornamental fountain which feeds a channeled stream (British Library, Harley Ms. 4425, f. 12v)

their edible produce as well as for building and fuel or as habitat for animals which could be hunted; the physic garden, wherein would be planted various medicinal herbs; or the aesthetic garden, developed largely for ornament and pleasure. Yet we must not be overly rigid about categories, because to the gardener a plot of ground might blissfully intermingle recreational, aesthetic, and practical purposes. One of the things most appreciated about the flowers in a garden was their sweet fragrance. Because medieval gardens were frequently enclosed, the fragrances of flowers and herbs were confined and concentrated.

A description of an enclosed garden comes from the pen of Reginald, a monk of Durham, who wrote the 'Life and Miracles of St Godric'. Godric, who died in 1170, was a hermit at Finchale a few miles from Durham. In the 'Life' a square garden is described surrounded on all sides by a hedge. At the centre of the garden (where in other gardens one might expect to find a fountain, pool, or special tree or plant) there was a desk upon which rested a book from which a man was reading. The garden is described as being laid out on a quadrangular plan, suggesting that it was divided into four quarters, each of which was an area of planting, and that the quarters were marked off with some sort of dividing boundaries. Such qualities as aroma, especially if concentrated in an enclosure, together with visual beauty and practical use, gave value to garden plants.

USEFUL GARDEN PLANTS

Among the useful garden flowers might be mentioned those of the *artemisia* family. Southernwood's (*Artemisia abrotanum*) hair-like leaves were used to relieve fevers and wounds and, when dried, the plant was valued for its aroma. The ability to purge a person of worms and poisons was attributed to wormwood (*Artemisia absinthum*), which was also respected as a cure for constipation and stomach discomfort, to say nothing of its value as flea repellent (shared by pennyroyal, one of the mints, but not a garden flower). Wormwood has a bitter taste, unlike mugwort (*Artemisia vulgaris*), which was used to add flavour to drinks. The tansy flower was thought to be an insect repellent, but the entire plant is aromatic and bitter to the taste, and all parts of the plant were variously used in cookery. Another useful flower was the marigold, named St Mary's Gold to honour the Virgin Mary. Marigolds were used both as medicine, against stings and pestilence, and in cooking, as a bitter spice. The blue iris, still a greatly appreciated flower, had many uses. The iris root made a decent ink and, when dried, had a sweet aroma, reminiscent of violets. Iris leaves could be used in making mats, patching thatched roofs, or like rushes in covering floors. Furthermore, the iris flower was not only fragrant and pleasing to the eye, but yielded a dark blue juice that was used for spot removing, as a salve for teeth and gums, and as an ingredient in a dye for cloth. Beautiful, useful, and sweet smelling, it is no wonder that the iris was a favourite flower.

Another useful and favourite flower was the periwinkle. Periwinkle garlands and wreaths could be easily woven because of the long and supple stems, and the plant grew low, making it a useful and attractive ground cover. Medieval English people were not attracted to lawns that aspired to the appearance of the modern golf course. They liked flowery meads of scythe-mown grass, fragrant herbs, and flowers like violets, daisies, primroses, and periwinkles, which acted as a summons to walk, dance, and lie among the visual beauty and enveloping aromas. Violets were popular, but were appreciated for more than just their fragrance. They were associated symbolically with humility, freshness, purity, and innocence, and thus came to be associated with the Blessed Virgin. Products of the kitchen were sometimes garnished and coloured with violets, while the petals had medicinal use as an emetic and purgative, and the oil could scent a bath or soothe the skin. Like periwinkles, daisies were made into garlands and crowns, and were welcomed in gardens. The bright freshness of the daisy is suggested by its name, which comes from the Old English 'daezeseye' or eye of day. Among the varieties, the large ox-eye was the favourite. The primrose was also popular, and was appreciated in part, as it still is, because of its early appearance in the spring. The primrose was also very useful. It could be made into wine. The leaves were used on wounds to ease pain and on the skin to avoid blemishes, and they were eaten to ease muscle aches. The petals were also eaten for pain relief, cooked into tansy cakes and pottages, and floated in comforting baths.

The gillyflower, ancestor of the carnation, was another flower respected for its usefulness and attractiveness. It was used in cooking as a spice because of its aroma and clove-like taste, and was used to cover the bitter taste of some medical potions as well as a flavouring in wine and ale. The gillyflower apparently came to England with the Normans, and by the fourteenth century was to be found in the colour varieties of flesh pink, crimson, and white, while by the next century there was also a clove pink variety, the one with the most assertive aroma and colour. The peony, thought of today simply as an ornamental flower, had additional uses in centuries past. The seeds were used in flavouring meat, or were eaten raw to warm the taste buds and stabilize the temperament, they were also drunk in hot wine and ale before retiring at night to avoid disturbing dreams. The pink, red, and white flowers of the *Paeonia mascula* can be seen today essentially as they were centuries ago on the island of Steep Holme off the north Somerset coast at the site of an Augustinian priory which existed only for a few decades in the thirteenth century. The conditions on the island were clearly better for the peonies than for the Augustinians. Less spectacular by far than the flower of the peony was that of sweet woodruff, which can conclude our sampling of useful flowers. It was frequently used for garlands, with its fresh, sweet fragrance and white summery colour, and also to add subtlety to drinks, while the leaves, so scented that they were known as 'sweetgrass', were strewn when dry on floors and packed with clothes as a freshener.

FLOWERS FOR PLEASURE

Flowers were not required to be useful to be appreciated. Luke (12:27) said: 'Think how the flowers grow; they never have to spin or weave. . . .' Some flowers were enjoyed for the pleasure alone which they provided. In a flowery mead, it will be recalled, we would encounter mown grass in which were periwinkles, daisies, primroses, violets, gillyflowers, or whatever else gave colour and fragrance.

Ornamental gardening was flourishing in England by the late eleventh century, and may well have been of earlier origin. The general story of pleasure gardens began, apparently, with high ecclesiastics who arrived from Normandy in the reign of William the Conqueror. The story of English royal gardens and parks begins with the Conqueror's son, Henry I (reigned 1100–35). Henry I had a pleasure garden laid out to complement the castle his father had built to control the Thames Valley at Windsor, and there were other pleasure gardens established as well, although no details about these royal pleasances have survived. Later kings continued the practice. Henry III (reigned 1216–72) devoted considerable resources to the building of pleasure gardens at the Palace of Westminster, the Tower of London, Windsor Castle, Woodstock, Clarendon, his manors of Guildford (Surrey) and Kempton (Middlesex), Winchester Castle, Gloucester Castle, Nottingham Castle, and others. Henry III's patronage of things beautiful

Floral decorations (British Library, Additional Ms. 38126, f. 7)

extended far beyond his rebuilding of Westminster Abbey. When kings like Henry III led the way in the creation and development of pleasure gardens, the powerful and wealthy figures of the secular and ecclesiastical aristocracy followed. There exists, for instance, an account from this era of the garden at Holborn belonging to the Earl of Lincoln.

ROSES AND LILIES

An old tradition states that the Romans named the most north-western target of their imperialism Albion because of the white roses found growing in Britannia, but it is not in fact certain whether the *Rosa alba* was present when the Romans arrived or if they imported it. In any case, throughout the medieval period the white rose was available as an English garden favourite. Eleanor of Provence, who became the wife of Henry III in 1236, used a white rose as her emblem, and her son Edward I (reigned 1272–1307)

A loving couple stand on a flowery mead hedged in by a low trellis to which are tied roses, apparently the white *Rosa alba* on the left, and a striped red-and-white rose of the type of 'Rosa Mundi' on the right (British Library, Harley Ms. 4431, f. 376)

took as an emblem a rose with almost gold-coloured petals and a green stem. Edmund, Earl of Lancaster (died 1296), a younger son of Eleanor and Henry, adopted a red rose, the *Rosa gallica*, following his marriage to Blanche of Artois (died 1302), granddaughter of Louis VIII of France, whose emblem it was; and thus the red rose became the emblem of the house of Lancaster. Red roses, like white, were to be found in England throughout the medieval period, and were no new introduction at the time of the marriage of Blanche of Artois and Edmund 'Crouchback' in 1275. Richard, Duke of York (died 1460), used the white rose as a favourite badge, and it was taken up by his son, Edward IV (reigned 1461–83). The red rose was evidently not used as a badge by the Lancastrian king, Henry VI (reigned 1422–61), who was supplanted by his kinsman Edward IV. The catchy title 'Wars of the Roses', for the intermittent civil and dynastic conflict of the 1450s to the 1480s between the red rose of Lancaster and the white rose of York, was not invented until the eighteenth century, but the idea went back at least to the 'Crowland Chronicle', which was completed in the 1480s, and the two roses as symbols of the rival dynasties was given a wider audience in the Temple Garden scene in Shakespeare's *Henry VI, Part I*, Act II, scene iv. The first Tudor king, Henry VII (reigned 1485–1509), employed the propaganda symbol of a combined red and white rose to represent himself as unifier of the warring factions of Lancaster and York. The Tudor rose remains a very familiar symbolic flower.

The third rose generally cultivated in late medieval England, along with the red and white, was the damask rose. It will probably never be known if the pink rose of Damascus was brought to England by merchants, monks, pilgrims, or crusaders. Along with the cultivated roses mention must be made of the native wild rose, the *Rosa rubiginosa*, known also as the sweet briar or eglantine, which has a lovely smell, is a good climber for walls and fences, and was used in the making of mead and various medicines. Actually, medieval cultivated roses would look fairly wild to the modern eye, accustomed as it is to the products of scientific breeders. The flowers of medieval cultivated roses were smaller, more open, and more fragile than today's roses, and they were more delicate of fragrance. The medieval rose plants were more like rambling bushes than modern roses, and the thorns were longer and more plentiful, an even more noticeable presence. It was when the rose petals were dried and powdered that they had the most powerful fragrance, and it was usually the petals of the red rose that were used in the making of rose water, rose oil, rose preserves, petal garnishes, and rose sugar. It was the custom to employ roses as symbols of the Holy Spirit, and to scatter them in churches for this reason. The practice was associated with festivals when roses would have been in bloom, such as that of John the Baptist (24 June), St Peter (29 June), and the moveable feasts of Whitsun and Corpus Christi (which fell in May or June).

The lily ranked with the rose as a special flower, and to the medieval mind roses and lilies were the devotional flowers without rival. The lily was associated especially with the Virgin Mary. The Venerable Bede (died 735), the glory of Northumbrian monastic culture, knew the Madonna lily as an emblem of the Virgin Mary, the white petals representing her bodily purity and the golden anthers the light of her soul. The lily was an ancient fertility symbol, and it suited the Mother of God. An association of the Virgin Mary with *The Song of Songs* also suggested itself to many medieval minds: 'I am the Rose of Sharon, the lily of the valleys'. The biblical Rose of Sharon may have been the crocus or narcissus, and the lily of the valleys could have been the Palestine anemone, but that is of no importance for medieval symbolism. The lily represented purity, innocent beauty, and chastity, a neat parallel for the virgin birth of Christ. It is worth recalling as well, that the central image of *The Song of Songs* is that of a garden. This means that the example of sensual literature most widely known to medieval people was centred upon a garden.

MONASTIC GARDENS

The inhabitants of monastic houses were among the most diligent of medieval gardeners. It is told in Genesis, the first book of the Old Testament, that God created a garden in Eden, a lovely place with multitudes of plants and trees. Adam and Eve's sin of disobedience which caused their exile became for Christians the Doctrine of the Fall of Humanity, and the tradition grew in succeeding human generations that one avenue for seeking association with God was by gardening. An obvious venue for spiritual gardening was the monastery. The monastic rule of St Benedict, drawn up in the sixth century for his community at Monte Cassino in Italy, was profoundly influential in England, and the Benedictine Rule specifically enjoined the cultivation of gardens.

Any monastery, Benedictine or otherwise, would require a kitchen garden, or gardens, depending on the size of the house. The kitchen garden would probably lie within a hedge or wall and

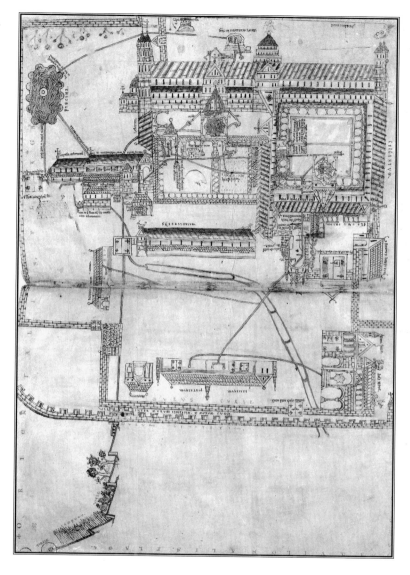

A plan of the water-supply system to the great Benedictine monastery of Christ Church, Canterbury. North of the church and east of the great cloister is the herb-garden ('Herbarium'), with rows of plants and a trellis fence. Outside the precinct are the vineyard ('Vinea') and the orchard ('Pomerium,'), between the city wall and the open fields (Trinity College Cambridge)

would produce the peas and beans required for the daily pottage, together with leeks, onions, and garlic. Larger gardens might also produce apples and other fruits, have beehives for the production of honey, and grow hemp. Hemp (cannabis) was introduced into England by the Romans, not as a drug but for the making of rope and canvas, and was for this reason vital to a useful medieval industry.

The garden for a monastic infirmary would probably have been smaller than the kitchen garden and more specialized. Here would have been grown the ingredients required for medicines, salves, and tonics. The modern word 'drug' is derived from the Old English verb 'driggen' meaning to dry, reflecting the preparation undertaken by the infirmarer of the herbs that he would store for use in his service to the sick. The infirmary garden at Westminster Abbey covered an acre, and would have offered space for convalescents to stroll among the beds of assorted herbs and flowers grown for their medicinal properties while enjoying gentle exercise in scented air. It may be noted in passing that the substantial garden maintained by the cellarer of Westminster Abbey was at a distance from the main buildings of the abbey at a location now known as Covent Garden, from the Norman French 'Le Couvent' or 'The Convent', while the orchard of the abbey is memorialized by Abbey Orchard Street.

In London by the reign of Edward I there existed a nursery trade to supply the needs and desires of gardeners. One could buy such things as seeds of leek, mustard, hemp, colewort, and onions, as well as onion sets, other small plants, and grafted fruit trees. An organized nursery trade was also appearing around the same time in such places as Oxford, Norwich, and York. Itinerant seedsmen moving about from place to place with their packhorses filled in the gaps between organized commercial centres. A trade in the surplus produce of household gardens also existed. One market for such surplus and for the produce of market gardens in the later Middle Ages was in London in front of the church of St Augustine, Watling Street, close by St Paul's churchyard.

Pleasure gardens, too, were a feature of some monasteries, planted with trees, shrubs, and vines. The cloister garth of a monastery would commonly be planted with trees, herbs, and flowers to make them more pleasant for contemplative recreation. Even more appropriate to contemplation would have been a paradise, inspired by the Garden of Eden described in Genesis 2:8–9. It was the custom that paradises were enclosed and used for prayer and meditation. The sacrist of the monastery saw to it that the paradise produced the flowers needed to decorate the church for various occasions, and such devotional flowers as roses and lilies would certainly have been grown there. When a monastery was able to establish a paradise, it was usually placed beside the monks' cemetery, normally north of the church, and itself decorated with trees, flowers, and fountains, together with a central cross or crucifix. Even heads of monastic institutions sometimes established private gardens, which reflected personal tastes and interests in favourite fruit trees, shade-giving trees, herbs, flowers, or vegetables.

CARTHUSIAN GARDENING

The cloistered religious orders of England made an ongoing contribution to the tradition of gardening, but among the monks and nuns a special niche in the history of English medieval gardening was filled by Carthusian monks. Because of the disciplined nature of their lives all Carthusians were gardeners. The Carthusian Order began in 1084 when Bruno, a priest and head of the cathedral school and chancellor of the diocese of Rheims, in his mature years founded the Grande Chartreuse in Provence. In Carthusian houses, or charterhouses as they were called in England, the monks lived lives of strict asceticism and solitude, each one residing in a separate cell, very much like a private house, within the monastery precincts. The brethren gathered each day to participate in collective worship, but they ate together only on important feast days. They followed a common daily schedule, but lived essentially as recluses. They prayed, studied, ate, and worked for the most part within the small world of their cells and gardens, each one following his own programme of cultivation.

VEGETABLES

An earlier generation of historical researchers determined that the medieval diet consisted mainly of bread and the flesh of beast, fish, and fowl, and that few if any vegetables were eaten. That conclusion was based upon the absence of vegetables in the purchasing accounts of households. Later generations of historians have realized that of course households did not buy many vegetables, because there was no need: they were available from their gardens. Household gardens were ubiquitous in medieval society. Staples for the day-to-day diets of ordinary English people in the Middle Ages were bread, ale, and pottage, which, contrary to a common misunderstanding, was not oatmeal. Pottage was the stuff cooked in the large pot hung over the fire, and was the basic hot dish served on most tables. The liquid medium of pottage was water, perhaps flavoured with meat stock, or that of poultry or fish, and enriched with the ever-changing addition of whatever was available. Any number of vegetables were included: leeks, onions, chibols, shallots, field peas, broad beans, and the leaves of colewort, which was planted often enough by any conscientious householder that its leaves could be cropped throughout the year. Parsley was a standard flavouring, as were garlic and hyssop. In the later Middle Ages, better gardens would have been contributing to the pottage

The flavoursome leek was widely grown in medieval Europe (Österreichische Nationalbibliothek)

such root crops as carrots, parsnips, skirrets (a species of water parsnip), rapes, and turnips. To sit down to a meal of bread, ale, and vegetable soup is, therefore, to do exactly as our medieval ancestors did.

FRUITS

Cider was a popular drink in medieval England, and consequently apple trees were common to orchards. Bitter-sweets, Pearmains, and Costards were among the most appreciated varieties. Crab apples grew wild and were seldom cultivated or appreciated; a medieval simile was 'as sour as a crab'. Pears were nearly as extensively enjoyed as apples, and the most common varieties were Wardens, Caleols, Sorells, and Gold Knopes. St Rule pears were élitist and expensive. While apples were often eaten raw, pears were usually cooked up into preserves, puddings, and pies. Pears yielded perry, but apple cider was more widely esteemed. Cherry trees often stood with apple and pear trees in orchards, and cherries

A young boy stealing cherries
(British Library, Additional Ms.
42130, f. 196v)

were eaten raw as a rule. Another medieval simile was 'cherry red', suggesting that cherries were enjoyed ultra-ripe. Nut trees were also a common feature of orchards. Walnuts, hazelnuts, filberts, and chestnuts were both eaten raw and used in cookery. Nut trees were also common to the woodlands of the countryside, and most people simply gathered nuts from the wild.

Before departing from cultivated fruits, mention should be made of the quince, a member of the pear family. Quinces were loved for their tangy taste, but as they are too hard to eat raw and yield no pleasant juice, they were cooked and made into jelly, pastries, and pies, while the seeds were used as medication. Peach trees were cultivated, but not without difficulty, and peaches were a noble fruit. Plums were grown with greater ease, and were therefore more available. The mulberry was another popular fruit and was frequently cultivated, but people turned to the wilds to gather fruits like raspberries, elderberries, blackberries, gooseberries, bilberries, and strawberries.

GRAPE-VINES

It is an old tradition that the grape-vine was introduced into Britain by the Romans, and there are thirty-eight vineyards

e li vns le fait bien lautres hardiement
e puinaus z despees fierent menuement
n hances z en testes sont plaie durement
villain les esgardent trop merveilleusement
dient que ce sont anemi z serpent
e nus ne sofferroit si grans cops longement

a reprendre salaine
oit le tesmoignent grieu de proece souuraine
cassamus escrie a clere vois hautaine
u est betis mes nies de nature germaine
hi aual nest il pas ie vout quon ne lenmaine
ar soi ce dist porrus cest i nouiaus ensaine

Collecting and treading the grapes for the preparation of wine, *c.* 1340 (Bodleian Library, Oxford, Ms. Bodl. 264, f. 133r)

mentioned in 'Domesday Book' (1086) as taxable assets. Mostly they were noted in the southern counties from Dorset and Gloucestershire in the west to Essex, Kent, and East Anglia in the east. Grapes were grown in the later Middle Ages in England, but the wine produced was not held in the same high esteem as that which was imported from the Continent. The southern counties and especially Kent had the best record for English wine production. However, medieval English viticulture was geared to the production of verjuice (grape vinegar), a staple for cooking and physic, as well as to the production of wine. Thus if the growing conditions and the expense of maintaining vineyards did not meet the expectations of a fine vintage, there was the compensation of marketable verjuice.

HERB GARDENS AND HERBAL MEDICINE

A substantial household or a monastery might have a separate herb garden, but most cottagers would merely have some herbs growing among the flowers, fruits, and vegetables of their utilitarian gardens. The medieval concept of herbs was more general than the modern. A medieval herb was a useful plant, generally one handy for flavouring or having medicinal properties. It is worth noting that non-academic medieval medicine could best be described as herbal medicine. What might be a herb for medicine or cooking in one context might also be for ornament in another, as with sage, hyssop and camomile, which were used in infirmary and kitchen, and also added their fragrance and prettiness to pleasure gardens. Rue was thought of as an especially useful herb. As a medication it was judged a strong purgative with which to attack phlegms in the sick or to purge the intestines. Tempered with rosewater, rue was used as an eyewash or as a strewing herb to clean the air by virtue

Making medicines, from Roger
Frugardi's *Chirurgia*, England,
mid-thirteenth century (Trinity
College Cambridge)

of its aroma. In cooking it was employed in the making of pickles or, like dill, to add tang to a broth. The seeds of dill, cumin, and anise were used medicinally as aids to digestion. Fennel was more commonly grown than anise, and was used in many sorts of digestive tonics. Tavern-keepers were inclined to grow the herb borage so that the leaves could be added to claret or cider, while borage was used medicinally to make cool cordials, bath oils, and other antidotes for hot ailments. Angelica (*Angelica archangelica*) was an exceedingly versatile herb. Strongly aromatic, its leaves could be chewed to relieve flatulence (as with the seeds of coriander and caraway), the oil derived from the roots and seeds was used to flavour drinks and distilled into perfume, and the bright green stalks were candied and eaten as sweets. Lavender, because of the oil it contained, was used in similar ways to angelica. Other herbs greatly appreciated for their strong scents as well as for other properties would include balm, sweet basil, marjoram of various types, thyme, purslane, and mints of different sorts, among which pennyroyal was the apparent favourite. Among the herbs that were most inclined towards kitchen usage would be parsley, chervil, lovage, which has a celery-like taste, and the sweetly aromatic and bitter-tasting tansy, which was an ale gruit, a fly repellent, and an ingredient in the tansy cakes eaten at the end of Lent.

THE FOUR HUMOURS

The medieval medical concept of the four humours was derived from classical antiquity, and was associated with the authoritative names of Hippocrates and Galen. To comprehend the humours it is

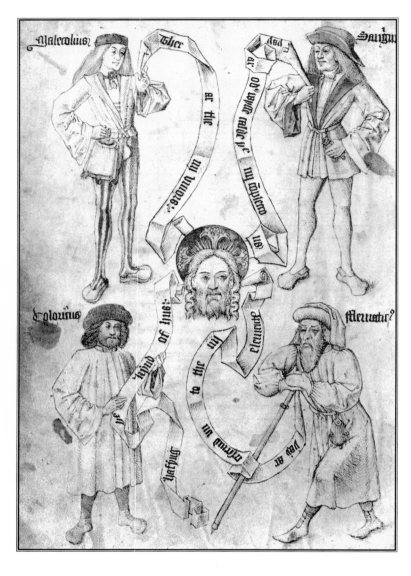

The four humours, blood, phlegm, choler, and black bile, are associated with stages of life and seasons of the year (From the fifteenth-century *Guild Book of the Barber Surgeons of York*, British Library, Egerton Ms. 2572, f. 51v)

helpful to know the complementary concept of complexion, and also to remember the notion of the four elements of which matter was composed. The four elements were earth, air, fire, and water. Each element had its quality: earth was dry, air cold, fire hot, and water wet. Complexion derived from the Latin term *complexio*, meaning temperament, and it was viewed as the balance of the qualities of dry, cold, hot, and moist. In this wonderfully rational, analytical system the goal for the regimen of health was the maintenance, or balance, of the qualities in an individual, because sickness occurred when the balance was upset. Every person was endowed with their own innate complexion. Furthermore, the complexion of every individual was affected by the circumstances in which they lived, their age, their diet, and other factors. The humours, which we are trying to conceptualize, were understood to be the bodily fluids essential to the functioning of every organism, and there were four of them: blood, phlegm, bile (also called choler or red bile or yellow bile), and black bile (also called melancholy). The humour of blood combined the qualities of hot and moist, phlegm was cold and moist, bile was hot and dry, and black bile was cold and dry.

Even this elementary analysis of the concept of the four humours begins to make clear various suppositions. The heat and moisture of youth suggested an excess of the humour of blood, a sanguine condition (perhaps requiring a phlebotomy), while old age suggested the cold and dry qualities of black bile moving to the ultimate cold and dry state of death. Different organs of the body were thought to have predominant complexional qualities, such as the brain's tendency towards cold and the heart's towards heat. An individual whose temperament appeared to acquaintances to be cold and moist would be described as phlegmatic, while one who seemed to be cold and dry would be described as melancholic. It seemed entirely obvious that ingested food became the humours of the body, and thus foods were often described as having the quality of hot or dry or cold or moist, and physicians would prescribe diets or medicines according to the qualities their contents were understood to have that would influence the balance of humours in patients. If one understood evil not to be a thing in itself but rather an absence of goodness, which was real and a gift from God, then sickness by analogy was a lack of health, a falling away from the proper balance of forces that made up the condition of being healthy. The wisdom of medicine, then, was not to teach ways to fight a thing called sickness so much as to teach ways to maintain health.

GARDENING WRITERS

A number of Englishmen made contributions to the body of medieval literature on gardening. Alexander Neckam (died 1217) is usually remembered as an English luminary on the scene of international scholarship around the start of the thirteenth century, but Neckam needs also to be remembered in the context of English gardening literature. He devoted a chapter of his 'De naturis rerum' to the flowers, herbs, and trees which grew in gardens, while in his lengthy poem, 'De laudibus divinae sapientiae', one section deals with plants and another with trees and crops. Altogether, Neckam mentioned some 140 species in these writings. Bartholomew the Englishman, whose observations on cats were quoted earlier in this chapter, devoted the seventeenth book of his encyclopaedia to plants, and mentioned 115 species altogether. A poem in English by, or at least attributed to, Master John Gardener, 'The Feate of Gardening', dealt with practical horticulture, and seemingly dates from the first half of the fourteenth century. The 'Feate' has been called 'the first English garden book', and 'Mayster Jon' should have an honoured niche in the history of English gardening. The poem demonstrates a solid practical knowledge of grafting fruit-trees, tending grape-vines, and in general discusses more than a hundred trees, herbs, and vegetables. In the same era Richard of Bury (died 1345), Bishop of Durham, wrote the 'Philobiblon', in which horticulture and aboriculture were accorded the highest respect.

Later in the fourteenth century Geoffrey Chaucer made garden references, suggesting a respectable knowledge of plants and trees, in such writings as *The Merchant's Tale* and *The Franklin's Tale*. Among fruit trees he mentioned, for instance, the medlar, peach, pear, plum, cherry, apple, and quince; and as forest trees such examples as holly, fir, plane, poplar, oak, linden, birch, maple, ash, beech, box, dogwood, willow, and yew. John Bray (died 1381) was a botanist as well as a physician, and his contemporary, the surgeon John Arderne, was a keen observer and classifier of plants. Henry Daniel, a Dominican friar, was a learned herbalist, and his main botanical writing survives (British Library Additional MS 27329), although the manuscript itself was completed after Daniel's lifetime. An earlier version of his work also survives (Arundel MS 42). Daniel studied plants both as a medical man seeking the benefits that different plants might provide, and as one who found pleasure in gardening. He was interested in naming and classifying plants, and noticed how variations in soil and site affected the growth and development of plants. He made several references to the garden he developed in the London area at Stepney, and asserted that he grew no fewer than 252 sorts of herbs in his garden. This comment was probably made in around 1385, by which time the friar was an elderly man. Daniel is also noteworthy for having written about the cultivation of rosemary.

Rosemary was a significant botanical introduction into England, and it was imported in about 1340 as a gift for Queen Philippa. Licorice, clary, mandrake, and the cypress probably arrived in the same century, while basil, monk's rhubarb, and true spinach appeared a bit later; asparagus and the kidney bean would not have been found in a medieval garden. Rosemary was a difficult evergreen shrub to establish and maintain, but as it became more common it came to be highly respected. It took up considerable space in a garden, and did well cascading down walls. Its uses were numerous: rosemary flower tea had a calming and purging effect upon the body; the flowers and stems when powdered became an ingredient in one type of toothpaste; brushing the hair with a branch of rosemary was regarded as beneficial for the scalp; the pale blue flowers attracted bees; the dried flowers were a fragrant strewing herb; it was used to flavour roasting meats; and was associated with remembrance – placing a sprig on the body of a departed friend was a way of affirming enduring memories. It might appropriately be mentioned, incidentally, that another introduction to England, saffron, was being grown at Saffron Walden in Essex by the end of the 1350s.

Another contribution to garden literature was written toward the end of the fourteenth century in Latin by an anonymous Englishman, and entitled the 'Agnus Castus'. It was translated into English in around 1440, and the Latin original is in the British Library (Sloane MS 2498). Medieval writers in Latin had the vocabulary to make horticultural distinctions in their writings. The common Latin words for any sort of garden were *hortus* or *ortus*, while common words for a gardener were *gardinarius* or *ortolanus*. A kitchen garden was a *gardinum*, while any specialized type of garden, for example a medicinal herb garden or a rose garden, became a *herbarium*. A utilitarian orchard could be called a *pomerium*, and a pleasure ground a *viridarium*, while the strict word for orchard, *vergier*, was the medieval equivalent of what we might call a pleasure garden. This was a place for taking the fresh air, finding shade in the summer heat, and was often surrounded by a hedge, wall, or moat.

SEVEN

Diet, the Tavern and Codes of Behaviour

An appreciation of food, the festivity of banqueting and convivial meal-taking were a common feature of medieval life. The sharing of food and drink with friends and people with whom friendship was sought fits into the conventions of gift-giving etiquette. Because of the nature of surviving evidence, we know much more about the food and cookery of the upper strata of society, with their abundant banquetting cuisine, than we do about the less grand. It was an accepted standard that the higher a person stood on the social scale the greater quantity and finer quality of food that person should have available. Cookery books surviving from the Middle Ages are unfortunately useless as a guide to what people generally ate, because they discuss the sophisticated dishes prepared for the tables of the moneyed.

Diet

The diet of English people in the later Middle Ages is not easily summarized. The type and quantity of food varied with the abundance of the harvest, the season, and the wealth of the consumer. To spread the food supply into seasons of scarcity, the only methods of preserving food were drying (which includes smoking, the easiest to do), salting (very commonly done with fish), and fermenting. The diet of most people, which means the agrarian population, was characterized in the thirteenth century by carbohydrates mostly in the form of bread made of barley and oats or grain brewed into ale. There would be dairy produce such as cheese or milk on a seasonal basis. Meat and eggs to supply protein for the diet were probably sparse in the thirteenth century, and the household garden provided fruits, herbs, and vegetables. The consumption of meat increased in the course of the fourteenth and fifteenth centuries, which made for an improvement in the diet. The quality of bread also improved, with wheat largely replacing barley and rye in the course of the fourteenth century. Another generalization of the scattered information surviving is that the late medieval diet became more balanced, from an earlier heavy dependence upon bread, cheese, some salted or smoked meat (most often pork) or preserved fish, together with ale, water and milk to drink, to a diet in the fifteenth century of wheat bread, abundant ale, and substantial portions of meat or fish.

THE MONKS OF WESTMINSTER ABBEY

One case study on the diet of a late medieval community that has been attempted is that of the monks of Westminster Abbey. It was the diet of a segment of the gentry, for Westminster was a wealthy monastery. Fish formed a substantial item in the monks' diet and it is what they ate for dinner, the meal taken around 11.00 to 11.30 a.m., on about 215 days each year. This was fairly evenly divided between fresh (mostly sea- as opposed to fresh-water) varieties and fish which had been preserved by smoking, drying, salting, or pickling. Cod was the most commonly served fish, and after that, whiting. Conger eel was a treat. Flesh-meat (that is, muscle tissue) could be expected by a monk about seventy-five days a year, and at both dinner and supper on most of those days. Nearly half the meat eaten by the Westminster monks was mutton, a quarter was beef, and the rest was pork, veal, poultry, and lamb. Most of the meat was fresh, not preserved. The methods of preparation varied from roasting to boiling to stewing. The monks also ate what were distinguished as 'meaty dishes', made from the offal and entrails of the animals from which they obtained flesh-meat. 'Meaty dishes' were classed as not being in opposition to the restrictions against the eating of meat found in the Benedictine Rule.

In addition to fish and meat, the monks of Westminster consumed quantities of bread and ale. The quality of both was high. The basic daily loaf of bread for each monk was baked from wheaten flour, and was likely to have weighed about 2 lb. Special occasions or extra labours would have seen an increase in the amount of bread eaten. The basic daily ration of ale was a gallon,

and if the monk was engaged in labours that engendered thirst, or there was a special occasion, additional ale would be drunk. It must be supposed that the alcohol content was low, or the monks' work would have often been impaired. On many solemn and convivial occasions, the monks drank wine, perhaps as much as a quart for an important event.

Fruit and vegetables were also part of the diet of the Westminster monks at the end of the fifteenth and early into the sixteenth century. The quantity of these items is difficult to estimate because most were grown in the gardens and orchards of the monastery and tended, rather than leaving traces in purchasing accounts, not to be recorded faithfully by the kitcheners. The impression is that vegetables like peas, beans, onions and leafy greens were commonplace, but that fruits were rather a treat for the monks. Dairy products, eggs as well as milk products, also had a solid place in the monks' diet.

The monks' diet was deficient in Vitamin C and probably also Vitamin A. They got more than enough protein, and seemingly enough fats and carbohydrates. Given the amounts of food (and alcohol) available, it is entirely possible that many of the monks of Westminster were plump fellows.

Cooking operations in the open air (above and opposite), using the mortar (large and small), pots being heated over different parts of the fire to give different levels of heat, basting food over a spit, and the spit being turned by hand, *c.* 1340 (Bodleian Library, Oxford, Ms. 264, part 1, f. 170v)

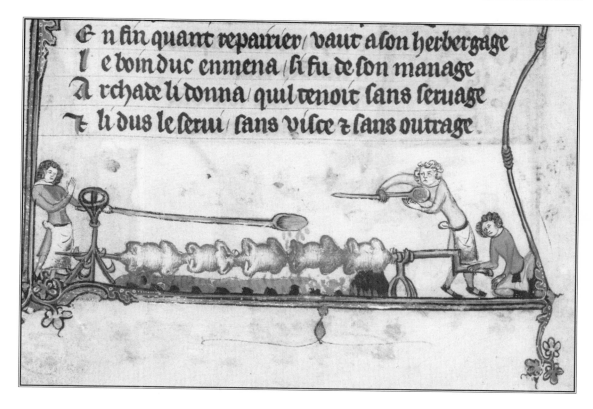

En fin quant repairier / vaut a son herbergage
Le boin duc enmena / si fu de son manage
Archade li donna / quil tenoit sans seruage
E li dus le serui / sans vilte e sans outrage

The Inn, the Tavern and the Alehouse

Food and drink were part of the ambience of inns, taverns, and
alehouses. Inns, the larger and more dignified of these
establishments, appeared in England in the twelfth and thirteenth
centuries, and were apparently fairly common, especially in towns,
by the fifteenth century. The earliest buildings still standing today,
such as New Inn, Gloucester, or King's Head, Aylesbury, date from
this time. While inns provided lodgings for travellers, taverns were
drinking houses seeking to cater for the more prosperous levels of
society. The leading taverners in larger towns were themselves
vintners or acted as agents for vintners. The Vintners' Company of
London, for instance, secured an essential monopoly of the retail
trade in the city in 1364. A tavern of the later medieval period
might be imagined as a fairly substantial building of several rooms
and a generous cellar. Taverns had signs to advertise their presence
to potential customers, and branches and leaves would be hung
over the door to give notice that wine could be purchased. Some
taverns sold wine as their only beverage, and a customer could also
purchase food brought in from a convenient cook-shop. Taverns
seldom offered lodgings or very elaborate feasting, such as would

This Ludlow misericord shows a
tapster drawing drink from a cask
(Conway Library, Courtauld
Institute of Art)

This activity cannot be identified, but it appears to be a drinking game in which the drinker attempts to swallow quantities of drink as quickly as possible with the help of a comrade who is pouring drink through a funnel-like apparatus (British Library, Additional Ms. 42130, f. 157v)

be expected at inns. Pastimes like gambling, singing, and seeking prostitutes were a more common part of the tavern scene.

While taverners strove to maintain respectable establishments for customers of the upper and middle classes, keepers of alehouses seem not to have been so inspired. Establishments for ale-brewing and selling were common in Anglo-Saxon times, if not also in Roman, and the proprietors – variously called brewsters (from a word of feminine gender in Old English), ale-wives or polewives (clearly women), bribsters, hucksters, or regrators of ale – established their businesses in rural or urban settings, wherever the prospects looked good. More humble alehouses opened for business intermittently to dispose of surplus household product for profit or when the materials for brewing were available, while wealthier alehouses would have been permanent drinking establishments. The quantity of ale brewed as well as its quality undoubtedly varied enormously among alehouses. The basic procedure was to use barley (though wheat, oats, and millet were also tried) which was steeped in water until germination took place. The germinated seeds were then dried, ground, and infused in water to await fermentation. Various spices, like long-peppers, might be added for taste and as preservatives. The resulting ale was apparently rather like a thick soup, even chewy if the grinding stage had been lazily done, and the taste can hardly have been deeply satisfying. Ale could not be effectively preserved, and had to be consumed within a few days of brewing. Wine, too, was difficult to keep for any length of time until it began to be bottled in the sixteenth

Opposite: Tavern scene showing cellar (British Library, Additional Ms. 27695, f. 14)

century. Dreams of substantial brewings of ale at considerable intervals to supply a wide geographical area were beyond the possible. Ale was the most common alcoholic beverage available to the lesser economic orders of society, but in some regions cider, mead, and piment were to be found. Various kinds of wine when augmented with honey and spices were known as piment, apparently from the word for apothecaries, *pigmentarii*, as it was they who had originally prepared the concoctions. Hippocras, spiced with cloves, ginger, cinnamon, nutmeg, and other spices as well as with honey, was a favourite piment, served as a rule at the conclusion of banquets with wafers and dessert.

COMMUNAL DRINKING

Ale was so commonplace in society that the king attempted to impose some standards on the trade through the Assize of Ale in 1266. Communal drinking was a common feature of social life, and perhaps should even be considered an essential part of some of the rituals that held society together. The institutions of the church-ale, to help meet parish expenses, and the bride-ale, to benefit a newly married couple, are mentioned elsewhere. Another common sort of charity ale was the bid-ale or help-ale, where ale would be brewed and friendly folk would gather around to drink, contributing the money collected from selling the ale to a worthy cause. It was a communal drinking session to raise funds, often to help friends and neighbours through a crisis time, without compromising the dignity of the recipient. It was also an opportunity to socialize, and contributed to the social solidarity of the participants. Bid-ales seem for the most part to have been informal, held at times of the year when pleasant weather could be

A misericord from St Lawrence's Parish Church, Ludlow, showing a dishonest ale-wife cast into hell for serving short measure

expected. The beneficiary, a respected and usually popular person, would actively participate in putting on the event, and people were expected to be generous. Charity ales existed in many parts of England as a convivial way to raise money for a cause. For instance, the quay called the Cobb, vital to the prosperity of Lyme Regis, was maintained by annual infusions of cash through the Cobb Ale.

Discussion of drink must also include the fact that, in medieval usage, the sin of gluttony meant not only excessive eating, but excessive drinking as well. The two plagues that William fitz Stephen identified in London in about 1180 were the possibility of fire and immoderate drinking. An additional substance entered the drinking habits with the introduction of beer into England. The use of hops in the brewing process in place of spices resulted in a drink that did not deteriorate as quickly as ale and was, to many drinkers, more palatable. Hopped beer was in England by the late thirteenth century but did not become widely available until the fifteenth century.

Advice on Courteous Behaviour

In the later Middle Ages several books dealing with etiquette at meals and related matters were written for young people with prospects and a desire to get on in the world. Such works give an idea of the deportment expected of a youth in a respectable household.

Suggestions from 'The Babees' Book' of about 1475 include: at a meal, when bid to be merry, be ready with pleasant words. On entering the presence of your lord, greet him with 'God speed', and then humbly greet others present. Enter at an easy pace, not rushing, and with head up. Kneel on one knee, but only to your lord. If spoken to, listen carefully and look directly at the speaker without wandering eyes. When answering, say useful things and avoid chattering. Do not sit until bid to do so. Keep hands and feet still: no fidgeting, scratching, handling objects placed about, or leaning against a post. Stand like a stone unless your lord speaks, and then answer with a courteous bow. If a social superior complements you, stand and thank him. If your lord and his lady are speaking of private matters, do not interrupt, but be ready to do service if you are needed by fetching your lord a drink, holding a light, or whatever needs doing. If your lord offers you a drink from his cup, take it graciously in both hands to avoid dropping it, drink, and return it without offering it to anyone else. When your lord is eating, be ready to fetch clear water and a towel so that he can wash his hands, and remain close until he is seated and grace has been said, and stand before him until he tells you to sit. Be sure your hands are clean when serving your lord. Make sure your own knife is clean and sharp so that you can eat decorously. Use your knife to cut your bread rather than breaking it. Eat your pottage quietly, and do not leave your spoon in the dish. Do not lean on the table. Avoid soiling the table-cloth. Do not lean over your dish. Do not drink with your mouth full. Do not pick your nose, teeth, or nails during a meal. Do not so fill your mouth with food that you cannot answer if spoken to. After drinking, wipe your mouth and hands with a cloth, so that the cup will not be offensive to the companion who shares it with you. Do not dip meat into the salt-cellar, but put some salt on your trencher for your use.

The curious 'A B C of Aristotle' of about 1430 used most of the letters of the alphabet, suggesting for each letter three things that should be avoided. The flavour is captured with the admonitions that 'thou shalt not be too Amorous, too Bold, too Cruel, Drink too much, be too Earnest, too Fierce, too vainGlorious, too Harebrained', and so on. In about the middle of the fifteenth century the book 'Urbanitas' suggested that when coming before a lord, doff your cap or hood and hold it until told to put it back on, and kneel on your right knee. Look your lord in the face when speaking to him, and stand still. When taking a meal in a hall or chamber, be sure your hands and knife are clean. Cut your bread and your meat. Let your social superiors serve themselves first; no reaching straightaway for the best piece (no matter how much you like it). Keep your hands as clean as possible so you do not soil the towel. Do not wipe your nose on the table-cloth. 'The Little Children's Little Book' of about 1480 adds: do not eat too fast. Do not pick your ears or nostrils. Do not drink with food in your mouth. Eat small bites. Do not be confrontational in company. Do not spit over the table or in the wash water. Do not lay your elbow or fist on the table while eating, and do not belch. Carve bites with your knife rather than tearing pieces off with your teeth, and do not pick your teeth with your knife. Around 1460 'The Book of Curtesy' suggests, among other things: do not pet the dog or the cat while at table. If you clean your nose at table, wash your hand afterwards. Do not slurp your pottage. Tell no shameful tales during the meal. Do not wipe your knife, or clean your teeth, or wipe your eyes with the table-cloth, and do not blow on your food or drink to cool it.

Of a slightly different cast is 'How the Good Wife Taught Her

Opposite: This fourteenth-century manuscript shows indulgence in feasting along with other pastimes as a major inducement to sin (British Library, Royal Ms. 19 C1, f. 204)

Daughter' dated about 1430. Addressing a young woman, it says if you look forward to being a wife, look lovely, love God and Holy Church, and attend services as often as possible. Give tithes and offerings; help the poor and sick. In church, attend to your beads and do not gossip or scorn others. When a man begins honourably to court you, do not conceal the fact from your friends, but be careful of doing anything that might raise slanderous comments. Love the man who marries you with a ring before God. Be your husband's dear darling, not a shrew. Do not haunt taverns and, if you drink, do so with measure for your reputation will suffer if you are often drunk. Do not watch wrestling or shooting at the cock, because that is the conduct of a strumpet. Stay at home and attend to your work. Supervise your servants even-handedly, not too harsh or too gentle; and give them clear work assignments. If your husband is away, do not let the servants slack off. Set your servants a good example by working energetically yourself. Check the work of your servants. Keep the keys to the storage areas yourself, or be sure that the person to whom you must give them is trustworthy. Be content with what God has provided, and do not be mocking or jealous if your neighbour's wife has more expensive attire than your own. If your children are refractory and disobedient, do not curse or scold them, but take up a rod and beat them until they cry for mercy; they will love you for it in time. The complementary 'How the Wise Man Taught His Son' is based upon old teachings. Be busy not idle; do not nourish sloth. Do not make a bargain you cannot keep. Avoid tavern-haunting, dice, and lechery. Do not stay up too late at night. Do not marry for money, but look for a woman of good character. Rule your wife with an even hand, and cherish her for the good things she does. If your wife is at ease, your life will be more peaceful. Do not defame your wife, because if she gets a poor reputation it will reflect upon you. Live peacefully with your neighbours. If you gain much of the world's goods, be grateful and not boasting. Pay your debts. Remember that life is transitory, and the salvation of your soul is more important than the things of this world.

The last two books mentioned, as well as the others, are essentially etiquette books for noble children to help them learn about the adult world into which they will be entering as heads of households. A book with a different slant, written to help train those who would enter into service in a household, is the 'Boke of Nurture' by John Russell, who was marshal and usher in the household of Duke Humphrey of Gloucester (died 1447). In the beginning the author meets a young man while walking in a forest

Carving and serving for the lord's table (British Library, Additional Ms. 42130, f. 207v)

on a fine May morning, and the young man indicates that he would like to be in service but has not been trained. The author then proceeds to give instruction in the arts of being a panter or butler. The first tools needed are three sharp knives: one to chop the loaves, another to trim them, and the third to shape the trenchers. The lord gets fresh bread, other bread at the table can be a day old, the general household gets bread three days old, and trenchers are made from bread four days old. Make sure the salt is dry, white, and fine, and that the lid of the salt-cellar does not touch the salt (silver will tarnish). Be sure the table linen is clean and fresh, and the knives and spoons for the table are washed and polished. When you broach a pipe of wine with an auger to fit in a tap, make the hole four fingers' space from the bottom rim to avoid disturbing the lees.

Russell continues his practical advice by saying that in the buttery the pots and cups must be kept clean. Ale should not be served until it is five days old. When laying a table, wipe the table before spreading the table-cloth. A salt-cellar should be placed at your lord's right hand, to the left of it one or two trenchers, then a knife, then white rolls, then a spoon resting on a folded napkin. The trencher, knife, and spoon are then covered. The lord's rolls might also be attractively wrapped in a towel. Other tables and places must be set with trenchers and cups and spoons and napkins. Basins and ewers for washing must be readied, together with hot and cold water, which can be blended to get the correct temperature. (Washing hands before and after meals was no idle ceremony: the fingers were actively employed in eating.) Be sure the serving-pots for wine and ale are clean, and that no flies or dirt get into the drink. Assist your lord with his washing, and carry a towel around your neck when serving. Bow your knees whenever you pass your lord. Be sure everyone is abundantly served so they do not grumble, and be cheerful and soft spoken. Make sure your hands and nails are clean, and that your clothes are neat. Do not put your fingers into cups to remove dust, and do not cough, spit, or belch too loud. Do not scratch as if you have fleas, or stroke your hair as if you have lice, or do anything that might seem to be showing off. Do not pick your nose, or blow it too loud, or let it drip mucus. Do not lick your lips or drool. Do not make faces, spit too far, wring your hands, yawn, stare, or wipe the dust out of a dish with your tongue.

To be a carver, Russell continues, one must have a clean knife and clean hands. The knife is to be held with two fingers and the thumb of the right hand, with the haft firmly in the hand. Food is to be touched only with the left hand, and then with thumb and two fingers. Wipe your knife on your napkin, not the table. Give your lord the upper crust of the trencher you cut and trim for his use. Russell then goes on with instructions for the carving of various foods.

The young man then asks for instruction in the office of sewer, that is, a servant who uses a ewer or basin filled with water for the washing of hands at meals. Instruction follows thereafter for the office of chamberlain, with instructions on how to serve the lord in his chamber or bedroom. The chamberlain is to see that the lord has clean clothes to put on in the morning, even warmed by a fire if the weather is chilly, and that he is to be cheerful and quick to please his lord. The lord's hair must gently be combed as the lord sits in a chair by the fire, which should be burning clean and not smoky, and in this cosy way the lord is assisted in washing his face and hands and in dressing. Should the lord wish to have a bath, sheets scented with flowers and herbs are to be hung from the ceiling around the tub, and big sponges are needed for him to sit upon, lean against, and be scrubbed with. After he is washed and rinsed with warm rose-water, he is to be dried with a clean cloth. Before the lord goes out of the house, busy about and see that he is clean and tidy. Then go to his chamber, fluff the feather-bed, see that the bed clothes are clean when the bed is made up, and that all is readied for the next use. Attention must be given to the care of the lord's clothes. They must be brushed, and woollens and furs must be shaken or brushed at least weekly to guard against moths. In the evening, the lord must be assisted in undressing, and his hair must be combed and his bed readied. When he is in bed, draw the curtains around the bed, provide a light, put out the dog and cat, and withdraw.

Russell turns next to the office of usher and marshal, telling his young auditor that the hierarchy of the Church and of the secular world must be known, as well as how they relate one to the other, because persons of each rank, their families, and servants must be treated appropriately by the marshal of the household when they turn up as guests. Russell is very aware of matters of rank and honour: 'a bishop is the equal of an earl, the Speaker of the Commons and the Mayor of London may be seated together, but the Archbishop of Canterbury and the Archbishop of York must be served apart'. The intricacies of these matters, it need hardly be said, require careful attention if all concerned are to be pleased with the marshal's service.

John Russell's 'Boke of Nurture', while primarily a book of practical advice, is also a useful confirmation of the hierarchical nature of English society in the late-medieval period. It reminds us too that people took comfort and found stability in their particular position. The household mentality had familial, economic, social, political, and religious ramifications, and was a powerful force in providing security and well-being for the servant and the householder.

Honour

It was important to have a good reputation and to be 'of good fame' if one wished to be of consequence. The preservation of personal repute was important for all ranks of society, for the politically powerful to avoid the frustration of their ambitions and for the more humble to avoid the summoner. Insights into the notions of personal honour which prevailed in the fifteenth century can be extracted from an analysis of the extensive surviving correspondence of the Paston family of Norfolk.

The Pastons were fully aware of, and in many ways influenced by, the chivalric notions of honour, encompassing such matters as war, tournaments, public renown, and family pedigree, but the honour system found in the Paston letters is one more suited to the world of the provincial gentry. Honour could be derived through having a demonstrated record of giving assistance and protection to members of one's family and other persons with whom interaction occurred – servants and tenants as well as friends. It would bring shame to a man or woman if, for instance, their servants could not rely on them for ongoing employment and comfortable retirement, or if their friends could not rely upon them for support in cases at law and to speak good of them.

An honour code of the Paston sort was grounded in the

possession of sufficient landed wealth that there would be an ongoing supply of the wherewithal to support family, servants, and friends. An honourable reputation also required businesslike attention to the maintenance of that property; it would bring derision to be judged a waster of the vital livelihood. This honour system also valued personal integrity, expecting that a person's outward actions were a reflection of inner convictions. Unlike the chivalric notion of honour, which was almost exclusively masculine through its martial ethos and concern for male descent in family identity, the honour system which touched a family like the Pastons was accessible to women as well as to men by such means as supporting servants, assisting in arranging worthy marriages, personal integrity, speaking worshipfully of worthy friends, and developing useful alliances with influential families. Margaret Paston even gained honour within her family by her martial organization in 1465 of the defence of Hellesdon Manor against the henchmen of the Duke of Suffolk.

The chivalric values of knightly honour, as mentioned, tended to be martial and masculine. A tight bond existed between chivalry and contemporary Christian attitudes. In the code of chivalry, the primary function of knighthood was the defence of the Church, and thus it is no wonder that the crusading ideal died so slowly. The sorts of attribute that would bring honour to caste-conscious knights were rich, even extravagant display, hospitality, liberality, prowess, justice, largesse, courtesy, and a willingness to defend the Church, protect the weak, such as women, widows, and orphans, and a determination to improve upon one's achievements, and not rest upon one's laurels. Knightly values included loyalty to one's lord (earthly and heavenly), to one's fellow knights, and to one's promised word. Knights cultivated a certain bearing and appearance that suggested virtue and good breeding.

How individuals confronted one another was also linked to honour. There was a symbolic vocabulary of body language in place. Rules were understood, for instance, that persons of different social ranks should keep set distances one from the other, and that persons of equal rank would keep their heads uncovered when conversing with each other. When persons of similar rank encountered one another, kissing would be expected. Kissing, most likely on the cheek rather than on the mouth, was a common polite gesture on greeting and taking leave of someone. It was rather the equivalent of the modern custom of shaking hands, which was not done. Erasmus of Rotterdam in 1499 seemed almost annoyed when he made the observation about England that kissing was ubiquitously abundant. A social inferior could indicate respect for a superior upon encounter in a variety of ways that formed a graduated scale of lower physical positioning, from the bending of a knee while moving, like a genuflection or curtsey, to kneeling on one knee (the right knee was the proper one), to kneeling on both knees, which clearly indicated dependency (as in prayer or when giving homage), to prostration as an absolute gesture of inferiority. Further signals of abasement included penitents going barefoot and wearing white sheets, felons going barefoot in white shirts, or abjurors of the realm going barefoot wearing white sack-cloth featuring a red cross. A woman letting her hair hang loose could be signalling self-abasement, as could a felon petitioning for his life to be spared by wearing a halter around his neck.

Confrontation in disagreement also had its rituals. Jean Froissart, a native of Hainault, was struck as an outside observer by the, to him, volatile and excitable nature of the English. An admittedly opinionated Frenchman could write in his journal in 1436 during the English occupation of Paris: 'the English, essentially, are always wanting to make war on their neighbours without cause. That is why they all die an evil death . . . .' These outsiders may simply not have understood insular manners. Conserving honour in confrontation was a matter of enormous concern. A man was inclined to guard jealously his social dignity, and loss of face might be thought intolerable. An insult had to be noticed and counteracted, and that might lead to further aureate oaths and extravagant threats and counter-threats and attempts at verbal intimidation. Taunts and insults were not necessarily taken as challenges requiring immediate recourse to physical violence or reaching for edged weapons. Verbal bluster seems, in fact, to have been an honour-saving ritual which anticipated the intervention (perhaps desperately longed for) of a mediator who would restore harmony. There seems almost to have been an understood ritual as gentlemen approached a confrontation: the possibility of violence needed to be suggested through extravagant language, symbolic sabre-rattling, threats of violence, and assorted physical gestures. The receiver of the threat could either back down, seek to appease, or respond in kind. If there was noisy response in kind, some blows might be exchanged or, at a distance, some arrows ostentatiously shot, and a mediator could now inject calm without compromising the honour of either party. But if no opportune peacemaker appeared to interrupt the proceedings, fighting would need to continue, the antagonists beating on one another and using the flat side of the sword (flatling, as it was known) to bruise and perhaps render one of the parties unconscious. It was bad form to injure terribly or kill another gentleman in this honour-laden sort of confrontation. This kind of ritual confrontation was apparently socially acceptable while, for example, a surprise assault upon a gentleman with whom one was having a disagreement was to behave in an egregiously vile fashion, which would bring dishonour to the perpetrator.

EIGHT

Religion

If we need now and again to be reminded of the obvious, then we might recall that Christianity was central to medieval culture, and that the Bible was the most influential of all books. That said, it is something else to grasp what religion meant in the later Middle Ages, and to realize that a variety of answers would have been forthcoming from different people when asked what it meant to them to be Christians. That many spent significant amounts of satisfying time in church activities is, however, a certainty.

Parish Guilds

Some men and women in small towns and in the countryside of late medieval England could become members of social-religious confraternities broadly known as parish guilds. Those who made up these voluntary associations gave special attention to praying for the aid and benefit of the souls in purgatory of fellow members. Parish guilds also did other things, such as provide charity for needy members and other poor, put together processions or feasts for appropriate holy days and funerals, supply candles for religious ceremonials and attend to the repair of their associated parish churches. There were approximately 9,000 parishes in England and affiliated with each there could have been possibly one, or several parish guilds. Because of the required entry fees and annual dues, parish guilds were more accessible to those women and men (both laymen and ecclesiastics) of higher social and economic status, reflecting the hierarchical nature of society. Nevertheless, a great many people could have participated in the works of the parish guilds.

Their names reflect the names of the saints they were formed to venerate or the Christian concept they concentrated upon: All Saints, John the Baptist, the Virgin Mary (the most popular of all), the Holy Trinity, Corpus Christi, and so on. On special days guild members would participate in feasts and processions, and take pleasure in viewing the candles, altar-cloths, garlands, banners, liturgical books, or whatever had been provided for the occasion. The celebration of the day or events for which the guild had been established was the primary mission of its members, but also of immense importance was the provision of suitable funeral services for deceased members together with prayers and Masses for the departed souls. By supporting prayers and Masses for these souls, parish guilds were complementing the Church's doctrine of purgatory.

Members of parish guilds could also derive satisfaction from charitable work, such as supporting schools, contributing to the support of the sick and deserving poor, funding hospitals, and repairing roads and bridges. The parish guilds supplemented the established activities of the parish priest and church, and were not viewed as an alternative or competition for the traditional parish structure. They also tried to make social life a bit more pleasant by promoting decorous behaviour and good fellowship among members and by arbitrating disputes should members fall into conflict.

The Annual Calendar

People living in medieval England were not so different from most people living in other times and places in having a craving for order in their lives. All of life was not orderly, to be sure, but pleasure was to be found in what system was available, and one source of comforting routine was the annual calendar evolved for society by the Church. It provided a subtle anchoring in familiar stories, teachings, and events which people could share as they moved through the seasons of the year and sought explanation and purpose in their existence. There were many days of the year that the Church enjoined should not be for labour but for attending church. Sunday was always such a *festa ferianda*, but even with respect to Sunday, charity and necessity could modify compliance for an indisposed parishioner. There was no absolute calendar of feast days set for the church, and local variations existed for minor festivals in particular. However, for the sake of having a model for understanding the annual calendar, we can use that legislated for the province of Canterbury in 1362 when Simon Islip was archbishop. The modern year is taken to begin on 1 January, and we can begin there with the celebration of the Circumcision of the Lord. The legislation of 1362 went on to call for, in chronological

Shrove Tuesday, back to back with Ash Wednesday, epitomized the conflict of youth with authority, the notion of a 'last fling' before Lent. The cock shown held in the cleft stick is a target for the grim-faced boy about to hurl a stick (see pp. 100–1). (Bodleian Library, Ms. Douce. 6, f. 156v)

order, the observance of Epiphany (6 January), Purification of the Virgin (2 February), St Mathias the Apostle (24 February), Annunciation to the Virgin (25 March), Good Friday (the Friday before Easter), Easter (and the three days following), St Mark the Evangelist (25 April), the Apostles Phillip and James (1 May), the Discovery of the Holy Cross (3 May), the Ascension of the Lord (the Thursday following Rogation Sunday, which was the fifth Sunday after Easter), Pentecost (the seventh Sunday after Easter) and the three days following, Corpus Christi (the Thursday after Trinity Sunday, which was the sixth Sunday after Easter), the Nativity of John the Baptist or Midsummer Day (24 June), the Apostles Peter and Paul (29 June), the Translation of St Thomas of Canterbury (7 July), St Mary Magdalene (22 July), St James (25 July), St Laurence (10 August), the Assumption of the Virgin (15 August), St Bartholomew (24 August), the Nativity of the Virgin (8 September), the Exaltation of the Holy Cross (14 September), St Matthew the Apostle (21 September), St Michael the Archangel (29 September), St Luke the Evangelist (18 October), the Apostles Simon and Jude (28 October), All Saints (1 November), St Andrew the Apostle (30 November), St Nicholas (6 December), the Conception of the Virgin (8 December), St Thomas the Apostle (21 December), Christmas or Midwinter Day (25 December), St Stephen (26 December), St John (27 December), Holy Innocents' Day (28 December), and St Thomas of Canterbury (29 December). The magnitude of this list of legislated festivals impresses us with how constantly, together with Sunday observances, the minds of the faithful would be brought to focus on the stories and teachings of the Church, and we gain an impression of the commitment of personal time to communal worship in the parish church. On a local basis, it was the feast-days of the saint or saints to whom the parish church was dedicated that would be celebrated. Other traditionally accepted local feast-days were authorized as well.

The Christmas Season

The season of the Christian year that called for extended celebration was that of Christmas. At the time when Christianity came into existence, the winter solstice was marked at 25 December. It was the occasion when the sun appears, from the perspective of northern Europe, to stand low and still on the southern horizon before rising with the passing days in anticipation of spring. The sun briefly standing still (*sol stitium* in Latin) was a noteworthy event for a heavenly body that was itself deified in some religious systems. Mithraism, a vigorous competitor with early Christianity, was a salvationist religion popular among soldiers in the Roman world, which incorporated the 'Unconquered Sun' (*Sol invictus*) into its belief system and celebrated the feast day of the sun on 25 December.

As Christianity developed, the debates about the divinity of Jesus of Nazareth were resolved with the acceptance that he was fully God and fully human; that God had inhabited a period of historic time as the man Jesus. There was an urgent desire to celebrate God become man, but none of the Christian gospels or any other writers had given a date for the birth of Christ. The urge to celebrate Jesus' birth (*nativitas* in Latin), the winter solstice, ancient midwinter rites reflecting a yearning for the return of the

Mary with the baby Jesus in the manger (Corpus Christi, 26.15v)

fertility of the earth, and other elements (including the Roman winter Saturnalia, a celebration for the god Saturn), all converged by the fourth century to fix the Christian Feast of the Nativity on 25 December. By the late medieval period, then, the Nativity was an established part of the Christian festival calendar.

Our word Christmas is derived from the Middle English usage 'Christ's Mass', and central to the celebration of the Nativity was the liturgical activity which had been established by the year 600, and did not change in the Middle Ages. In medieval England there were, in fact, three Masses celebrated on Christmas day. The first and most characteristic was at midnight (the Angel's Mass), catching up the notion that the light of salvation appeared at the darkest moment of the darkest date in the very depth of winter. The second Christmas Mass came at dawn (the Shepherds' Mass), and the third during the day (the Mass of the Divine Word). The season of Advent, the forty days leading up to Christmas, was being observed in the Western Church by the year 500. St Nicholas was a very popular medieval saint, and his feast day came in Advent (6 December), but he did not play his part in Christmas as Santa Claus until after the Reformation.

Also important in the celebration of Christmas was the banquet, which necessarily varied in sumptuousness with the resources of the celebrants. The menu varied with soups and stews, birds and fish, breads and puddings, but a common element was the Yule boar, an animal for those who could afford it or a pie shaped like a boar for more humble tables. Churches and houses were decorated with ivy, mistletoe, holly, or anything green, which remained up until the eve of Candlemas. The gift-giving of the season was represented by the New Year Gift, which continued a tradition of Roman origin. The later Christmas present was not part of a medieval Christmas. The sorts of things that people might have done to entertain themselves at Christmas apart from eating is succinctly summarized in a letter written by Margaret Paston on Christmas Eve 1459 after she had inquired how her Norfolk neighbour, Lady Morley, had conducted her household in mourning the previous Christmas, just after Lady Morley had been widowed: '. . . there were no disguisings [acting], nor harping, luting or singing, nor any lewd sports, but just playing at the tables [backgammon] and chess and cards. Such sports she gave her folk leave to play and no other'.

Mention of disguisings calls to mind the Christmas cycle of the mystery plays, which were part of late medieval urban entertainment in different parts of England. The Shepherd Plays

A misericord from Gloucester Cathedral showing the three shepherds (Jack Farley)

from Wakefield would be a specific example. Mention by Lady Morley of 'lewd sport' is possibly a reference to the carol-dance. The leader of the dance sang a verse of the carol, and a ring of dancers responded with the chorus. Carol-dances were often suggestive of their pagan ancestors where, for instance, holly and ivy had fertility associations with male and female. Further music for the celebration of the season was provided by the Latin hymns of the Church.

A medieval Christmas celebration was not over in a day, but continued until 6 January (the Egyptian winter solstice), the Feast of the Epiphany on the twelfth day after Christmas Day. Epiphany celebrated the visit of the wise men, the Magi, around whom many layers of legend accumulated as they came to be conceptualized as three oriental kings who visited the infant Christ at Bethlehem in Judaea. Epiphany also symbolized the manifestation of Christ to the Gentiles. The Monday after Epiphany was called Plough Monday, and it was then that ploughing began.

The day after Christmas recalled St Stephen, the martyr mentioned in the New Testament book of Acts. The following day was that of John the Apostle and Evangelist (not to be confused with John the Baptist), and 28 December was Holy Innocents' Day

Opposite: Feasting at Christmas time (British Library, Additional Ms. 35215, f. 97)

or Childermas Day, commemorating the male children killed by Herod (Matthew 2: 16–17), who was king of the Jews when Jesus was born. It was superstition that the day of the week upon which Holy Innocents' Day fell would be unlucky for the coming year.

One of the most curiously entertaining customs of the Christmas season, associated with Holy Innocents' Day, was that of the boy-bishop. The origins of the temporary substitution of a boy into the role of an adult ecclesiastical authority are obscure, but in part it was apparently the result of an effort by the Church to emphasize the significance of children, together with the pagan Roman feast of Saturnalia in December with its topsy-turvy aspect of relaxing social and moral restraints. Another ingredient was St Nicholas, Bishop of Myra (in modern Turkey), among whose roles was being patron saint of children and whose feast-day was in December. The unsavoury story that tied Nicholas to children related that in a time of famine an innkeeper, short on his inventory of food, killed three schoolboys, then pickled their flesh and stored it in a barrel. Bishop Nicholas later happened by, and restored the three boys to life, and in medieval iconography St Nicholas is often portrayed with a cask by his side from which three boys are climbing.

The boy-bishop was to be found in England by the first quarter of the thirteenth century, and the custom was not finally abolished until 1559. The boy-bishop custom was observed, among other places, in the cathedrals of Canterbury, York, Durham, Exeter, Gloucester, Hereford, Lichfield, Lincoln, London, and Salisbury, and at other churches like St Nicholas, Bristol and Magdalen College, Oxford, the collegiate churches at Rotherham and Winchester, as well as Eton College, whose founder, King Henry VI, had been born on the feast day of St Nicholas, whom he took as his patron saint. At Salisbury, to select a case, the boy-bishop was chosen by the cathedral choristers from among their number on St Nicholas Day, and performed his pseudo-episcopal office for just over three weeks, until the night of Holy Innocents' Day. During this time the hierarchy of cathedral officers was turned upside-down, with the chosen boy acting as bishop, his fellow choristers as cathedral canons, and so on. The culmination came at the high Mass of Holy Innocents' Day. For that Mass the boy-bishop would wear full episcopal vestments, including the cope, mitre, and ring provided for the occasion in immitation of the bishop, and the boy-canons would also wear copes in serious and comic imitation of the elders for whom they were substituting. The boy-bishop also preached a sermon, and a favourite text was certainly Matthew (18: 3): 'Then

He [Jesus] said, In truth I tell you, unless you change and become like little children you will never enter the kingdom of Heaven'.

Following the culminating ceremonies in the church, the boy-bishop, like a true bishop, would set out with his attendants on a visitation, though without the episcopal authority to impose correct doctrine and discipline as he travelled. The 'visitation' of the boy-bishop and his retinue to ecclesiastical establishments and noble households in the vicinity might last several weeks and involve being given many gifts and being generously entertained. Many of the gifts would necessarily go to cover expenses. The whole carnival of the boy-bishop was splendid entertainment, sometimes overly irreverent and unruly, but it suited its era by allowing ritual protest against an authority structure integral to the existing social order.

THE END OF THE CHRISTMAS SEASON

While the boy-bishop set out on his visitation, the celebration of the Christmas season moved ahead. The first day (or Kalends) of January had been the day in the Roman Empire when administrative officials holding appointments for a year entered into office, and this festival of long standing became the commemoration of Christ's circumcision, whereby the boy Jesus conformed to Hebrew law. This first day of the Roman civil year was also known as New Year's Day, and the western ecclesiastical year began on the same day, although the Church sustained a rearguard action in favour of the feast of the Annunciation to the Virgin Mary (or Lady Day), 25 March, so that in some instances the new year was dated from 25 March.

There was no absolute standard about ending the Christmas season with Epiphany, and many carried it through to forty days after Christmas, the date of an ancient pagan festival on 2 February. This is now celebrated as Candlemas, or the feast of the Purification of the Virgin, or alternatively as the Presentation of the Infant Jesus in the Temple. In one of the most elaborate processions of the year, all parishioners came to Mass with a penny and a candle blessed before the procession, both of which were offered to the priest as part of the parochial dues of the faithful. Other candles were blessed and taken away by the faithful to be used for such things as giving comfort during thunder storms or while sick or even dying. Such candles were thus important for giving people a light of solace in the face of hostile forces and stressful events. And thus Candlemas was a closure for the long season commencing with Advent that drew medieval Christians to concentrate on the miraculous gift to humanity of Christ, and the promise of salvation, while leaving at the same time space for fun, feasting, and socializing.

Pilgrimage

Although not essential in Christian life, pilgrimage was a popular and spontaneous activity which the Church desired to supervise and direct towards acceptable spiritual ends. A jolly outing of pleasurable travel was not seen to have any special spiritual merit, but a suitably directed pilgrimage could be of great spiritual value, and was sometimes enjoined as penance. Some pilgrimages were quests for healing miracles or help of other kinds, and others were genuine acts of devotion as the pilgrim strove to enhance his spiritual life. Just as it was helpful to have the patronage of a powerful lord in this life, the protection of a saint was appreciated for this world and beyond. There is also a very natural human curiosity about seeing the places where things of significance took place or viewing the physical residue of past events. Different people would be attracted by different places. For medieval Christians, there was an understandable desire to visit the sites and artefacts of Christian heroism, and pilgrimage was devotion in action, as opposed to contemplation. Jerusalem and the Holy Land were the most lofty pilgrimage centres for medieval Christians, and in the West Rome drew many pilgrims.

Potential objectives for pilgrims were numerous. The second Council of Nicaea in 787 decreed that no church should be consecrated unless it housed some holy relic – this was simply official recognition of an already established idea. Within England there were many places of local pilgrimage. Canterbury and Our Lady of Walsingham, moreover, were two English shrines which ranked among the most attractive for general European pilgrimage. Canterbury was not only the administrative centre of Christianity in England as the seat of the senior of the two archbishops, but was also a pilgrimage site as the location of the shrine of St Thomas Becket, the murdered archbishop.

A pilgrim to the shrine of St Thomas of Canterbury not long after his murder in 1170 was a London shoemaker named Gilbert. Gilbert suffered from *fistula* (a type of draining ulcer), but a visit to the shrine and a drink of the miraculous Water of St Thomas enabled him to walk the sixty-plus miles home, whereupon he stripped off his shirt and challenged his London neighbours to a

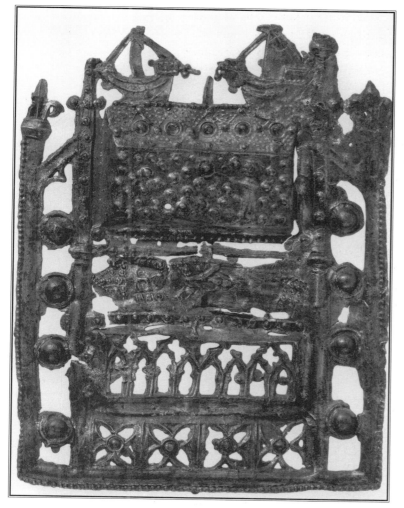

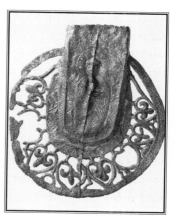

Above: A thirteenth-century lead
ampulla for the Water of St
Thomas, inscribed in Latin
'Thomas is the best healer of the
holy sick' (Museum of London)
Left: A lead pilgrim badge of the
shrine of St Thomas Becket, richly
decorated with gems. A small
figure (under the ship on the
right) points to the large ruby
given by the King of France
(Museum of London)

foot race to demonstrate his cure. Such was the power of St
Thomas' relics and water, which was a mixture of gallons and
gallons of water drawn from the Well of St Thomas in the
precincts of the cathedral and a tiny bit of the archbishop's blood.
Phials (*ampullae*) cast from lead or tin containing Water of St
Thomas became one of the most popular badges or tokens acquired
by Canterbury pilgrims and were often worn hanging by a cord
around the neck. On well-travelled routes, such as the pilgrims'
way between London and Canterbury, there existed a system for
hiring horses. The horses were branded on the flank for easy
identification, and travellers would rent a sequence of horses at
different stages of their journeys.

The other highly popular shrine, which drew pilgrims from afar, was that of the Virgin Mary at Walsingham in eastern England. In the eleventh century, just before the Norman Conquest, following a petition made by the Virgin herself in a vision to a wealthy widow, Richeldis de Faverches, a reproduction was built of the Holy House of Nazareth where the Annunciation had taken place. Until the Reformation, Walsingham on the north coast of Norfolk was England's Nazareth, and pilgrims would come to contemplate the ancient wonder of the annunciation to the Virgin Mary that she would be the mother of Christ.

St Swithun did not rank in fame with the Virgin Mary. His exact dates are difficult to determine, but he was an associate and tutor of King Alfred the Great, and was Bishop of Winchester in the 850s and early 860s. Swithun was remembered for his humility and goodness, and asked to be buried in the churchyard where his grave would be under the rain from the cathedral eaves and the feet of pedestrians. The story goes that after some years it was planned to move his relics into Winchester Cathedral, but forty days and nights of rain prevented the carrying out of the plan, and thus in

Fourteenth-century pewter pilgrim badges from the shrine of Our Lady of Walsingham, Norfolk (Museum of London)

received tradition a rain on St Swithun's Day, 15 July, becomes a prediction of forty days of damp. A shrine to St Swithun stood on a raised platform behind the high altar of Winchester Cathedral and, having gained a reputation for miraculous cures of illnesses, was the objective of pilgrims from all over England.

The shrine of St Edward the Martyr was at Shaftesbury in Dorset. Edward became king in 975 and was assassinated by an unknown aggressor at Corfe Castle on 18 March 978. The body of the unmarried and childless king was buried at Wareham, but was taken a few years later to the Benedictine nunnery at Shaftesbury, which had been founded in the previous century by King Alfred. Royal endowments and gifts of the pilgrims to the shrine of St Edward, king and martyr, led ultimately to Shaftesbury Abbey becoming the largest nunnery in England. Another shrine in the county of Dorset that drew pilgrims was at Whitchurch Canonicorum where the parish church of St Candida and Holy Cross houses the shrine of St Candida (or St Wite). Little is known about the saint's life, but the tradition is that she was martyred by Danish Vikings. It happens that the relics of St Candida are still in the shrine, making Whitchurch Canonicorum the only parish church in Britain still in possession of the relics of its patron saint. Subsidence in the north transept of the church, where the shrine is located, caused a crack in the tomb, and consequently in 1900 a lead reliquary was found within bearing the words *Hic Reqesct. Sce. Wite.* The reliquary held the bones of a small woman estimated to

The shrine of St Candida (or St Wite) in the Parish Church of St Candida and Holy Cross at Whitchurch Canonicorum in Dorset (© RCHME Crown Copyright)

have been about forty when she died. The altar-like tomb, pierced by three oval openings through which the faithful could lean their heads to be in closer proximity to the saint's relics, is dated to the thirteenth century. It was a common conviction that saints would be especially responsive to prayers offered close by their relics, and pilgrims liked to get as near as possible, even if that meant crawling in or about shrines. There is also a holy well named for St Candida at nearby Morecombelake, and its water had a reputation as a cure for eye ailments. The saint is also commemorated in the popular local name for wild evergreen periwinkles: St Candida's Eyes.

A late medieval pilgrim going from Dorset to London might stop off at Salisbury. Bishop Osmund of Salisbury died in 1099, but he was not canonized until 1457. His shrine at Salisbury Cathedral was erected in 1456, and so was a focus for pilgrimage in the west country only in the last decades before the Reformation. A pilgrim would have sites to visit upon arrival in London. The shrine of St Erkenwald, Bishop of London, who died in 693, was in St Paul's Cathedral. The shrine, which was destroyed along with the cathedral itself in the Great Fire of 1665, attracted pilgrims because of the reputation of St Erkenwald for interceding with God on behalf of penitent sinners. The shrine in Westminster Abbey of Edward the Confessor, king from 1042 until his death in 1066 set

Pilgrims at the shrine of St Edward the Confessor in Westminster Abbey, creeping in and out of the apertures which permit them to touch the tomb; a monk supervises the activity (Cambridge University Library, Ms. Ee.3.59)

in motion the events of the Norman Conquest, was a great attraction for pilgrims. Edward, who was canonized in 1161, caused the monastic church to be built in his lifetime and was buried before the high altar. His relics, to which healing miracles were attributed, were attracting pilgrims before the official canonization by Pope Alexander III. St Edward at Westminster was viewed especially as England's royal saint, even more than St Edward the Martyr at Shaftesbury.

The canonization of Edward the Confessor was the first canonization of a saint by Pope Alexander III, and from Alexander's day onward the process of canonization was reserved to the papacy, although this did not make it impossible for someone to be regarded popularly as a saint. Such a person was John Schorne (died 1314), rector of North Marston in Buckinghamshire. In his lifetime Schorne achieved renown as a healer (especially of the ague and gout) and exorcist. One story about him is that in a contest with the Devil he drove his enemy into a boot, and in iconography Schorne is shown holding a boot with the Devil in it. It has in fact been said that Schorne's power over the Devil in the boot inspired the jack-in-the-box children's toy. At any rate, Schorne's reputation inspired visitors to his tomb in North Marston church and to Schorne's Well, and the attraction was sufficiently powerful for pilgrims that in the 1470s Schorne's relics were transferred to the newly built St George's Chapel at Windsor. In 1484 the remains of another putative saint, Henry VI (died 1471), were also moved from their original place of interment in Chertsey Abbey to St George's Chapel. Many pilgrims came to the tomb of the dead king but, like John Schorne, Henry VI never received official canonization.

In East Anglia one of the most popular saints of the later Middle Ages was St Etheldreda, whose shrine stood in the retrochoir of Ely Cathedral. Etheldreda, who died in 679, enjoyed prominence as the daughter of King Anna of East Anglia, and she married as her second husband King Ecgfrith of Northumbria. After a decade as queen of Northumbria, Etheldreda (or Aethelthryth) separated from her husband and became a nun. Etheldreda's saintly reputation was complemented by her sister St Sexburga, who had been the queen of King Earconberht of Kent, and their nieces St Ermenilda and St Werburga. A curious post-medieval legacy of St Etheldreda, who came also to be known by the name of St Audrey, was the result of the early modern female fashion of wearing silk or lace collars purchased at St Audrey's Fair in Ely as a substitute for more expensive necklaces. St Etheldreda had attributed the throat

John Schorne conjuring the Devil from his boot. A fifteenth-century painting on panel (Gainsborough House Museum)

tumour from which she suffered at the end of her life to her youthful delight in wearing precious necklaces. The substitute neck-wear came by association to be called 'St Audrey's Lace', then 'Tawdry Lace', and now tawdry remains as an adjective for pretentious but cheap finery.

One of the most attractive objectives in eastern England for pilgrims was the Benedictine abbey of Bury St Edmunds, which housed the shrine of King Edmund of East Anglia, who was killed by marauding Vikings on 20 November 869 (which fixed the feast day of St Edmund on that date) and whose relics were enshrined in the monastery in 903. A story about Edmund's martyrdom is that as a final degredation his killers struck off his head and concealed it in a thicket where a wolf guarded it until it was found by Edmund's men; a wolf thus became an emblem of St Edmund. Such was his fame that dozens of churches were dedicated to him, and his image was painted or sculpted in many places. Water of St Edmund acquired at Bury was respected for its healing powers and, for whatever reason, the saint's relics attracted married female pilgrims who wished to have children in the belief that fertility could be enhanced by a visit to the shrine. Some English children did become putative saints. There was, for example, a pilgrim attraction at Norwich Cathedral in St William, a boy supposedly murdered by Jews in 1140, a story similar to the anti-semitic legend of Little St Hugh of Lincoln.

An objective of pilgrims in the Midlands had its origins in early fourth-century Roman Britain. Approximately twenty miles north-

The wolf guarding St Edmund's head (British Library, Harley Ms. 2278, f. 64)

west of Londinium lay Verulamium, and it was here that the first British Christian martyr, St Alban, was executed for his faith by Roman soldiers. The Benedictine Abbey of St Albans that housed the shrine of the protomartyr was not established until the late eighth century, but pilgrims using the main road north from London for centuries paid reverence to St Alban by visiting his shrine, built in its latest construction in the early fourteenth century, destroyed during Henry VIII's dissolution of the monasteries, and reconstructed from many hundreds of fragments discovered during alterations to the church in the nineteenth century. Worcester Cathedral in the Midlands was the site of the shrines of St Oswald and St Wulfstan, both bishops of Worcester, who died in 992 and 1095 respectively. So highly regarded were the two episcopal saints that King John, who died in 1216, requested burial between the saints' shrines, and the saints are carved on either side of the king's head on his tomb effigy.

In the north of England no saint enjoyed more prestige than the missionary monk and, late in life, Bishop of Lindisfarne, St Cuthbert, who died on 20 March 687. Uprooted from Lindisfarne in the ninth century by Viking attacks, the monks who kept the shrine of St Cuthbert migrated with the relics, and after several generations a final home was found in the Benedictine abbey church at Durham. The fame of St Cuthbert was in part established

Building St Albans Abbey, early fourteenth century (British Library, Cotton Ms. Nero D I, f. 23v)

by Bede (died 735), the greatest scholar-monk of his age in Europe, whose relics today also lie in Durham Cathedral. St Wilfred, son of King Oswiu of Northumbria, was a contemporary of St Cuthbert and also a monk, a missionary, and a bishop. After Wilfred's death in 709, his body was buried in the church of the community of monks he had founded at Ripon in Yorkshire, and his relics attracted pilgrims as did those of St Cuthbert. Another northerner of the era of Wilfred and Cuthbert who was Archbishop of York before his retirement to the monastic community at Beverley, where he died in 721, was St John of Beverley. St John's relic drew pilgrims to Beverley, but an Archbishop of York whose relics attracted pilgrims to the cathedral church itself was William FitzHerbert, who died in 1154 and was canonized in 1226. Archbishop FitzHerbert is today gloriously depicted in the St William stained glass window in the north-eastern transept of York Minster, which was completed in the 1420s to display the miracles performed by St William. The saint's relics before the Reformation rested in a prominent shrine in York Minster, and today they lie in a recycled Roman sarcophagus in the crypt.

The targets for pilgrims in late medieval England were numerous, and it was not terribly difficult to enhance religious life by coming into the presence of the relics of a notable saint. The representatives of the heavenly community just mentioned are by no means the full complement, and others would include St Dunstan of Canterbury (died 988), St Hugh of Lincoln (died 1200), and St Thomas Cantilupe of Hereford (died 1282). Visits to the shrines of these and other saints and putative saints offered another approach to participation and pleasure in religious life.

Astrology

The study of astrology in England during the late medieval period was not a part of popular culture. It was a subject that attracted a selection of university scholars at Merton College, Oxford, who wanted to explore the actions of heavenly bodies and how they might influence the natural world. Some monasteries, because of the books in their possession, could also have been centres of astrological study, such as the Benedictine house of St Augustine at Canterbury, the Austin friary at York, and the Carthusian house at Syon.

If the course of future events was set by the stars, then God was not omnipotent and human beings were without free will, and the consequences of both of these notions were abhorrent to Christian

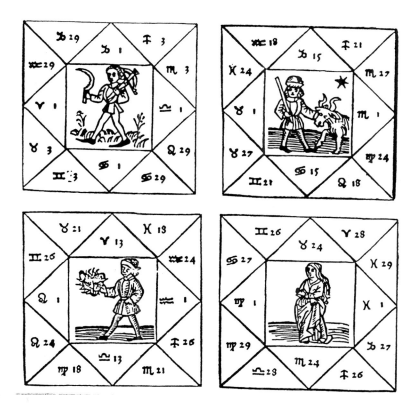

Astrological figures from the
'Opus Astrolabi Plani', 1488

theology. Such unacceptable ramifications meant that astrology was
approached with caution, following such examples as the famous
theologian, scientist, chancellor of Oxford, and bishop of Lincoln,
Robert Grosseteste (died 1253), who used astrology as a tool for
weather prediction, but who, in the main, rejected it for rational
and theological reasons. Astrology did, however, have an
established place in the practice of medicine, and was used in
conjunction with the concept of the four humours (see Chapter 6).
Thus medical texts as a rule included drawings of zodiac men,
naked figures linking parts of the body with specific astrological
signs to suggest, for instance, that it would be unwise to bleed a
patient from the neck during the ascendancy of the sign of Taurus.
Astrology had other uses beside medicine: the 'Secretum
Secretorum', which had considerable renown, was designed in part
as a handbook for princes, and counselled that it was prudent to
consult with astrologers and search among the occult sciences for
wisdom.

It is generally accepted that astrology enjoyed a revival in
Europe in the late fourteenth and fifteenth centuries, and that the
revival developed in the courts of rulers. This does not, however,

A medieval depiction of Euclid observing the moon and stars with a *dioptra*, and Hermannus holding an astrolabe (Bodleian Library, Oxford, Ms. Digby. 46, f. 8v)

seem to have been the case with the court of Edward III of England. Edward's chaplain, Thomas Bradwardine, was not friendly towards astrology or any other sort of divination. In Edward III's time, astrology appears to have been the activity of individuals who acted with circumspection for fear of ecclesiastical censure. On the other hand, Edward's grandson and successor, Richard II, was at least cautiously open to the activities of astrologers. The clearest evidence of Richard's interest in astrology, and the occult more broadly, is the king's own book of divination, which is generally dated 1391. A physically attractive book, in Latin, now in the Bodleian Library, Oxford (Manuscript 581), its chapter headings and index suggest that it was produced for the king's use. In fact, a drawing of the king wearing the royal regalia is to be found on folio nine. Richard's book was an anonymous compilation mainly of four texts: a portion of the very popular 'Secretum Secretorum' ascribed to Aristotle known as the 'De quadripartita regis specie'; the 'Phisionomia Aristotelis', a physiognomy also drawn from the 'Secretum Secretorum'; a dream-book attributed to Daniel known as the 'Philosophia Visionum cum sompniis Danielis'; and the 'Liber Judiciorum', which was a geomancy with associated astrological tables. King Richard's book would itself be most properly categorized as a guide for geomancy.

A drawing of Richard II wearing royal regalia, from the king's own book of divination (Bodleian Library, Oxford, Ms. Bodl. 581, f. 9r)

A ninth-century astrolabe from Iraq used to decipher the celestial mechanism that was said to govern life on earth (Bibliothèque Nationale, Paris)

An Arabic scheme for organizing astrology was to divide it into four subcategories: (a) revolutions, which were concerned with events of a broad scope, such as wars, epidemics, and political events, and grew out of a careful observation of the celestial bodies on the occasion of the sun entering Aries (thought of as the beginning of the year); (b) interrogations, which were predictions about particular questions, such as the victor in a battle or the appropriateness of a marriage, based upon an observation of the celestial bodies when a question was asked; (c) elections, which involved observation of the celestial bodies for aid in selecting the best possible time for performing an action, such as entering a battle or celebrating a marriage; (d) nativities, which involved predictions for an individual according to the circumstances of the celestial bodies at the time of the person's birth, suggesting the individual's future health, character, actions, fortune, and so on. The scheme of the heavens constructed by the astrologer seeking guidance from the celestial bodies was called a *schema* or a horoscope, and was calculated for a particular time. The astrologer then interpreted the horoscope in accordance with the relative positions of the various celestial entities. It was an extremely intricate process. The labour of casting a horoscope was eased by the appearance of astronomical tables and instruments such as the astrolabe.

A horoscope was prepared for King Henry V using an entirely incorrect birthdate in the year 1369. The treatise, known as the 'Nativitas nocturna', survives in the Bodleian Library, Oxford (Ashmole MS 393). The anonymous nativity confidently predicted, among other things, that Henry, who died at the age of thirty-five, would live to be fifty-two. The existence of the 'Nativitas nocturna' should not be taken to indicate that the pious Henry V was himself favourably disposed towards astrology, for indeed he had little sympathy for any of the occult sciences. There were those about the court, however, who had fewer reservations, and astrology in particular was beginning to attract a following at the English court similar to that which for some time past had been found at Continental courts. Astrology was not centrally implicated in a legal charge of sorcery in England, however, until 1477 when Thomas Burdett of Arowe was accused of treason, although some years earlier there had been charges directed at Eleanor Cobham and Joan of Navarre. It was alleged that Burdett had employed two astrologers to calculate the nativities of Edward IV and the king's eldest son, and that Burdett also sought by occult means to bring about the deaths of the king and the prince. Thomas Burdett was a friend of the king's maladjusted brother George, Duke of Clarence, and it might be said that Burdett's downfall presaged that of Clarence.

There were some notable practitioners of astrology to be found in England in the later Middle Ages: John of London was a monk of St Augustine's, Canterbury, and John Ergum was an Augustinian canon of York. Other names turn up like William Rede, Lewis of Caerleon, and Richard of Wallingford. John Ashenden, author of 'Summa judicialis de accidentibus mundi', was active in the middle decades of the fourteenth century and devoted his life to the study of astrology, with an emphasis on weather prediction. Dr John Argentine is probably most widely remembered as the last attendant actively to serve the sons of Edward IV, the 'Princes in the Tower', before their mysterious disappearance. Argentine was a doctor of medicine, perhaps trained at Padua, and a doctor of divinity from Cambridge, where his memorial brass can be seen in King's College Chapel. Argentine also carried astrology to the highest levels of patronage by casting the horoscopes of Edward IV and the child-king Edward V. The integration of the studies of astrology and medicine is readily apparent in this case. Moreover, Argentine was a learned man who drew together a substantial collection of books, among which was one suggesting how the doctor might have enjoyed passing his leisure time. This brief book, now in Balliol College, Oxford (Ashmole Ms. 344), is a compilation of four different discussions of board games: a set of chess problems, Bishop John Shirwood of Durham's 'Ludus Arithmomachie', an account of a variant on the same game under the title 'De ludo philosophorum', and lastly a 'Ludus astronomorum'. The game of astronomy employed a round board laid out in degrees with the signs of the zodiac, rather like the back of an astrolabe, and the pieces for the game were the seven planets which moved in the game as they were understood at the time to move in the heavens. It was a complex game, related to an Arabic game of the same name, in which one player sought to gain astrological dignity for his pieces while trying to diminish the dignity of the pieces of his opponent.

NINE

Mysticism and Personal Devotion

A longside public worship of the Church in late medieval England, there was a powerful element of religious sentiment that might be called lay piety, even if it was not restricted exclusively to the laity, and which was not always contained within the official ecclesiastical orbit. This development was not confined solely to England, and was particularly strong, for instance, in Germany and the Netherlands. The lay piety of the era placed emphasis upon personal morality and private spiritual life. A supreme moment of private spiritual contemplation for a Christian would be a mystical experience whereby the recipient is transported spiritually from earthly confines to insights into the higher realm of the divine. There was in the fourteenth century in England a flowering of mysticism illuminated by some distinguished contemplative individuals. The writings they left behind do not convey the impression of 'popeholyness', a word contemporaries used for pretended piety.

Rolle

Richard Rolle was a highly influential guide for the spiritually inclined as they sought to understand the contemplative and religious life. He is known as the hermit of Hampole, in Yorkshire, which is where he returned in due course after an academic sojourn at Oxford and perhaps at Paris as well. He died in 1349, having become one of the great names of English mysticism. One prominent theme in Rolle's writings is his devotion to the Holy Name of Jesus, and another is his association of the impact of spiritual love upon the individual as the sensations of *calor*, *dulcor*, and *canor* (that is, warmth or heat, sweetness, and melody or song).

Opposite: A cleric praying to Richard Rolle (Bodleian Library, Oxford, Ms. Laud Misc. Ms. 528)

Rolle wrote religious lyrics and devotional tracts in Latin and English, and translated the Psalter into English. The 'English Psalter', which enjoyed immense popularity, used the format of the Latin text of the psalm, followed by Rolle's English translation and a brief commentary in English. Rolle's 'Form of Living' was a guide to meditation and a work of instruction on the living of the Christian life, and was one of the highly regarded devotional tracts from Rolle's pen.

'The Cloud of Unknowing', Hilton and Love

'The Cloud of Unknowing' was a mystical tract composed after Richard Rolle's time by an unknown solitary contemplative, whose work reflected a knowledge of some of Rolle's writings and who also is credited with other writings such as 'The Book of Privy Counselling'. Walter Hilton, who was familiar with 'The Cloud of Unknowing', was an Augustinian canon of the priory of Thurgarton in Nottinghamshire where he died in 1396. Hilton's contributions to mystical spirituality included such works as the 'Eight Chapters on Perfection', 'Of Angels' Song', the 'Epistle on the Mixed Life', and his classic 'Scale of Perfection'.

'The Cloud of Unknowing' makes the case for the supremacy of affectionate desire and love over reason and intellect, as an avenue for the soul's ascent to God. The loving faculty is a much more potent mental power than the knowing faculty. Only the power of love is able, and only with great effort, to penetrate the dark cloud of unknowing that hides God from the soul. The mystical experience of union with God is intensely personal, and the writings of mystics are revelations of private emotional experiences of a sort difficult to express, especially in summary fashion. Walter Hilton's 'Scale of Perfection' is an unusual guide through the challenging levels of meditation and contemplation for those who wish to ascend to the light and love of God, which explains why the book had a wider circulation than 'The Cloud of Unknowing'. The audience for any book on mystical spirituality was under most circumstances select and small. Hilton also was convinced that love and intellect played interdependent parts in the contemplative experience.

Nicholas Love (died 1424) gained recognition early in the fifteenth century from Archbishop Thomas Arundel of Canterbury for his writings against heresy. Love was a Carthusian monk and prior of Mount Grace Priory in Yorkshire, and he was notable also as the abridging translator of 'Meditationes Vitae Christi'

('Meditations on the Life of Christ'), formerly believed to have been written by St Bonaventure but thought now by scholars to have been the work of a fourteenth-century Franciscan friar named John of Caulibus. Love's 'Mirrour of the Blessed Lyf of Jesu Christ', as his translation is entitled, brought a piece of devotional prose to a wider audience than could have been reached by the Latin source from which he worked, and it enjoyed wide popularity throughout England. Love's work was designed as a devotional tract to encourage meditation upon Christ's life, and it was written in a very direct and elegant way appropriate to the devout lay audience he wished to reach.

Shrouded Luminaries

Two writers require mention because they are today regarded as luminaries in the late medieval English mystical group of writers, although in their own time the writings of Julian of Norwich and Margery Kempe were shrouded in the utmost obscurity. We do not know the baptismal name of Julian of Norwich, but she adopted the name of St Julian and ended her life as an enclosed recluse at Norwich. On 13 May 1373, when Julian was thirty years of age and suffering from a life-threatening bout of illness, she experienced a series of fifteen 'schewings' of mystical rapture, and soon afterwards these were written down in what is called her Short Text. After fifteen or more years of prayerful meditation upon her experience of 1373 she set down a commentary that is known as her Long Text, which is by common consent an ascetic masterpiece. Margery Kempe was not a quiet recluse. She was the daughter of John Burnham, who had sat in the Commons for Lynn in Norfolk, and was married to a freeman of the same borough. Margery obtained agreement from her husband to take a vow to live chastely so as to be freer to cultivate her religious life. She became an enthusiastic pilgrim, even visiting Rome and Jerusalem, as well as Julian of Norwich, and her pilgrimages and other devotional activities finally encouraged in her a desire to record her experiences. She employed an amanuensis to take down her memoirs, a sort of spiritual autobiography, which is known as 'The Book of Margery Kempe'. This work has produced widely differing reactions in modern readers, from judging her hysterical to regarding her as a distinctive mystic. What is most relevant in this context is that she and Julian of Norwich, who were little known in their own day, indicate a fraction of the population that sought satisfaction in pastimes of private spiritual devotion.

Other Guides to Devotion

Hundreds of pieces of devotional literature and religious instruction in English survive from late medieval England, and the quantity alone gives the impression that a great many folk were anything but complacent about their religious lives. Devotional literature might be such things as confessions, meditations, prayers, or exhortations. Religious instruction might take the form of informational tracts on penitence or virginity, or copies of the Creed, the Lord's Prayer, or the Ten Commandments. Some devotional works were translations from the Latin works of Continental writers, such as 'The Booke of Gostlye Grace', a translation of the 'Liber Specialis Gratie' of the Benedictine nun Mechtild of Hackeborn (died 1298) or the 'Dialogo' by Catherine of Siena (died 1380), which was translated for the Bridgettine nuns at Syon as 'The Orcherd of Syon'. An Augustinian friar, William Flete, wrote a treatise of spiritual advice before leaving England for Italy in 1359, and his 'De Remediis contra Temptaciones' circulated in both Latin and in English translation to assist the faithful to find remedies against temptations. Henry Suso's 'Horologium Sapientiae' was available before the end of the fourteenth century as a work of pious devotion in an English version under the title 'Seven Points of True Love and Everlasting Wisdom'.

Works of religious instruction were extremely useful in Christian life. To take one situation, the Fourth Lateran Council of 1215 enjoined upon all Christians annual confession to one's parish priest. Confession of sin required knowing what sin was, and thus the proper employment of the sacrament of penance took on an educational dimension, for if the priest acted as instructor, the laity needed to be capable of analysing their behaviour. The instructional literature that resulted in England from the stimulus of the Fourth Lateran Council has yet to be evaluated and inventoried by modern scholarship, but the response was vast. The clergy realized the need for instruction, and various thirteenth-century bishops, like Walter Cantilupe of Worcester (died 1266) and William of Britton II of Bath and Wells (died 1274), urged the priests under their authority to teach the laity. A famous programme of instruction was the 'Ignorancia Sacerdotum', issued in 1281 among the statutes of the Council of Lambeth under the leadership of Archbishop Pecham of Canterbury. Subsequent instructional works like the 'Pore Caitiff' and the 'Speculum Christiani', both in prose, were compiled to answer the need for Christian education as outlined in the 'Ignorancia Sacerdotum'.

A group of prose works in Middle English from the West Midlands offers further confirmation of the attractiveness of writings of religious advice and instruction. An especially famous example is the 'Ancrene Wisse', a guide for anchoresses composed in the late twelfth or early thirteenth century. The term Katherine Group is applied to five works: 'Hali Meiðhad', which praises virginity; 'Sawles Warde', a homily of body and soul in allegorical form; and 'Saint Katherine', 'Saint Juliana', and 'Saint Margaret', all saints' lives. Another four items in rhythmic prose make up what is known as the 'Wohunge' or Wooing Group: 'þe Wohunge of Ure Lauerd', 'On wel swuðe god Ureisun of God Almihti', 'þe Oreisun of Seinte Marie', and 'On Lofsong of Ure Louerde'.

The Rosary

A very old tradition credits St Dominic (died 1221), founder of the Dominican Order, with the introduction of the rosary following an appearance to him of the Virgin Mary. However, there is no reliable record to indicate that Dominic had anything to do with the origination or promulgation of the rosary. The word derives from the Latin *rosarium*, meaning a garden, a rose wreath, a collection of flowers or, by extension, a collection of texts. The word came to be used for a collection of fifty salutations to the Virgin.

The rosary, which came in the later Middle Ages to be the most popular of all extraliturgical prayers employed by Christians, seems to have originated in the twelfth century. Rather than being conceived whole by an individual or a committee, it grew and developed in use by experiment and revision. In its earliest form, going back at least to the twelfth century, the rosary was a Latin prayer, Ave Maria (Hail Mary) based upon the salutation of the Angel Gabriel to Mary (Luke 1:28) and the greeting of Mary by her cousin Elizabeth (Luke 1:42). The first joining of these salutations in the West is attributed to Pope Gregory I (reigned 590-604), the apostle of the English. The combined scriptural greetings are familiar in modern English as: 'Hail, Mary, full of grace, the Lord is with thee; blessed art thou amongst women and blessed is the fruit of thy womb.'

The repetition of prayers was an effective form of private devotion, and the repetition of the Psalms was a part of Church life. Repeating 150 times the paternoster was a way of imitating the recitation of the 150 Psalms, and repeating the Ave Maria offered a way to merge

Marian devotion with the desire to imitate the chanting of the Psalms of the Divine Office. A way of keeping track of the repeated prayers was to divide the total into three groups of fifty, and use fifty beads on a string to keep count of how many prayers had been said, but a full string of rosary beads would have the same number of beads as Psalms. A string of beads used as prayer-counters appeals to common sense. The chronicler William of Malmesbury tells a story dated to 1040 that Lady Godiva of Coventry had a number of gems threaded on a string which she fingered one by one as she recited her prayers so that she might not fall short of the desired number of prayers. Strings of beads used for counting repetitions of Aves or paternosters were called Ave or, more commonly, paternoster beads. The craftsmen who made and sold the beads were also called paternosters, and the street in London where the craftsmen's shops were clustered was, and is, called Paternoster Row. Using beads to keep track, a proper rosary from the fourteenth century onwards, consisted of engaging mentally in meditations on the life of Christ while verbally repeating the Hail Mary.

An English gold rosary (The Board of the Trustees of the Victoria & Albert Museum)

A striking example of an English rosary survives from about 1500. Made of gold and the work of English goldsmiths, it consists of fifty small, oval beads, and six larger lozenge-shaped beads, with ten smaller beads between each of the larger. The string begins and ends with a larger bead, and is joined together by a large four-sided gold knop. The rosary would thus be described as a five-decade rosary with six pater beads. Every bead is engraved on each side with the figure of a saint or a religious symbol (such as the Lamb of God), and the engraving is made more dramatic by being filled with black enamel. The vast majority would not have had such a precious object to assist them with their devotions, but however humble the materials from which the beads were made they served the same purpose for individual prayer and contemplation.

Books of Hours

Like Paternoster beads, books of hours were employed as aids to personal devotion in late medieval England, as they were on the Continent. To many, the term 'book of hours' will bring to mind a beautiful illuminated and precious book, but many were modest little volumes with little or no decoration. This type of devotional book takes its name from the fact that its core content, the Little Office of the Blessed Virgin Mary, was made up of eight services designed to be recited at different times of the day. The services are modelled on the fuller Divine Office (*Officium divinum*), which is found in the service book called the Breviary, conducted by the clergy eight times a day at the canonic hours (*horae canonicae*): Matins (*matutinum*), before sunrise; Lauds (*laudes*), at sunrise; Prime (*ad primam horam*); Terce (*ad tertiam horam*); Sext (*ad sextam horam*); None (*ad nonam horam*) – the first, third, sixth, and ninth hours of the day would fall at different times by the clock at different times of the year – ; Vespers (*ad vesperam*), at sunset and Compline (*completorium*), before retiring. The services in books of hours share the same names as those of the Divine Office, but they are shorter and have less variation. A book of hours would normally contain materials in addition to the Little Office of the Blessed Virgin Mary, such as selected Psalms (which, of course, circulated as a complete collection in the form of book known as the Psalter), or other extracts from the Bible, a calendar of feasts for the liturgical year and saints' days, the Office of the Dead, and assorted prayers. Books of hours usually contained materials in Latin, but it was not out of the ordinary for some of the prayers to be in English.

The Annunciation, with scenes from the early life of the Virgin Mary. Example of an illuminated page from the Bedford Book of Hours, fifteenth century (British Library, Additional Ms. 18850, f. 32)

Devotional literature, especially in the form of psalters and books of hours, seems to have been particularly popular with women readers in the later Middle Ages.

'Le Livre de Seyntz Medicines'

Henry of Grosmont, first Duke of Lancaster (died 1361), was one of the most accomplished commanders in the wars of his friend, Edward III. He fought at sea, at Sluys (1340) and Espagnols-sur-Mer (1350), and on land, in Scotland, Prussia, and many French campaigns, including that where the French were defeated at Poitiers (1356). He was a diplomat, an administrator, a founding member of the Order of the Garter, and such a model of chivalry that young squires competed to train in his service. Yet this man who soldiered for nearly half a century was also the learned contributor to the Anglo-Norman devotional literature 'Le Livre de Seyntz Medicines' ('The Book of Holy Cures'). Although a warrior, Henry offers us another example of lay piety. His work, which he tells us he wrote in 1354, is a confession of his sins in the form of an extended allegory. He, for instance, compares his heart to a fox's hole, a whirlpool in a sea, the *donjon* of a castle, and a city market-place into which his many sins have become entrenched. He confesses himself to be mortally wounded in body, senses, and soul with the poison of the seven deadly sins, and he appeals for remedies to the divine physician, Christ, and to that *Douce Dame*, the Virgin Mary.

Piers Plowman

Another expression of the presence of religious conscience or intention in late medieval England is the widely read allegorical poem 'Piers Plowman', written in alliterative verse by William Langland (1330–86), a cleric in minor orders. In the allegory, Piers the Plowman, a symbol of good, and life as it should be lived, is the guide. The poet first paints a picture of the world as it is, followed by a picture of the world as it could be if the teachings of the Gospels were followed. The poet clearly believes that a righteous society is not impossible to create. In part, the maxims of allegorical figures must be followed if a better world is to be brought into being. The instructions of 'Do-Well' are to be God-fearing, honest, hard-working, charitable, and obedient to the Church; 'Do-Better' counsels to do those things but also to teach the ignorant, aid the suffering, and to set a righteous example; while 'Do-Best' proposes to move to a still higher level by achieving such a level of righteousness that the Church and society will be led to salvation.

TEN

Poaching, Sorcery and Prostitution

T his final chapter deals with all those pleasures and pastimes which were illegal or frowned upon in medieval society. There must have been as many occasions in medieval England when the buyer had to beware of the illegal activities of fellow citizens as there are centuries later. Merchants used illegal weights and measures, and victuallers attempted to sell tainted foods. Bogus relics were available for the faithful, and poor quality wool was buried under good in wool sacks to deceive buyers. Frail livestock was passed off as healthy. Junk was offered up as quality merchandise. Sanctimonious clerics tried to secure the sexual favours of parishioners. Charlatans posed as skilled in surgery or medicine to play upon the health fears of the citizenry with promises of infallible cures, and spurious apothecaries could doubtless be found who would promise to sell to the ailing (for the highest bearable cost) a potion or treacle (that is, a salve) for every bodily disfunction. How much displeasure resulted for some from the criminal pastimes of others we can only surmise.

Poaching

Stealing deer was the quintessential form of poaching. It was not limited to any special social group, and there was no typical poacher. For the gentry class and above, deer hunting may primarily have been a sport, perhaps a passion, even if it were done under illegal conditions. The prowess displayed in hunting had high prestige and a powerful association with male gender identity, and venison was the proper meat for a prominent table and a convivial occasion. Poaching for people of lower social status would have contributed substantially to their livelihood, and the lower on the economic scale a poacher fell, the more his interest lay in meat and skins and the less in the sport of hunting. Nonetheless, the excitement and delight in hunting was wonderfully appealing to all participants. For some it was a part of normal social life.

Gentlemen and peers were protective of their hunting rights in their private forests and parks. They were also keen on keeping poachers from taking game from their hunting franchises. A legal remedy against poachers was to sue them in a common-law court on an action of trespass. The first Game Law to be enacted by a parliament came in the reign of Richard II in 1390 and dealt with the circumstances in which hunting could be a crime. Hunting had long been a royal monopoly within the royal forests. Forest, it must be noted, was a legal concept brought to England with the Norman Conquest, and basically designated an area as a game preserve; the term did not convey our modern understanding of a woodland. The king could also license the right of others to designate lands as parks, chaces, and warrens for private hunting preserves. Places not designated as hunting preserves were free to everyone until the statute of 1390, which laid down that such

The fowler approaches a walled town carrying what may or may not be his legimate catch (British Library, Ms. YT 30, f. 11)

persons as artificers, labourers, and anyone whose lands and tenements produced less than forty shillings income a year or any priest or clerk whose benefice produced less than ten pounds annually should not, on pain of a year in prison, hunt 'gentlemen's game' such as deer, conies, or hares. The Game Law of 1390 was clearly an effort by the king and his more privileged subjects to control the right to hunt for themselves. Doubtless to some of our peasant ancestors the statute was a siren song to poach, but poaching was not limited to the peasantry.

What was so attractive about poaching? Poaching was more than a method to obtain food. For the excluded, it was a way to participate in deer-hunting culture, and a method of attacking aristocratic privilege. Poaching another man's game could be a way of venting hostility at one's enemy or a way of making the man unable to protect the game on his land look weak. The bonds of fraternity developed among poachers must have been gratifying to some who joined in the activity. Poaching was a dangerous and exciting game of manliness. It offered an opportunity to display the cunning required to outwit the lord of the land and his officials. It seems only appropriate that Robin Hood, one of the most enduringly appealing literary figures from medieval England, would have numbered poaching among his activities.

Upper-class Criminality

The criminal pastimes of the higher levels of society were not confined to the occasional poaching foray. The wealth and power of the upper classes, together with a certain amount of tolerance on the part of kings, allowed them to engage in illegal acts for which they were lightly punished or not punished at all. The ability of the powerful to distort the course of justice through bribes and intimidation, as is mentioned elsewhere, was one of the anxieties of the age. Extortion was another upper-class criminal pastime. It could be as crude as a bullying protection racket, using household members to threaten and beat victims into a willingness to pay for a reprieve. Abduction for ransom was another form of extortion. Battening on some neighbours and tenants while at the same time protecting others could gain at least some grudging supporters for nobles in a region. The prestige and safety of a regional lord was, after all, measured in part by the number of followers he had, and the pressure to support and develop a retinue must have been an incentive to criminal acts for some men of ambition.

Royalty tried to control upper-class crime but not eradicate it.

Disreputable japes (Bodleian Library, Oxford, Ms. Bodl. 264, f. 74)

Kings needed the services of the nobility in peace and war and in the governance of the kingdom, and had no incentive or instinct to upset the social hierarchy. That is not to say that on occasion matters did not get out of hand. There was, for instance, the case of the six scoundrel sons of John de Folville, lord of Ashby-Folville in Leicestershire. The worst of these lads was Eustace, who had at least five murders to his credit, together with all sorts of thefts, receiving, extortion schemes, assaults, and rapes. Another was Richard, rector of the parish church of Teigh, who was killed by a royal keeper of the peace, Sir Richard Colville. This unfortunate man suffered immense difficulties because of his execution of a priest, even though that priest was an outlaw many times over. Yet even the Folville thugs were pardoned as an act of royal magnanimity when Edward III became king in 1327, and were pardoned again for further crimes when they joined in the king's wars, and the notorious Eustace Folville died a peaceful natural death in 1346. There were other criminal gangs led and employed by nobles, such as that of the Coterel brothers, who worked with the Folvilles on occasion. These upper-class evil-doers were not professional criminals, but their activities as warriors, administrators, and men of local prominence opened the way for them to drift into patterns of part-time crime.

Sorcery

There are occasional references to men and women in late medieval England turning to sorcery or witchcraft such as that of the warlock, Richard Perkin, who confessed before Archbishop Rotherham of York in 1481. There is no mention of Perkin's motives for his supernatural activity. The concerns that most attracted people to sorcery appear to have been the desire to do injury to an enemy, the wish to recover lost or stolen property, and the longing for success in romance or marriage. The lesson of caution learned from the episodes described below tended to make medieval English sorcerers exceedingly circumspect in the practice of their art.

An especially famous case of political sorcery became a scandalous episode in 1441 involving the proud Duchess of Gloucester. The events had very clear political overtones, and are associated with the gradual easing of the king's uncle, Humphrey, Duke of Gloucester, from the centre of political power. (Humphrey insisted upon no compromise with the great enemy France, while Cardinal Beaufort and the Earl of Suffolk, who were on the political ascendancy, were looking for a way to cool the French war.) Gloucester's wife, Eleanor Cobham, inadvertently gave the duke's opponents a weapon with which to strike him, for she had been delving into the occult arts, a dangerous activity for the wife of the heir apparent to the throne. On the evening of 28 or 29 June it became known to Eleanor that certain of her associates had been conspiring against the life of the childless King Henry VI by means of sorcery. They were: Master Roger Bolingbroke, a priest and a member of the duke's household; Master Thomas Southwell, rector of St Stephen's, Walbrook, and canon of the king's palace chapel of St Stephen's, Westminster; John Home, Eleanor's chaplain and secretary to both Eleanor and her husband; and Margery Jourdemain, known locally in London as the 'Witch of Eye' (that is, Ebury, by Westminster). The accused were arrested and examined, and apparently it was Bolingbroke who implicated the duchess in a scheme that had included holding certain ceremonies for the prediction and encompassing of the king's death. Bolingbroke made a public recantation of his sorcery at St Paul's Cross on 23 July before an audience distinguished by the presence of many members of the king's council and other notables. The next day Eleanor was examined by a group of ecclesiastics on twenty-eight counts of treason and felony. Maintaining her innocence, she was allowed to return to Westminster Abbey where she had earlier fled for sanctuary. She was examined again the next day and, confronted by Bolingbroke, admitted to five of the charges which had been brought against her, though she stoutly denied attempting to kill the king by image-magic. Following the confession, Eleanor was imprisoned in Leeds Castle in Kent.

The next major event came in October 1441 when Eleanor – Gloucester was apparently able to do nothing to aid his wife in her time of distress – was brought from Leeds to Westminster for further examination in St Stephen's Chapel before an impressive gathering of ecclesiastics. The interview took place on 20 or 21 October, and once again Eleanor accepted some of the charges as

Witches riding their broomsticks, a marginal illustration from a manuscript of *c.* 1451 (Bibliothèque Nationale, Paris, B 67/295, f. 105v)

An effigy of Joan of Navarre from the tomb of Henry IV, Canterbury Cathedral (Geoffrey Wheeler)

true while denying others. The hearing was then adjourned until 23 October when Eleanor, Bolingbroke, Southwell, and Jourdemain were brought before their judges, and all were found guilty of heresy and necromancy. Before any sentence could be carried out, Southwell died in the Tower. The Witch of Eye, whose intended service to Eleanor was to provide potions to ensure a pregnancy and an heir for the Duke of Gloucester, was burned at Smithfield on 27 October. Bolingbroke died a traitor's death at Tyburn on 18 November, while Home, clearly a lesser figure, was pardoned the same day. Meanwhile, Eleanor had been enduring her own humiliations. Her marriage to Gloucester was terminated by a commission of ecclesiastics on 6 November, and she was later required to perform public penance. On three market days, 13, 15, and 17 November, she walked through London first to St Paul's Cathedral, then to Christchurch in Aldgate, and on the third day to St Michael's Cornhill, each time offering a candle at the altar of the designated church. She was then imprisoned, and remained in custody in various places until her death at Beaumaris Castle on 7 July 1452.

The case of Eleanor Cobham had an impact upon English law, for in 1442 it became statutory that peeresses indicted of felony or treason should be tried in the manner of peers. The Cobham case is reminiscent of that of Joan of Navarre in 1419, but there were differences. Joan was the widow of King Henry IV, and by 1419 Henry had been succeeded on the throne by his eldest son by his first marriage, Henry V (as of 1415 the hero of Agincourt). Joan was denounced by her Franciscan confessor, John Randolf, for encompassing the death of the king – her stepson – by sorcery and necromancy. Neither she nor her accuser, who was later murdered by a deranged priest, were ever tried, but Joan was kept in confinement until the end of the reign when she was restored to favour. Her accusation was almost certainly politically motivated because of the Breton connections that existed from her first marriage to Duke John IV of Brittany (her son by that marriage was a prisoner of war from Agincourt), and because of the constitutionally ambiguous position she occupied as stepmother to the king. It was also a means of reapportioning her 10,000 marks per annum dowry. Joan was an alien queen-dowager, rather than a possible queen as was the English-born Eleanor Cobham. Joan's imprisonment was soft and brief, while Eleanor's was firm and permanent, and Joan's case did not have such heavy political ramifications as those which burdened Eleanor's.

Sex and Prostitution

That our ancestors took some degree of pleasure in sexual activity is made evident by the fact that we are here to contemplate the matter. The pleasure of sex was in fact taken as so self-evident as to require no particular comment. Sexual activity in the form of prostitution was thought to be an evil thing, but at the same time necessary to keep sinful men driven by lust from corrupting respectable women, including their own wives, or from turning to homosexuality/If the established authorities of society could accept prostitution as an unfortunate necessity, the same equanimity was not extended to prostitutes, who most authorities believed had chosen their profession because of the innate lustfulness of womankind. They did not notice that it was extremely difficult for an unmarried woman, who had not adopted the religious life, to survive economically. Such women had few ways in which to support themselves: as servants in urban or rural households, as unskilled workers or hucksters (street-sellers) on the economic fringe in towns, or as prostitutes. Some fortunate women grew up in families where they learned a skill, such as weaving or embroidery, by which they could gain an income, but for many unmarried women prostitution was one of a small group of economic possibilities.

Prostitutes existed in a very awkward milieu. As people they were shunned by mainstream society, and yet their activity in society was recognized and regulated. It is reasonable to suppose that their activity put them at risk of physical and social abuse as a segregated group, and also at risk in terms of physical health. But, to reiterate, for an impoverished woman without a patron or marketable skill, prostitution could have been a singular means of survival. Why else would a woman follow a life that would not allow her a Christian burial in consecrated ground?

Much of the prostitution that was a part of late medieval English society was at the edge of the social underworld and has therefore left no trace in surviving records. How widespread prostitution was, as opposed to the ubiquity of illicit sex, cannot be known with certainty, but brothels in which some of the prostitution was concentrated are known to have existed. Brothels were not viewed in England, or on the Continent, as institutions for the protection of prostitutes, but as a means of preserving social order and protecting decent women in the face of the male demand for a sexual outlet. The only English example of officially regulated brothels, for which revealing documentation survives, is that of the brothels of Southwark. The only other place known to have had an officially sanctioned brothel was the port town of Sandwich in Kent. The environs of London probably offered a greater wealth of opportunity for sexual promiscuity than any other location in the kingdom, and City authorities did tolerate the operation of brothels in Cock Lane, in Smithfield. Southwark lay across the Thames from London and, as it was wholly outside the jurisdiction of the City, gained something of a reputation as the habitation of unsavoury characters. Court records indicate that the authorities were not successful in limiting prostitution to Cock Lane and Southwark. Territorially, Southwark Bankside was in the county of Surrey, giving it jurisdictional liberty, and was the London seat of the Bishop of Winchester, hence a familiar name for the prostitutes working there was 'Winchester Geese'. Since Southwark was a liberty of the Bishop of Winchester, residents sued one another not in the king's court, but the bishop's, and could be punished in the bishop's prison, the Clink. Winchester Geese were to be found in the stews, which could mean synonymously public baths or brothels, and the Bishop of Winchester benefited financially from rents and court profits.

A prostitute with her client (Bodleian Library, Oxford, Ms. Bodl. 264, f. 204r)

The fifteenth-century regulations that survive for the Southwark stews ordain that the stewholders be men. Throughout the kingdom, however, wherever there was some concentration of population, the keeping of brothels offered an opening for illegal entrepreneurship to women. In Southwark the business was legal, and was supposed to be under male direction. The regulations required also that the prostitutes did not live or board in the brothels. This requirement, that the women dwell and take their meals elsewhere would have allowed the prostitutes more freedom of movement than if they had lived and worked in the same place, and would have helped them to avoid being exploited by the stewholders. In the same light, stewholders were prohibited from lending money to the prostitutes, and from beating the women. Nor were the stewmongers to keep a boat or to sell food or other goods, probably to protect customers from being exploited. It was probably not to protect customers, but to cut down on people wandering the streets at night, that lay behind the requirement that a prostitute spend the entire night with a customer. Nightwalking was a common offense against public order. It was declared that customers were not to be harassed in the street, pulled into the brothels by their clothing, or to have themselves or their goods detained in the brothels for debt.

The Southwark regulations do not require prostitutes to wear any distinctive clothing, although striped hoods were often required in other places, such as Bristol. The Southwark

A wood carving, on a misericord in Westminster Abbey, of a prostitute with a client who dips his hand into his purse (Dean and Chapter of Westminster)

prostitutes, for no given reason, were not to wear aprons. The women were required to be away from the stews during most of the daylight hours on holy days between Michaelmas and Candlemas, and at night when a parliament happened to be in session. They were not allowed paramours, particularly men whom they supported, probably in an attempt to eliminate 'bawdry' or pimping. Prostitutes were not to be attached to any one man, lover or husband; they were 'common women' who belonged to the community. The brothel-keepers in Southwark did not technically employ the prostitutes, but simply rented rooms by the week to the women for their work. One intention of the surviving regulations was that the women were not compelled to remain against their will as prostitutes. The rents for prostitutes were high compared with the rent of similar space for other purposes, and this may indicate that the stewholders did not get a portion of the fees charged to customers.

Sadistic Entertainment

What was public humiliation for one person was entertainment to another, and public punishments were a common spectacle. In London, for instance, a man found to be a procurer or receiver of prostitutes would have his hair distinctively tonsured, his beard shaved off, and be taken with minstrelsy to a pillory where he would stand for so long as the mayor determined. For a second offence, he got the same punishment with a time in prison added, and for a third offence, he was expelled forever from the City. A woman guilty of the same offence was taken with minstrelsy to a 'thew', a pillory for women, and there her hair was cut in some unattractive way, and for further offences she would be treated as would a man. The Common Council of London decided in 1384 that a prostitute found guilty of residing other than in Cock Lane, where the residences of 'common women' were confined, would be taken from her prison to Aldgate wearing a striped hood and carrying a white wand in her hand, and from Aldgate to the thew escorted by minstrels, and at the thew (or 'cucking-stool') her offence would be publicly proclaimed. She would then be escorted through the City, along Cheapside, and out of Newgate to Cock Lane where she was expected to live. For a second offence, she would spend time on the thew in addition to the rest, and for a third offence, she would have her hair cut short and be expelled from the City.

Executions were public shows. Favourite meeting places, and therefore favourite execution places, were watering-holes. The

Maltreatment of prisoners (The Master and Fellows of Corpus Christi College, Cambridge, Ms. 16, f. 48v; photograph: Conway Library, Courtauld Institute of Art)

The gallows: prisoners being hanged outside Bedford Castle (The Master and Fellows of Corpus Christi College, Cambridge, Ms. 16, f. 64v; photograph: Conway Library, Courtauld Institute of Art)

principal source of water for London was Tyburn, and one important outlet from the stream was a pump called the Standard, built in Cheapside in 1285. A gallows stood near to where Marble Arch is now. Gruesome penalties were expected to serve as deterrents to crime. The sort of lesson the public was expected to derive from executions is captured in the lines prepared early in the sixteenth century by the grammar master Robert Whittinton for his students to translate into Latin:

Upon London Bridge I saw three or four men's heads stand upon poles. Upon Ludgate the forequarter of a man is set upon a pole. Upon the other side hangeth the haunch of a man with the leg. It is a strange sight to see the hair of the heads [fall] or [mould] away and the gristle of the nose consumed away, the fingers of their hands withered and clunged [that is, shrivelled] unto the bare bones. It is a spectacle for ever to all young people to beware that they presume not too far upon their own heedness (or, self mind).

Prisons and prisoners were much less hidden from public view in the Middle Ages than they are now. It would have been fairly common to see prisoners being led to gaol by guards, to be petitioned by prisoners begging for alms or food from within their place of confinement, or to witness convicted felons being executed. Newgate Prison was the primary prison for the City of London and for the county of Middlesex. It was also used by the king and royal justices as a place to keep prisoners, and so it tended to be occupied by the worst sorts of criminals, many of whom faced execution. It is little wonder that Newgate had a sinister reputation. Newgate was probably initially built in the first half of the twelfth century when a new gate was built into the City wall, and a building to be used as a prison was constructed on an adjacent site. In the 1230s a prison was established in one of the turrets of the gate itself, and it is at this time that the history of Newgate proper begins. It continued in use with little change until another new gate and gaol were constructed with a bequest from the famous mayor Richard Whittington (died 1423). Another prison easily viewed by Londoners was the Tun in Cornhill, a small gaol which architecturally resembled a barrel placed on end.

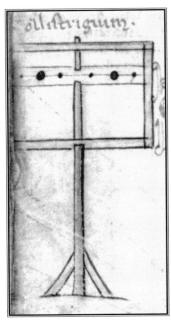

The pillory (The Master and Fellows of Corpus Christi College, Cambridge, Ms. 16, f. 25v; photograph: Conway Library, Courtauld Institute of Art)

Postscript

Sometimes the side of the past that appears to have given pleasure to those who experienced it left evidence in odd places, but it is very important that we take notice. There survives, for instance, the entry in a financial record for the expenses of Edward II that the king gave a cash reward to a painter in his service, Jack of St Albans, who danced upon a table before the king and made him laugh heartily ('qui daunsa devant le Roi sur une table et lui fist tresgrantment rire'). It would be wonderful to know how lacking in decorum the dance was. Another bit of royal humour is found in the terms of service by which Rolland le Pettour was to hold from the king the manor of Hemingstone in Suffolk. The service was to

'Duck discourse' from the Gorleston Psalter (British Library, Additional Ms. 49622, f. 190v)

appear at the king's court annually on Christmas Day where he was to perform a leap, a whistle, and a fart. A motto used by King Edward IV was 'Confort et liesse', comfort and mirth. An image painted in a margin of the Gorleston Psalter between about 1310 and 1320 is that of a fox which has just snatched a duck, and the duck is exclaiming 'queck', which so far as anyone has noticed is the first time that an English hand had written that a duck said 'quack'! We are inclined to think of history as the study of politics, war, diplomacy, economics, administration, family strategy, great deeds of powerful men, and the like. But if we want to fully understand our ancestors we must know what made them smile and laugh and relax, just as surely as what supported their family economies or drew them into conflict.

Two boys whip their tops
(Bodleian Library, Oxford, Ms.
Douce. 62, f. 72v)

Sources

Chapter One: Literature

Baskervill, C.R. 'Dramatic Aspects of Medieval Folk Festivals in England', *Studies in Philology* 17 (1920), pp. 19–87.

Bennett, H.S. 'Caxton and His Public', *The Review of English Studies* 19 (1943), pp. 113–19.

———. *Chaucer and the Fifteenth Century*, Oxford, Clarendon Press, 1947.

———. 'Science and Information in English Writings of the Fifteenth Century', *Modern Language Review* 39 (1944), pp. 1–8.

Bornstein, Diane. 'Military Manuals in Fifteenth-Century England', *Mediaeval Studies* 37 (1975), pp. 469–77.

Brewer, Derek. *Chaucer and His World*, 2nd edn, Woodbridge, Brewer, 1992.

Chambers, E.K. *English Literature at the Close of the Middle Ages*, Oxford, Clarendon Press, 1947.

Evans, Joan. *Magical Jewels of the Middle Ages*, Oxford, Clarendon Press, 1922.

Field, P.J.C. *The Life and Times of Sir Thomas Malory*, Woodbridge, Brewer, 1993.

Genet, J.P. (ed.). *Four English Political Tracts of the Later Middle Ages*, London, Camden Fourth Series, 18, 1977.

Gransden, Antonia. *Historical Writing in England II: c. 1307 to the Early 16th Century*, Ithaca, Cornell University Press, 1982.

Green, R.F. *Poets and Princepleasers*. Toronto, University of Toronto Press, 1980.

Heffernan, T.J. (ed.). *The Popular Literature of Medieval England*, Knoxville, The University of Tennessee Press, 1985.

Howard, D.R. *Chaucer: His Life, His Works, His World*, New York, E.P. Dutton, 1987.

Lacy, N.J. (ed.). *The Arthurian Encyclopedia*. New York, Garland, 1986.

Lyon, Bryce. *A Constitutional and Legal History of Medieval England*, 2nd edn, New York, W.W. Norton, 1980.

Olson, Glending. *Reading as Recreation in the Later Middle Ages*. Ithaca, Cornell University Press, 1980.

Ramsey, L.C. *Chivalric Romances: Popular Literature in Medieval England*, Bloomington, Indiana University Press, 1983.

Reeves, A.C. 'The Careers of William Lyndwood', in *Documenting the Past: Essays in Medieval History presented to George Peddy Cuttino*, J.S. Hamilton and P.J. Bradley (eds), Woodbridge, Boydell, 1989.

———. 'Thomas Hoccleve, Bureaucrat', *Medievalia et Humanistica*, New Series, 5 (1974), pp. 201–14.

———. 'The World of Thomas Hoccleve', *Fifteenth Century Studies* 2 (1979), pp. 187–201.

Rhodes, Michael. 'A Pair of Fifteenth-Century Spectacle Frames from the City of London', *Antiquities Journal* 62 (1982), pp. 57–73.

Chapter Two: Art, Architecture, Music and Dancing

Binski, Paul. *Painters*, London, British Museum Press, 1991.

Brown, Sarah, and O'Connor, David. *Glass-Painters*, London, British Museum Press, 1991.

Bullock-Davies, Constance. *Menestrellorum Multitudo: Minstrels at a Royal Feast*, Cardiff, University of Wales Press, 1978.

Caldwell, John. *Medieval Music*, Bloomington, Indiana University Press, 1978.

Cosman, M.P. 'Machaut's Medical Musical World', in *Machaut's World: Science and Art in the Fourteenth Century*, ed. M.P. Cosman and Bruce Chandler, New York, Annals of the New York Academy of Sciences 314, 1978.

Durant, D.N. *The Handbook of British Architectural Styles*, London, Barrie and Jenkins, 1992.

Eams, Elizabeth. *English Medieval Tilers*, London, British Museum Press, 1985.

Evans, Joan. *English Art, 1307–1461*, Oxford, Oxford University Press, 1949.

Harrison, F.L. *Music in Medieval Britain*, 2nd edn, London, Routledge and Kegan Paul, 1963.

Harvey, J.H. *The Master Builders*, London, Thames and Hudson, 1971.

——. *The Perpendicular Style, 1330–1485*, London, Batsford, 1978.

McGee, T.J. *Medieval Instrumental Dances*. Bloomington, Indiana University Press, 1989.

Marks, Richard. *Stained Glass in England during the Middle Ages*, Toronto, University of Toronto Press, 1993.

Montagu, Jeremy. *The World of Medieval and Renaissance Musical Instruments*, Woodstock, Overlook Press, 1976. .

Platt, Colin. *The Architecture of Medieval Britain: A Social History*, New Haven, Yale University Press, 1990.

Saunders, O.E. *A History of English Art in the Middle Ages*, Oxford, Clarendon Press, 1932.

Southworth, John. *The English Medieval Minstrel*, Woodbridge, Boydell, 1989.

Wilkins, N.E. *Music in the Age of Chaucer*, Ipswich, Brewer, 1979.

Wilson, D.F. *Music of the Middle Ages*. New York, Schirmer Books, 1990.

Chapter Three: Fashion, Ornament and Craftsmanship

Baildon, W.P. 'Three Inventories: (1) The Earl of Huntingdon, 1377; (2) Brother John Randolf, 1419; (3) Sir John de Boys, 1426', *Archaeologia* 61 (1909), pp. 163–76.

——. 'The Trousseaux of Princess Philippa, Wife of Eric, King of Denmark, Norway, and Sweden', *Archaeologia* 68 (1915–16), pp. 163–88.

Blair, John, and Ramsay, Nigel (eds). *English Medieval Industries: Craftsmen, Techniques, Products*, London, Hambledon, 1991.

Brooke, Iris. *English Costume of the Later Middle Ages*, London, Adam and Charles Black, 1935.

Cherry, John. *Goldsmiths*, London, British Museum Press, 1992.

Evans, Joan. *A History of Jewellery, 1100–1870*. 2nd edn, London, Faber and Faber, 1970.

Haslam, Jeremy, *Medieval Pottery in Britain*, Aylesbury, Shire Publications, 1978.

Hogarth, Sylvia. 'Ecclesiastical Vestments and Vestmentmakers in York, 1300–1600', *York Historian*, 7 (1986), pp. 2–11.

Houston, M.G. *Medieval Costume in England and France*, London, Adam and Charles Black, 1939.

Myers, A.R. 'The Jewels of Queen Margaret of Anjou', *Bulletin of the John Rylands Library* 42 (1959–60), pp. 113–31.

Newton, S.M. *Fashion in the Age of the Black Prince*, Woodbridge, Boydell, 1980.

Spencer, Brian. 'Fifteenth-Century Collar of SS and Hoard of False Dice with their Container, from the Museum of London', *Antiquaries Journal* 65 (1985), pp. 449–53.

Stratford, Jenny. *The Bedford Inventories*, London, Society of Antiquaries, 1993.

Veale, E.M. *The English Fur Trade in the Later Middle Ages*, Oxford, Clarendon Press, 1966.

Chapter Four: Games, Drama and Heraldry

Benham, W.G. *Playing Cards: History of the Pack and Explanations of its Many Secrets*, London, Spring Books, 1956.

Brody, Alan. *The English Mummers and Their Plays*, Philadelphia, University of Pennsylvania Press, 1970.

Brooke-Little, J.P. *An Heraldic Alphabet*, rev. edn, London, Robson Books, 1985.

Davenport, W.A. *Fifteenth-Century English Drama: The Early Moral Plays and their Literary Relations*, Woodbridge, D.S. Brewer, 1982.

Hanawalt, B.A. *Growing Up in Medieval London*, Oxford, Oxford University Press, 1993.

Helm, Alex. *The English Mummers' Play*, Woodbridge, D.S. Brewer, 1981.

Hutton, Ronald, *The Rise and Fall of Merry England: The Ritual Year, 1400–1700*, Oxford, Oxford University Press, 1994.

James, Mervyn. 'Ritual, Drama and Social Body in the Late Medieval English Town', *Past and Present* 98 (1983), pp. 3–29.

Lewis, N.B. 'The Anniversary Service for Blanche, Duchess of Lancaster, 12th September, 1374', *Bulletin of the John Rylands Library* 21 (1937), pp. 176–92.

Lindenbaum, Sheila. 'The Smithfield Tournament of 1390', *Journal of Medieval and Renaissance Studies* 20 (1990), pp. 1–20.

Micklethwaite, J.T. 'On the Indoor Games of School Boys in the Middle Ages', *Archaeological Journal* 49 (1892), pp. 319–28.

Moran, J.H. *Education and Learning in the City of York, 1300–1560*, York, Borthwick Paper 55, 1979.

Osberg, Richard. 'The Jesse Tree in the 1432 London Entry of Henry VI: Messianic Kingship and the Rule of Justice', *Journal of Medieval and Renaissance Studies* 16 (1986), pp. 213–32.

Post, J.B. 'The Obsequies of John of Gaunt', *Guildhall Studies in London History* 5 (October 1981), pp. 1–12.

Richardson, Christine, and Johnston, Jackie. *Medieval Drama*, London, Macmillan, 1991.

Stewart, I.J., and Watkins, M.J. 'An 11th-Century Bone Tabula Set from Gloucester', *Medieval Archaeology* 28 (1984), pp. 185–90.

Wagner, A.R. *Heralds and Heraldry in the Middle Ages*, 2nd edn, Oxford, Oxford University Press, 1956.

Woolf, Rosemary. *The English Mystery Plays*, London, Routledge and Kegan Paul, 1972.

Chapter Five: Sport, Hunting and Tournaments

Barker, J.R.V. *The Tournament in England, 1100–1400*, Woodbridge, Boydell, 1986.

Barker, Juliet, & Keen, Maurice. 'The Medieval English Kings and the Tournament', in *Das ritterliche Tournier im Mittelalter*, ed. Josef Fleckstein, Gottingen, Vanderhoeck & Ruprecht, 1985.

Carter, J.M. 'The Ludic Life of the Medieval Peasant: A Pictorial Essay', *Aethlon* 3/2 (Spring 1986), pp. 169–88.

——. *Medieval Games*, Westport, CT, Greenwood, 1992.

Cummins, John. *The Hound and the Hawk*, New York, St Martin's Press, 1988.

Edge, David, & Paddock, J.M. *Arms and Armor of the Medieval Knight*, New York, Crescent, 1988.

Evans, Dafydd. 'The Nobility of Knight and Falcon', in *The Ideals and Practice of Medieval Knighthood, III*, ed. C. Harper-Bill & R. Harvey, Woodbridge, Boydell, 1990.

Fitz Stephen, William. *Norman London*, New York, Italica Press, 1990.

Hands, Rachel (ed.). *English Hawking and Hunting in 'The Boke of St Albans'*, Oxford, Oxford University Press, 1975.

Hardy, Robert. *Longbow*, 3rd edn, New York, Bois d'Arc Press, 1992.

Henricks, T.S. *Disputed Pleasures*, Westport, CT, Greenwood, 1991.

——. 'Sport and Social Hierarchy in Medieval England', *Journal of Sport History* 9/2 (1982), pp. 20–37.

Hoffmann, R.C. 'Fishing for Sport in Medieval Europe: New Evidence', *Speculum* 60 (1985), pp. 877–902.

MacGregor, Arthur. 'Bone Skates: A Review of the Evidence', *Archaeological Journal* 133 (1976), pp. 57–74.

Magoun, F.P. 'Football in Medieval England and in Middle-English Literature', *American Historical Review* 35 (1929–30), pp. 33–45.

The Master of Game, By Edward, 2nd Duke of York, ed. W.A. & F. Baillie-Grohman, London, Chatto & Windus, 1909.

Oggins, R.S. 'Falconry and Medieval Social Status', *Mediaevalia* 12 (1989 for 1986), pp. 43–55.

Orme, Nicholas. *Early British Swimming, 55 BC–AD 1719*, Exeter, Short Run Press, 1983.

Owst, G.R. 'The People's Sunday Amusements in the Preaching of Medieval England', *Holborn Review* 68 (1926), 32–45.

Vale, Malcolm. *War and Chivalry*, Athens, University of Georgia Press, 1981.

Chapter Six: Nature, Pets and Gardening

Backhouse, Janet. *The Luttrell Psalter*, London, British Library, 1989.

Coulton, G.G. *Social Life in Britain from the Conquest to the Reformation*, Cambridge, Cambridge University Press, 1918.

Farmer, D.H. *Saint Hugh of Lincoln*, London, Darton, Longman & Todd, 1985.

Hanawalt, B.A. *The Ties That Bound*, Oxford, Oxford University Press, 1986.

Harvey, J.H. 'The First English Garden Book: Mayster Jon Gardener's Treatise and its Background', *Garden History* 13/2 (1985), pp. 83–101.

——. *Mediaeval Gardens*, London, Batsford, 1981.

——. 'Vegetables in the Middle Ages', *Garden History* 12/1 (1984), pp. 89–99.

Jeneid, Michael. *Chaucer's Checklist*, Capitola, CA, Pandion, 1993.

Labarge, M.W. *A Baronial Household of the Thirteenth Century*, London, Eyre & Spottiswoode, 1965.

McLean, Teresa. *Medieval English Gardens*, London, Barrie & Jenkins, 1989.

Myers, A.R. 'The Captivity of a Royal Witch', *Bulletin of the John Rylands Library* 24 (1940), pp. 263–84; 26 (1941–2), pp. 82–100.

Nicolas, N.H. (ed.). *Privy Purse Expenses of Elizabeth of York*, London, William Pickering, 1830.

Norris, Malcolm. *Brass Rubbing*, London, Studio Vista, 1965.

North, J.D. *Chaucer's Universe*, Oxford, Clarendon Press, 1990.

Orme, Nicholas. *Exeter Cathedral as it Was, 1050–1550*, Exeter, Devon Books, 1986.

Platt, Colin. *Abbeys of Yorkshire*, London, English Heritage, 1988.

Power, E.E. *Medieval English Nunneries*, c. *1275–1535*, Cambridge, Cambridge University Press, 1922.

Siraisi, N.G. *Medieval and Early Renaissance Medicine*, Chicago, University of Chicago Press, 1990.

Chapter Seven: Diet, the Tavern and Codes of Behaviour

Bennett, J.M. 'Conviviality and Charity in Medieval and Early Modern England', *Past and Present*, no. 134, May 1992, pp. 19–41.

Clark, Peter. *The English Alehouse: A Social History, 1200–1830*, London, Longman, 1983.

Dyer, C.C. 'Change in Diet in the Late Middle Ages: The Case of Harvest Workers', *Agricultural History Review* 36 (1988), pp. 21–37.

Hammond, P.W. *Food and Feast in Medieval England*, Stroud, Alan Sutton Publishing Ltd, 1993.

Harvey, B.F. *Living and Dying in England, 1100–1540: The Monastic Experience*, Oxford, Clarendon Press, 1993.

Keen, Maurice. *Chivalry*, New Haven, Yale University Press, 1984.

Maddern, Philippa. 'Honour Among the Pastons: Gender and Integrity in Fifteenth-Century English Provincial Society', *Journal of Medieval History* 14 (1988), pp. 357–71.

Mennell, Stephen. *All Manners of Food: Eating and Taste in England and France from the Middle Ages to the Present*, Oxford, Blackwell, 1985.

Mertes, Kate. *The English Noble Household, 1250–1600*, Oxford, Basil Blackwell, 1988.

Phythian-Adams, C.V. 'Rituals of Personal Confrontation in Late Medieval England', *Bulletin of the John Rylands University Library of Manchester* 73/1 (1991), pp. 65–90.

Rickert, Edith (ed.). *The Babees' Book: Medieval Manners for the Young*, New York, Cooper Square, 1966.

Shirley, Janet (trans. and ed.). *A Parisian Journal, 1405–1449* [Journal d'un Bourgeois de Paris], Oxford, Clarendon Press, 1968.

Chapter Eight: Religion

Adair, J.C., & Cheze-Brown, P. *The Pilgrims' Way: Shrines and Saints in Britain and Ireland*, London, Thames & Hudson, 1982.

Blench, J.W. *Preaching in England in the Late Fifteenth and Sixteenth Centuries*, Oxford, Blackwell, 1964.

Carey, H.M. *Courting Disaster: Astrology at the English Court and University in the Later Middle Ages*, New York, St Martin's Press, 1992.

Cheney, C.R. 'Rules for the Observance of Feast-days in Medieval England', *Bulletin of the Institute of Historical Research* 34 (1961), pp. 117–47.

Collins, Marie, & Davis, Virginia. *A Medieval Book of Seasons*, New York, Harper-Collins, 1992.

Duffy, Eamon. *The Stripping of the Altars: Traditional Religion in England, 1400–1580*, New Haven, Yale University Press, 1992.

Finucane, R.C. *Miracles and Pilgrims: Popular Beliefs in Medieval England*, London, Dent, 1977.

Hall, D.J. *English Mediaeval Pilgrimage*, London, Routledge & Kegan Paul, 1966.

Hanawalt, B.A. 'Keepers of the Lights: Late Medieval English Parish Gilds', *Journal of Medieval and Renaissance Studies* 14 (1984), pp. 21–37.

Heath, Peter. *The English Parish Clergy on the Eve of the Reformation*, London, Routledge & Kegan Paul, 1969.

Hole, Christiana. *English Shrines and Sanctuaries*, London, Batsford, 1954.

LeGoff, Jacques. *The Birth of Purgatory*, London, Scolar Press, 1984.

Mackenzie, Neil. 'Boy Into Bishop', *History Today* 37 (December 1987), pp. 10–16.

Mason, Emma. 'The Role of the English Parishioner, 1100–1500', *Journal of Ecclesiastical History* 27 (1976), pp. 17–29.

Meade, D.M. *The Medieval Church in England*, Worthing, Churchman, 1988.

Murray, Alexander. 'Medieval Christmas', *History Today* 36 (December 1986), pp. 31–39.

Owst, G.R. *Literature and Pulpit in Medieval England*, 2nd edn, Oxford, Blackwell, 1961.

Rodwell, W.J. *English Heritage Book of Church Archaeology*, rev. edn, London, Batsford, 1989.

Swanson, R.N. *Church and Society in Late Medieval England*. Oxford, Blackwell, 1989.

Thurston, Herbert. *Familiar Prayers: Their Origin and History*. Westminster, MD, Newman Press, 1953.

Wedel, T.O. *The Mediaeval Attitude toward Astrology, particularly in England*, New Haven, Yale University Press, 1920.

Chapter Nine: Mysticism and Personal Devotion

Arnold, E.J. 'Henry of Lancaster and His "Livre des Seintes Medicines"', *Bulletin of the John Rylands Library* 21 (1937), pp. 352–86.

Backhouse, J.M. *Books of Hours*, London, British Library, 1985.

Colledge, Eric (ed.). *The Mediaeval Mystics of England*, New York, Charles Scribner's Sons, 1961.

Du Boulay, F.R.H. *The England of Piers Plowman*, Cambridge, D.S. Brewer, 1991.

Labarge, M.W. 'Henry of Lancaster and Le Livre de Seyntz Medicines', *Florilegium* 2 (1980), pp. 183–91.

Maclagan, Eric, and Oman, C.C. 'An English Gold Rosary of about 1500', *Archaeologia* 85 (1935), pp. 1–22.

Shaw, J.G. *The Story of the Rosary*, Milwaukee, Bruce, 1954.

Winston, Anne. 'Tracing the Origins of the Rosary: German Vernacular Texts', *Speculum* 68 (1993), pp. 619–36.

Chapter Ten: Poaching, Sorcery and Prostitution

Baldwin, F.E. *Sumptuary Legislation and Personal Regulation in England*, Baltimore,

Studies in Historical and Political Science, 44, Johns Hopkins University Press, 1926.

Bassett, Margery. 'Newgate Prison in the Middle Ages', *Speculum* 18 (1943), pp. 233–46.

Birrell, Jean. 'Who Poached the King's Deer? A Study in Thirteenth-Century Crime', *Midland History*, 7 (1982), pp. 9–25.

Erickson, Carolly. *The Medieval Vision*, New York, Oxford University Press, 1976.

Hanawalt, B.A. 'Fur Collar Crime: The Pattern of Crime Among the Fourteenth-Century Nobility', *Journal of Social History*, 8/2 (1975), pp. 1–17.

——. 'Men's Games, King's Deer: Poaching in Medieval England', *Journal of Medieval and Renaissance Studies*, 18 (1988), pp. 175–93.

Johnson, D.J. *Southwark and the City*, Oxford, Oxford University Press, 1969.

Karras, R.M. 'The Regulation of Brothels in Later Medieval England', *Signs*, 14 (1989), pp. 399–433.

Manning, R.B. *Hunters and Poachers: A Cultural and Social History of Unlawful Hunting in England, 1485–1640*, Oxford, Clarendon Press, 1993.

Post, J.B. 'A Fifteenth-Century Customary of the Southwark Stews', *Journal of the Society of Archivists,* 5 (1977), pp. 418–28.

Pugh, R.B. *Imprisonment in Medieval England*, Cambridge, Cambridge University Press, 1968.

Reeves, A.C. *Lancastrian Englishmen*, Washington DC, University Press of America, 1981.

Register of Thomas Rotherham, Archbishop of York, 1480–1500, The, ed. E.E. Barker. 1 Volume to date, Torquay, Canterbury and York Society, 1976–.

Salusbury-Jones, G.T. *Street Life in Medieval England*, 2nd edn, Oxford, Pen-in-Hand, 1948.

Bibliography

Abram, Annie. *English Life and Manners in the Later Middle Ages*, London, G. Routledge & Sons, 1913.

——. *Social England in the Fifteenth Century*, London, G. Routledge & Sons, 1909.

Alexander, Jonathan, & Binski, Paul. *Age of Chivalry: Art in Plantagenet England, 1200–1400*, London, Weidenfeld and Nicolson, 1987.

Astill, Grenville, & Grant, Annie (eds). *The Countryside of Medieval England*, Oxford, Basil Blackwell, 1988.

Du Boulay, F.R.H. *An Age of Ambition*, New York, Viking Press, 1970.

Edwards, A.S.G. (ed.). *Middle English Prose: A Critical Guide to Major Authors and Genres*, New Brunswick, Rutgers University Press, 1984.

Ford, Boris (ed.). *The Cambridge Guide to the Arts in Britain: Volume 2: The Middle Ages*, Cambridge, Cambridge University Press, 1988.

Hanawalt, B.A. (ed.). *Chaucer's England: Literature in Historical Context*, Minneapolis, University of Minneapolis Press, 1992.

Harrison, Frederick. *Medieval Man and His Notions*, London, John Murray, 1947.

Jacob, E.F. *The Fifteenth Century, 1399–1485*, Oxford, Clarendon Press, 1961.

Keen, Maurice. *English Society in the Later Middle Ages*, Harmondsworth, Penguin, 1990.

McKisack, May. *The Fourteenth Century, 1307–1399*, Oxford, Clarendon Press, 1959.

McLean, Teresa. *The English at Play in the Middle Ages*, Windsor Forest, Kensal Press, 1983.

Mathew, Gervase. *The Court of Richard II*, London, John Murray, 1968.

Medcalf, Stephen (ed.). *The Context of English Literature: The Later Middle Ages*, London, Methuen, 1981.

Millar, E.G. *The Luttrell Psalter*, London, printed for the Trustees of the British Museum, 1932.

Nelson, William (ed.). *A Fifteenth Century School Book*, Oxford, Clarendon Press, 1956.

Orme, Nicholas. *From Childhood to Chivalry: The Education of the English Kings and Aristocracy, 1066–1530*, London, Methuen, 1984.

Poole, A.L. (ed.). *Medieval England*, rev. edn, 2 vols, Oxford, Oxford University Press, 1958.

Quennell, Marjorie, & Quennell, C.H.B. *A History of Everyday Things in England, 1066–1499*, 2nd edn, London, Batsford, 1931.

Reeves, A.C. *Delights of life in Fifteenth-Century England*, New Orleans, Richard III Society, 1990.

Salzman, L.F. *English Life in the Middle Ages*, Oxford, Oxford University Press, 1926.

Saul, Nigel (ed.). *Age of Chivalry*, New York, St Martin's Press, 1992.

Scattergood, V.J., & Sherborne, J.W. (eds). *English Court Culture in the Later Middle Ages*, London, Duckworth, 1983.

Strutt, Joseph. *Sports and Pastimes of the People of England*, 2nd edn, London, White & Co., 1810.

Virgoe, Roger (ed.). *Private Life in the Fifteenth Century*, New York, Weidenfeld & Nicolson, 1989.

Williams, Daniel (ed.). *England in the Fifteenth Century*, Woodbridge, Boydell, 1987.

Wright, Thomas. *The Homes of Other Days: A History of Domestic Manners and Sentiments in England*, London, Trubner & Co., 1871.

Index

Index